The Star that Astonished the World

by
Ernest L. Martin, Ph.D.

PUBLICATIONS

This book is dedicated to
the memory of my father and mother:
Joel C. and Lula M. Martin

From the cowardice that shrinks from new truth,
From the laziness that is content with half-truths,
From the arrogance that thinks it knows all truth,
O God of Truth, deliver us.
-- Ancient Prayer

2nd Printing, 1998

PUBLICATIONS

P.O. Box 25000, Portland, OR 97225, USA
The Star that Astonished the World
(Second Edition)
Copyright © Ernest L. Martin, 1996
ISBN 0-945657-87-0

Contents

Introduction 1
Chapter
1   The Star of Bethlehem in History 3
2   Who Were the Wise Men? 22
3   Was the Star a Real Star? .33
4   The Real Star of Bethlehem 46
5   The Time of Jesus' Birth .67
6   The Birth of Jesus and the Day of Trumpets 92
7   That Dark Decade in History 103
8   Astronomy and the Death of King Herod 119
9   The Lunar Eclipse of Josephus 138
10   The War that No One Can Find 156
11   The Two Governorships of Quintilius Varus 169
12   The Census of Quirinius 181
13   The Chronology of Josephus 200

Appendix One   Quintilius Varus and the Lapis Tiburtinus 232
Appendix Two   The Question of Gaius Caesar 235
Appendix Three   The Banishment of Julia 237
Appendix Four   The Sabbatical Years and Chronology 239

The Star that Astonished the World

Through a telescope, the magnificent conjunction of June 17 would have looked like this to the magi. The perspective is from near the equator. As seen from Babylon, Venus barely missed moving in front of Jupiter. (James Roth, Griffith Observatory, based on calculations by DeYoung and Hilton)

Used with permission of Griffith Observatory

INTRODUCTION

This book seeks to identify the Star of Bethlehem mentioned in the New Testament. This is not a religious book. It is a book of science and history to demonstrate what was the star that led the Wise Men to Bethlehem. The new evidence that is given will make the story of the Nativity a much more reasonable and interesting account than most historical narratives have provided up to now. The historical and astronomical research in this book is why many planetariums are now showing what was astronomically happening at the crucial time in history when Jesus of Nazareth was born. The planetarium staffs are not making judgments on these celestial phenomena, and this is the correct procedure for such observatories. Planetariums are scientific establishments and are not intended to give opinions on historical or biblical matters. But they are aware of the fascinating and spectacular astronomical relationships that were occurring in 3 to 2 B.C., the period history reveals Jesus was born. Because these celestial events were so remarkable and symbolically significant, many planetariums have considered it worthwhile to show them as a service to the general public because of the widespread interest in this "star."

Since the introduction of computers in the study of astronomical phenomena that occurred within past history, great strides have been made in the last twenty years in determining the actual chronology of those historical events of the past. These facilities were not available to earlier historians and theologians trying to identify what the Star of Bethlehem really was. That is why this new evidence, that comes from up-to-date scientific evaluations, has made it much easier to find the "star" that led the Wise Men to the infant Jesus. The identification of the Bethlehem Star is an event that astronomy can provide. This book gives the historical and biblical evidence (along with the astronomical) that makes the identification possible.

There is one thing for certain. The astronomical and historical information given in this book makes the period of Jesus' nativity come alive as never before. Whether people today wish to view these planetary/stellar events (that I will present in this book) from the early Roman, Mesopotamian or a Palestinian perspective, or even from a modern secular one, we now have clear evidence that there was once (at the very beginning of our era) a unique appearance of a magnificent "Star that Astonished the World."

Chapter 1

THE STAR OF BETHLEHEM IN HISTORY

It was the early evening of June 17, 2 B.C. All the cities around Babylon in Mesopotamia were aglow with talk about a spectacular astronomical event being witnessed in the western sky. What had been monitored for several weeks was the planet Venus moving eastward among the stars on what appeared to be a collision course with the planet Jupiter. Now the expected event had happened right in front of their eyes.

This astronomical drama being enacted in the western part of the sky showed the "collision" of the two brightest planets in the heavens. So small was the separation between them that to the naked eye they would have appeared not as two stars, but as one brilliant star shining far brighter than any other star or planet. Though the two planets were millions of miles away from one another, to observers in Babylon in the year of 2 B.C., they appeared as a single star dominating the twilight of the western sky in the direction of Palestine.

The use of superlatives is appropriate in describing this conjunction. Such an awe-inspiring display was unique in the lifetimes of the people watching the event. It would have been especially important to those in Babylon where astronomy and astrological interpretations had been studied and analyzed for centuries. It was celestial pageantry at its best. Such closeness of the planets had not happened for centuries and would not occur again for hundreds of years. At this time in history, such an astronomical phenomenon would have made "front page news" not only in Babylon but in most regions of the world. The sight would have been observed with a great deal of brilliance in all areas of the habitable earth. Truly, it would have astonished the world.

Modern Astronomers are Impressed

This conjunction of Jupiter and Venus has evoked the astonishment of modern astronomers. The use of computers has given astronomers today the ability to have easy reference to all the solar, lunar, planetary and stellar motions and their relationships with one another over the past five thousand years. And within the last twenty-five years no astronomical event of the past has caused more discussion between astronomers and historians than this conjunction of Jupiter and Venus on June 17, 2 B.C. It was Roger W. Sinnott, writing in the astronomical journal "*Sky and Telescope*," who was the first to draw attention to this unusual conjunction of Jupiter and Venus. He said it was a brilliant "double star" which finally gave the appearance of merging into a single "star" as the planets drew nearer the western horizon. Sinnott showed that only the sharpest eyes would have been able to split them. The twinkling caused by the unsteady horizon atmosphere would have blended the two planets into one "star" for almost all viewers. "The fusion of two planets would have been a rare and awe-inspiring event."[1]

Other modern astronomers have said the same thing. Professor D.C. Morton, the Senior Research Astronomer at Princeton University, said this particular fusion of Jupiter and Venus on that day in history was "a notable astronomical event."[2]

Chapter 1 - The Star of Bethlehem in History

This occurrence also impressed the astronomers at Griffith Observatory in Los Angeles. In the year 1980 a symposium was held at Griffith attended by various scholars and the staff of the observatory. The meeting was convened to discuss the historical significance of several astronomical events that occurred in the years 3 and 2 B.C. It was led by the noted chronologist and biblical historian Professor Jack Finegan of Berkeley, California. At the meeting it was determined that the unique conjunction of Jupiter and Venus and other astronomical events covering an 18 month period from May, 3 B.C. to December, 2 B.C. were of such historical and astronomical significance that there was need for modern scholars to reappraise the historical accounts associated with these outstanding astronomical occurrences.

This prompted the astronomer John Mosley of Griffith to program the Zeiss instrument in the observatory theater to show the heavens from 3 to 1 B.C. When this was done, there was a private viewing to the observatory staff of this interesting period in astronomical history. The technicians who directed the planetarium instrument back to that period projected the appearance of the sky on the theater dome of the planetarium. When the twilight period of June 17, 2 B.C. came into view, the planets Jupiter and Venus were seen in a magnificent conjunction. All the audience expressed wonderment over this rare sight.

What was being observed was what the astronomers at Griffith had already determined by calculation would happen. The visual effect, however, was stunning. Everyone in the planetarium theater was now seeing it as those in Babylon and Jerusalem would have observed it almost 2000 years ago. What was being witnessed was one of the most spectacular astronomical displays of two planets merging together that the planetarium staff had ever observed. Without doubt, this conjunction of Jupiter and Venus on June 17, 2 B.C. would have caused astonishment and awe to people living in in the world in 2 B.C.

5

Events in Roman History

When dramatic celestial events are referred to in the historical records, it is often possible to understand what significance the ancients saw in them. Within the last 3000 years, the period from May, 3 B.C. to December, 2 B.C. is one of the most fruitful to investigate in this regard. There were several astronomical events within this period of eighteen months that must have inspired many wonderful interpretations by the priests and religious people who witnessed them. This is especially so since celestial interpretations by official religious authorities were reckoned at the time to be of supreme worth in evaluating historical events. There were probably as many or more people percentage-wise interested in astronomical occurrences and their interpretations at this period of history than at any other in western civilization. Historical documents show how serious people were in regard to what they called the science of astrology. One event can give us an example of this. According to Julius Marathus, a personal confidant of Augustus Caesar, the Roman Senate in the year 63 B.C. ordered all boy babies to be killed who were born in that year because prophetic dreams and astrological signs suggested that a "King of the Romans" was to be born.[3] The Senate ostensibly considered a "King of the Romans" to be anathema to the government of the Republic. So concerned were some of the senators of this astrological interpretation, whose wives were pregnant, that they refused to register births from their wives in hopes that the signs applied to them. We are informed that in that very year (23 September, 63 B.C.), the person who later became the first emperor of the Romans (Augustus) was born.

Sixty years later these beliefs among rulers on the supposed veracity of astrological interpretations had not diminished. Recall that the New Testament records that King Herod killed the innocent children in and around Bethlehem when Magi (astrologers) informed him that a King of the Jews had been born. The Magi were serious with their interpretations, and they made a long and

Chapter 1 - The Star of Bethlehem in History

arduous journey to show homage to the newborn king.[4]

Astrological matters at this time in history were reckoned by most people as being first-class scientific indicators to present and future events. Whether one today believes in astrology or heartily disapproves has nothing to do with the matter. If modern historians wish to evaluate in a correct manner the historical events in this early period of the Roman Empire, they must possess a considerable knowledge of the astrological concepts that governed the people who lived in that generation. At no time in the history of Rome was a belief in astrology more fervently believed and practiced than in the early Empire period. The Roman emperors were particularly addicted to a belief in its efficacy. As for Tiberius: "His belief in astrology having persuaded him that the world was wholly ruled by fate."[5]

Simply put, near the first century of our era the majority of people considered astrological interpretations as reliable scientific guides in understanding most historical events, especially those involving the rulers of the various lands. What a joy it must have been from 3 to 2 B.C. for the astrologers of the classical world (such as the Chaldeans and the Magi) to be witnessing the planetary and the stellar relationships that were happening within the background of that historical environment. The period of 3 to 2 B.C. was especially important to Rome. In the Roman Empire, all political sections of the imperial domains were then in festival and in celebration. Let us look at this particular time.

The Glory of Rome

This time was one of the most glorious periods in the history of Rome. In 2 B.C. Augustus celebrated his 25th jubilee year of being emperor of the Romans (from the time he was proclaimed "Augustus" on January 16, 27 B.C.).[6] This year also coincided with the 750th year of the founding of Rome as determined by the chronological records of the Roman priests.[7] In August of 2 B.C.

(the month named after Augustus himself and still a month we recognize today) there were festivities in Rome and throughout the provinces and client kingdoms. People came to the festivities from all over the Empire and even beyond. In Rome during this year there were magnificent displays and carnival activities. There were sham sea-fights on the flooded Tibertine fields, gladiators in abundance and wild beast hunts. The Roman Empire was in great celebration. Along with this, Augustus, in 2 B.C., finally dedicated the new Forum bearing his name after many delays and he sanctified the Temple of Mars Ultor (Mars the Avenger).[8]

The year 2 B.C. was almost as if a Roman millennium had commenced. The Roman poet Virgil, in his *Fourth Eclogue* a few years before, had given a prophetic revelation that a child was destined to bring in a new Golden Age of peace and prosperity sometime within this period. Sir Ronald Syme mentioned the importance of this special year 2 B.C. Peace and security seemed everywhere in the air. "East as well as west and north, the horizon was clear of menacing clouds."[9] "The third closing of Janus belongs about this time, so it may with some confidence be conjectured."[10] The shutting of these gates at the temple of Janus was the signal that peace was now on the borders and within the Roman Empire. Political tranquility was everywhere in evidence. Active war had ceased and large numbers of legionary soldiers had been released from military service from 7 to 2 B.C.[11]

Truly, it seemed at the time that every man would "sit under his vine and fig tree." It seemed that the Roman state under the leadership of the emperor Augustus had secured this for the Roman Empire. By the year 2 B.C., the world saw in Augustus a type of "Prince of Peace" who was then in charge of the greatest empire on earth. Virgil's prophecy of a Golden Age was seemingly coming true.

Chapter 1 - The Star of Bethlehem in History

The Father of the Country

Another important matter occurred in 2 B.C. Augustus was given his most prestigious title: *Pater Patriae* (Father of the Country). In the previous year a decree went out from Augustus that required "*the entire Roman people*" scattered over the Empire to register their approval that Augustus should be given the most prestigious title of his career, the *Pater Patriae*.[12] This registration of people in all areas of the Empire was an oath in which individuals proclaimed the emperor Augustus as the "Father of the Country." This oath took place in the summer of 3 B.C. and it was required of all Roman citizens and others of distinguished rank among the client kingdoms associated with Rome.[13] This universal census of allegiance to Augustus was demanded of those who claimed any kind of authority within the Empire. The whole of the Roman Empire responded, and Augustus was gloriously proclaimed the *Pater Patriae* (the Father of the Country).

This award itself was given to Augustus by decree of the Senate and the people of Rome on February 5, 2 B.C. This was the festival day dedicated to *Concord*. It was the traditional day that honored peace and reconciliation among all classes of people all over the Roman Empire.[14] Throughout the year 2 B.C. Augustus was being recognized as the one who brought peace, security and tranquility to the world. In the festivities and banquets that occurred during that year it was common for people to drink to the health of Augustus with the toast: "Father of the country, Caesar, the best of men."[15]

The Astronomical Events of 3 to 2 B.C.

The period of 3 and 2 B.C. was an important one for political and social festivities within the Roman Empire. Several important political anniversaries in Rome's history were merging together at that very time. And joining in celebrating the praises of Rome, Augustus and the Roman people, the heavens themselves burst forth with great fanfare. The heavenly bodies celebrated with a

The Star that Astonished the World

variety of conjunctions and stellar/planetary relationships that would have inspired imagination and admiration to the people and astrologers at that time. These celestial events have certainly astonished modern astronomers.

It is known that astrological interpretations can vary with each astrologer and with those of different countries or ethnic groups. But there are some universal concepts that many astrologers of the past generally accepted as indicative of important historical events. To the Romans, these interpretations associated with the period from 3 to 2 B.C. seemed to be showing a heavenly approval of the greatness and sovereignty of Rome and its Empire.

For one, there was the extremely close conjunction of Jupiter and Venus on June 17, 2 B.C. This was when the planets appeared as one gigantic "star" in the western sky. It is interesting that this conjunction occurred at the exact time of the full moon. While the western quarter of the sky was being adorned by this brilliant planetary spectacle, the dome of the sky itself was being illuminated from the east by the resplendence of the full moon. In that early evening scene, the whole sky was aglow with celestial brightness. These heavenly demonstrations no doubt inspired wonder in Rome and elsewhere throughout the world. This is especially so because, added to this, the conjunction of Jupiter and Venus appeared within the constellation of Leo, the Lion. As I will soon show, the constellation of Leo was the *chief* or *head* sign of the Zodiac both in the secular and the biblical Zodiac. This sign was especially important in astrological circles.[16] It *began* the year for astrologers to interpret prime historical and astrological events.

Leo, the Central Sign of Royalty

The sign of Leo was not only reckoned as being the head of the Zodiac but it was thought to be ruled by the Sun (the chief "star" of the heavens). It was a "Royal Constellation." Leo was dominated by Regulus which was known by astrologers as the "King Star." To

10

Chapter 1 - The Star of Bethlehem in History

the Romans who lived at the time of Augustus, the significance of this conjunction of Jupiter and Venus in the constellation of Leo had associated with it the symbol of Roman "rulership" and "domination."

This celestial event on June 17, 2 B.C. would have appeared fortunate to the people of Rome because Jupiter was also reckoned as the guardian and ruler of the Empire and it was supposed to determine the course of all human affairs.[17] Besides this, Venus (which was now in conjunction with Jupiter) was believed to be the mother (*Genetrix*) of the family of Augustus.[18] So, here were the two planets dedicated to the origins of Rome and reckoned as special to Augustus now merging together into a "marriage" union during one of the most glorious years in the history of Rome.[19]

That this conjunction of Jupiter and Venus on June 17, 2 B.C. happened at the precise time of the full moon was also important to the Romans. Full moon day was especially sacred to Jupiter and a sheep was led along the Via Sacra to be sacrificed to Jupiter. The day itself was called "the Trust of Jupiter."[20] It was celebrated as a time when faith and trust were supposed to be given to the guardian and ruler of the Empire of Rome, whether human or divine.

A Massing of the Planets

There was, however, yet another rare astronomical event in 2 B.C. that developed 72 days after the conjunction of Jupiter and Venus. This was a massing of four planets into a close longitudinal relationship. They all appeared in the same region of the sky. This happened in the month of August when most of the Roman festivities for that unusual year were taking place. This massing of the planets took place near the conclusion to the celebrations at Rome, on August 27, 2 B.C. Jupiter and Mars were only .09 degrees from one another with latitude considered while Venus and Mercury were also in close longitudinal proximity to them. Note this. Jupiter was situated along the ecliptic (the path of the Sun in its journey

11

through the heavens) at 142.6 degrees; Mars at 142.64; Venus, 141.67; and Mercury at 143.71. The massing of planets was important to astrologers in the sense that the planets located "together" were astrologically reckoned as being in a "common agreement of purpose."

To astrologers, a massing of planets signalled a new beginning in historical affairs. And look at this. These planets were clustering near one another in the important constellation of Leo, the Lion. This was the beginning zodiacal sign for the astrological year and it was considered to be denoting royalty and power for any of the planets found within it. A massing of planets in the constellation of Leo could have given astrologers much to talk about. It would have signalled a new and powerful beginning for Rome and the world.[21] It could have suggested to many that Virgil's Golden Age was now commencing.

More Astronomical Signs

There were other astronomical signs at that period that would have strengthened the concept that a new Golden Age was dawning. A little over a year earlier (May 19, 3 B.C.) the planets Saturn and Mercury were in close conjunction (.67 degrees from each other). Then Saturn moved eastward through the stars to meet with Venus on June 12, 3 B.C. At this conjunction they were only a mere .12 degrees from each other. And, as if this were not enough, two months later (August 12, 3 B.C.) Jupiter and Venus appeared together in a pre-dawn conjunction which was even closer (just .07 degrees from each other as viewed from earth). Though the planets at this conjunction did not appear to "touch" one another as they did some ten months later on June 17, 2 B.C., they were very close in this meeting. Then look at what happened. What began as a pre-dawn "morning star" union on August 12, 3 B.C. for Jupiter and Venus, then developed into their "evening star" reunion some ten months later.

Chapter 1 - The Star of Bethlehem in History

There is more. The "morning star" conjunction of Jupiter and Venus on August 12, 3 B.C. occurred when the planets were in the last degrees of the zodiacal sign of Cancer which was the *concluding* sign for interpreting the astrological year. Yet the "evening star" conjunction of the same planets in their reunion ten months later happened in the first degrees of Leo, the *beginning* sign of the astrological year. The zero degree line for beginning astrological calculations was between the signs of Cancer and Leo.[22]

This means that the "morning star" conjunction of Jupiter and Venus in August 12, 3 B.C. happened at the conclusion of the astrological year, while the "evening star" reunion some ten months later occurred in the *beginning* of a new astrological year. These two unions of Jupiter and Venus could well have been interpreted as showing the *close* of one age in history and the *beginning* of another age in 2 B.C.

Regulus, the King star

There are even more significant events from the astrological point of view that happened in 3 B.C. and into 2 B.C. Just 33 days after the Jupiter and Venus "morning star" conjunction in August 12, 3 B.C., an observer would have seen Jupiter in union with Regulus (a star of the first magnitude). Regulus is the chief star in the constellation of Leo, the Lion, and because it lay practically on the path of the Sun, it was reckoned as a "Royal Star." Jupiter and Regulus came into juxtaposition on September 14, 3 B.C. and as viewed from earth they were only .33 degrees from each other. Here was the "King planet" (Jupiter) now coming in contact with the "King star" (Regulus) and in the "Royal Constellation" (Leo the Lion). If viewed in isolation to other astronomical occurrences, this single event may not have been significant to astrologers, but combined with the other celestial displays of 3 to 2 B.C., it soon took on great symbolic meaning. This is because this first conjunction began a series of three meetings of Jupiter and Regulus that occurred in a precise sequential pattern. Note what happened.

The Star that Astonished the World

Jupiter first united with Regulus and then it continued on its normal course in the heavens. On December 1, 3 B.C., Jupiter stopped its motion through the fixed stars and began its annual retrogression. In doing so, it once again headed toward the star Regulus. Then on February 17, 2 B.C., the two were reunited, .85 degrees apart. Jupiter continued in its motion (still in retrogression) another 40 days and then it reverted to its normal motion through the stars. Remarkably, this movement placed Jupiter once again into a third conjunction with Regulus on May 8, 2 B.C. They were then .72 degrees from each other.[23]

The visible effect of these three conjunctions of Jupiter (the King planet) with Regulus (the King star) would have shown Jupiter making a circling effect over and around Regulus. Jupiter was "homing in" on Regulus and pointing out the significance of the King star as it related to the King planet. Notice the following drawing that illustrates what observers would then have witnessed. The drawing is exaggerated. The actual "loop" was more linear. This circular maneuver of Jupiter over Regulus would have signalled to astrologers that a great king was then destined to appear.

Looking Toward the Southern Horizon

Regulus
(The King Star)

Path of Jupiter
(The King Planet)

East   West

Diagram is for illustration only. It is not to scale.

This motion effect of Jupiter circling over Regulus brings up a most important astrological observation. As mentioned earlier, the zero line for beginning and ending the 360 degrees of the Zodiac

Chapter 1 - The Star of Bethlehem in History

was reckoned by some astrologers as existing between Cancer and Leo.[24] This means that this motion effect shown by Jupiter circling around Regulus (like a "crown" over the star) was happening in the heavens just east of the zero degree line for astrological measurements. It occurred at the *beginning* section of the astrological Zodiac in the view of some Gentile astrologers. This interpretation is similar to that adopted by Moses in his arrangement of the armies of Israel in the fashion of the Zodiac around the Tabernacle in the wilderness. The biblical Zodiac designed by Moses also began with the royal sign of Leo, but its zero degree line was located in the middle of the constellation, not at its beginning. Whatever the case, these indications would surely have shown to the people of that era that a great king or ruler was then being introduced to the world.

And who was the greatest ruler then in existence? It was Augustus Caesar, emperor of Rome. When were these celestial events happening? Note the chronological significance. They coincided with the 25th year of Augustus' elevation to supreme power over the Romans, the 750th priestly anniversary of the founding of Rome, and the exact year the people and Senate of Rome gave Augustus his supreme title: *Pater Patriae* (the Father of the Country). To those in Rome, it seemed like heaven itself was giving approval for the emperorship of Augustus and that the government of Rome had the divine right to world sovereignty. Hardly a person in Rome would have disputed that interpretation and most people would have agreed that the astronomical evidence in support of it was overwhelming.

But in another part of the world those outstanding astronomical signs were viewed in a different way. As an example of this, some Magi (Wise Men or Astrologers) from the eastern world were also watching these wonderful celestial phenomena denoting the advent of "royalty." These Magi decided to skip Rome and its festivities and celebrations. Instead, they headed in the direction of Jerusalem and Judaea looking for this special child whom they considered to be a very important newborn "King of the Jews."

The Interpretation of the Magi

This historical and astronomical information I am giving in this book provides a clue in identifying the "star" that led the Magi to Jerusalem and then to Bethlehem. The evidence is impressive enough that historians and biblical scholars have to give it serious consideration. After all, modern astronomers have recognized that "a notable astronomical event" occurred at that very time in history. It was one that would have astonished the world. Thankfully, attention to these matters is now being given by modern scholars.

In December 1980, Griffith Observatory in Los Angeles was the first in modern times to show the new astronomical drama that was occurring in the 18 month period from May, 3 B.C. to December, 2 B.C. Much of this historical and astronomical information was shown in my article in *Christianity Today* titled "The Celestial Pageantry Dating Christ's Birth" which appeared in 1976 and also in my research study called *The Birth of Christ Recalculated* (first edition, 1978). Because of this historical research, Griffith Observatory decided it was time to introduce a new December Show at their planetarium. Up to this time most planetariums throughout the world normally featured the astronomical happenings from 7 to 4 B.C. as the possible ones associated with Jesus' nativity which brought the Magi to Jerusalem and then to Bethlehem. This new astronomical information made the celestial events of that earlier period fade into insignificance. The period of 3 to 2 B.C. both historically and astronomically is far more impressive, and it coincides with the majority of the early historical records as well as those in the Bible.

The accounts in these early records make this period interesting. There are historical reasons for this. It is important to note that *the majority of early Christian scholars up to the fourth century placed the birth of Jesus in this very period of 3 to 2 B.C.* This is a power-

Chapter 1 - The Star of Bethlehem in History

ful witness that deserves emphasis. In this book, I will show that the historical and astronomical evidences truly support the basic conclusions of these early Christian fathers.

Since Griffith Observatory recognized the astronomical and historical value of this new information, they began to show these celestial events at their planetarium for educational purposes. Other planetariums also altered their annual December showings to accord with this outstanding display of stellar activity. The *Los Angeles Times* reported on the change made by Griffith Observatory in December, 1980 by stating: "At least 10 planetariums in the United States, Germany and Greece are revising their shows this Christmas season to correspond with the dating theories of Ernest Martin. Scores of others are considering a shift."[25] And by 1990, some ten years later, there were over 600 planetariums showing the 3 to 2 B.C. astronomical occurrences.

And no wonder. These displays of astronomical events have astonished modern astronomers, and it is now recognized that they would have also astonished the ancient world that personally observed them in the heavens. To modern astronomers, the central event was that of June 17, 2 B.C. So magnificent was this astronomical exhibition by two of the brightest planets that Isaac Asimov was impressed to mention it. Since the celestial phenomenon appeared to observers in Mesopotamia as occurring toward Palestine, it prompted Asimov to ask the question: "Is the fact that the unusual 'star' was seen in the direction of Judaea enough to make them think of a Messiah?"[26]

Indeed, this may have been the very conjunction that led the Magi to Palestine to give gifts to the one they believed to be the king of the Jews. There were serious beliefs even among the Romans that somewhere in this period a mighty ruler was destined to come out of the eastern parts of the Empire.[27] People may well have wondered if the astronomical signs in 3 to 2 B.C. were heaven's signal that the new prophetic ruler was imminent. The heavens were certainly making a grand display and the Magi may well have interpreted the signs accordingly, especially in witnessing the conjunction of Jupiter and Venus on June 17, 2 B.C.

The Star of the Wise Men

When the full story is known about these matters and what happened astronomically from May, 3 B.C. to December, 2 B.C., historians and astronomers may now be able to discover the very "star" that led the Wise Men to the infant Jesus at Bethlehem. Isaac Asimov asked the right question about the conjunction of Jupiter and Venus on June 17, 2 B.C. We may share our inquisitiveness with him. Was *this* the "Star of the Messiah" that the Jews and others were looking for? Was *this* the "star" mentioned in the Gospel of Matthew and supported by the account in the Gospel of Luke?[28] The word "star" in the first century could refer to a planet as well as a fixed star. Could the "star" have been the planet Jupiter? The historical events recorded in the New Testament about the "Star of the Messiah" chronologically occurred precisely at this time, and this is the period early Christian scholars said Jesus was born.

These matters need serious investigation and the academic world recognizes the importance of this astronomical activity. Historians and classical scholars are aware of this new information that was recorded in my earlier article and book. Let me give a few reviews of this new research. Dr. Thorley in England wrote in the classical journal "Greece and Rome." "New light has been thrown on the date of the nativity.... Martin tackles the [historical] problems convincingly. It does seem that Luke's account of the nativity is turning out to be essentially accurate in its historical details [and that] Luke did not mislead Theophilus, not even historically."[29]

The *National Catholic Register* also reported on this new information. "Dr. Martin directs a Pasadena-based organization devoted to research on biblical subjects. He has had considerable archaeological experience, and the Education section of *Time* [magazine]

Chapter 1 - The Star of Bethlehem in History

for September 3, 1973 was devoted to him and his excavations in Jerusalem. He not only knows his subject but can write simply and understandably. [His work] does seem to afford a solemn astronomical basis for calculating the birth of Christ."[30]

In the 1987 publication *The Christmas Star* published by Griffith Observatory we read: "Martin has rewritten the history of this period, clearing up a slew of nagging problems. Prominent classical historians are taking his work very seriously, and although it will be years before a consensus is reached, an impartial referee would probably conclude that Martin's chronology is correct."[31]

This new information inspired *Guideposts* magazine in its December, 1988 issue to state (having been given the astronomical evaluations of those on the staff of Adler Planetarium in Chicago) that this historical evidence represents the best explanation of the "Star of Bethlehem" yet presented.[32]

This was followed in November, 1992 with a presentation and discussion of this research on the Star of Bethlehem at the Center for Constructive Alternatives Seminar at Hillsdale College in Michigan. Among those attending was Prof. Owen Gingerich, Professor of Astronomy and Science at Harvard University and several other prominent professors in other scientific disciplines. The astronomer Dr. Craig Chester gave the lecture at the Seminar on the new research, and in December, 1993 he wrote a full report about these astronomical and historical findings in *Imprimis* magazine in which he said that among astronomers the First Edition of this book (*The Star that Astonished the World*) "has become the authoritative source on the subject."[33]

There is no question that the astronomical occurrences which took place from 3 to 1 B.C. did in fact happen, and they represent some of the most spectacular celestial displays that either astronomers or the general public could ask for to introduce a newborn king into the world. If there were any design to it at all (and I

19

believe that there was), most people would think that someone of great importance was then being announced to the world. This is because the whole of the heavenly host was bursting forth into a brilliant panoramic exhibition that would have certainly astonished those who witnessed it.

The Star of Bethlehem Has Now Been Found

When Sinnott over twenty years ago (concentrating on the astronomical events of this period) suggested that the "Star of Bethlehem" could be found with the planetary union of Jupiter and Venus in 2 B.C., the door was opened that made it possible to identify that biblical star in an astronomical and historical sense. What Sinnott suggested began to make sense to other astronomers. The results of his research was impressive to several astronomers. C.A. Federer, editor-in-chief of *Sky and Telescope*, said that "Sinnott's results make the Star of Bethlehem more plausible astronomically than it has seemed heretofore."[34] In addition to that astronomical appraisal, this present book will show that the same identification also becomes plausible in a historical sense as well. When the records of history are combined with the results of astronomy, it now becomes possible to identify the "Star of Bethlehem" that many people for the past 1900 years have been trying to discover.

What is needed is a serious scholarly consideration for this scientific approach in identifying the "Star of Bethlehem." Evaluating the data will result in a much better understanding of that historical era of time. The astronomer John Mosley wrote in the *Griffith Observer*: "It is not often that we see the demise of an astronomical theory that dates back to pre-telescopic times. Yet a theory first proposed by none other than the famous astronomer Johannes Kepler himself, and generally accepted as correct for more than 3 and ½ centuries, is now being discarded... [by] new historical research of Dr. Ernest L. Martin."[35]

This historical and astronomical research in this book is why

Chapter 1 - The Star of Bethlehem in History

many planetariums (well over 600 in the United States alone) are now showing what was astronomically happening at the crucial time in history when Jesus of Nazareth was born. They are, correctly, not making judgments on these phenomena. Planetariums are scientific establishments and are not intended to give opinions on historical or biblical matters. But they are aware of the fascinating and spectacular astronomical relationships that were occurring in 3 to 2 B.C., the period that history as revealed in this book shows Jesus was born. Because these celestial events were so remarkable and symbolically significant, many planetariums have considered it worthwhile to show them as a service to the general public because of the widespread interest in this period of time.

There is one thing for certain. This astronomical information given within this book makes this period in the history of the world come alive as never before. Whether people today view these planetary/stellar events from the early Roman, Mesopotamian or the Palestinian perspective, or even from a modern secular one, we now have clear evidence that there was once (at the very beginning of our era) a unique appearance of a magnificent star which must be called the "Star that Astonished the World."

Chapter 2

WHO WERE THE WISE MEN?

One of the most important points in understanding what the New Testament states about the Star of Bethlehem is to realize the social and political status of the Wise Men who came to Herod. The word that was used to describe them was "Magi." This was a title and in the first century it signified that they were professional astrologers. This fact is so well-known in scholarly circles that many modern translators of the New Testament simply render "Magi" as "astrologers" without explanation.[36] Once this primary point is realized, we are provided with reliable information that can make the account of the Magi's visit to Herod understandable.

The simple teaching of the Gospel of Matthew states that astrologers came from the eastern part of the world to pay homage to the newborn "King of the Jews" and to present him with the customary gifts that were generally accorded to new kings. The account in the New Testament does not mean that the writer of the Gospel of Matthew was endorsing the principles of astrology because there are biblical verses condemning its religious practice which he no doubt was aware of.[37] But, in mentioning their trek to

Chapter 2 - Who Were the Wise Men?

Jerusalem, Matthew shows that the Magi themselves were being motivated by symbolic principles which were taken seriously by people in the world at the time.

The recording of this account in Matthew makes it clear that Matthew did not view these Magi as quacks or charlatans. When the Magi came to Jerusalem with their announcement that the star of the newborn Jewish king had been seen, Herod was "troubled and all Jerusalem with him."[38] Since the Magi were professional astronomers as well as astrologers, the mention of their visit to Jerusalem was Matthew's way of securing the testimony of top scientific authorities to authenticate the royal birth of Jesus.

The Importance of the Magi

These Magi came from the east bearing rich gifts for the newborn king. They could not have been reckoned as certain classes of sorcerers and confidence men who roamed the Roman world under the name "Magi." Herod and all Jerusalem would hardly have been troubled by what they considered impostors. But if the Magi had come from the court of the Parthian kings who employed Magi in the religious affairs of their government, or from the respected Magian colleges of the east, then that would have been a different matter in the view of Herod and the Jewish authorities in Jerusalem.

In order to have an audience with Herod and for him to have members of the Sanhedrin (the Supreme Court of the Jews) to hear the interpretations of these Magi must show that they were held in high esteem by the people of Jerusalem. In their deportment, it was customary for the Magi to dress in magnificent priestly attire to indicate their professional status. In presenting themselves before royalty the historical records show that the Magi did this with pomp and circumstance.[39] In travelling or on official business in areas where their influence was felt, it was normal for the priestly Magi to proceed in a processional mode with various ranks of them appropriately positioned in the caravan. This must have been the manner in which they approached the city of Jerusalem to present their gifts to the newborn king of the Jews. This would account for the respectful attitude of Herod and the Jewish authorities to them.[40]

It is important to realize that this type of travel for respected Magian priests is not a fantasy story. They travelled in majestic style. The account recorded by Matthew fits well with other journeys of Magian priests when they were presented to kings or emperors. When Tiridates of the order of the Magi was made king over Armenia by the emperor Nero, the new Magian king went to Rome with the other Magi to present gifts to Nero. A great deal of ceremony was associated with this visit of the Magi.[41] This must also have been the case with the Magi who came to Herod. He would have given them a proper ceremonial protocol. This is why "all Jerusalem" knew of their coming and why members of the Sanhedrin were summoned to hear their interpretations on the "star" which they had seen. The account in Matthew harmonizes perfectly with other historical events involving Magi in the time of the early Roman Empire.

The Professional Role of the Magi

There is a considerable amount of early information about the Magi of the east. We are told by Herodotus that they were originally one of the six tribes of the Medes,[42] a priestly caste similar to the Levites among the Israelites. In their early history their occupation was to provide the kings of the Medes, Persians and Babylonians with what they considered to be divine information about the daily matters involving government affairs. Because of the high religious and political esteem accorded them by the peoples of the east,[43] they were able in the sixth century B.C. even to overturn some royal powers.[44]

Their role in interpreting divine matters for kings and rulers is mentioned in the Bible. The prophet Daniel in the time of King Nebuchadnezzar became the "master of the magicians [master of

Chapter 2 - Who Were the Wise Men?

the Magi], astrologers, Chaldeans, and soothsayers."[45] The prophet Jeremiah mentioned that a chief authority among the Magi was called the *Rab-Mag*.[46] The prophet Daniel must have been assigned to this high office. Perhaps the fraternization of Daniel with the early Magi in Babylon helps to explain why those in the Magian profession expected a Jewish king to arrive near the end of the first century. This is the very thing that Daniel prophesied would happen. Recall that Daniel prophesied the rebuilding of Jerusalem after the Babylonians destroyed it in the sixth century B.C. He also said that 490 years would pass from a command to rebuild Jerusalem until a world-embracing messianic kingdom would emerge on the earth in the region of Palestine.[47] The prophecy had numerous unknown factors associated with it. For example, Daniel did not clearly explain which command to rebuild Jerusalem was meant. He did not say whether his year-lengths were lunar or solar. Regarding the Messiah, Daniel did not indicate if the 490 years would end with his birth, his bar mitzvah, when he would become twenty years of age and able to go to war, when he would become thirty (the year of spiritual adulthood), or whenever the Messiah would be proclaimed king which could happen at any time during his life.

Because Daniel did not detail these points, the prophecy was vague to Jews and others at the time. It was subject to a variety of interpretations. Most Jews, however, were certain enough about the prophecy to believe that it would occur sometime near the first century. Josephus, the Jewish historian who lived in the last part of the first century, mentioned a conviction among the Jews that this prophecy of Daniel would have its fulfillment within the first century. Josephus said that it was shown in the "sacred writings that about that time one from their country [Judaea] should become governor of the habitable earth."[48]

There can be no doubt that the Magi in Mesopotamia would have been aware of these prophetic indications among the Jews. In

25

The Star that Astonished the World

fact, scholars today are able to see that there was a great deal of mingling of beliefs between the Jews and the Magi at this period of time. This was because of their connections with one another since the sixth century B.C.[49]

Even the Romans were aware of the prophecies of Daniel. Suetonius in the early second century said: "A firm belief had long prevailed through the east that it was destined for the empire of the world *at that time* to be given to someone who should go forth from Judaea."[50] Tacitus also said: "The majority of the Jewish people were very impressed with the belief that it was contained in ancient writings of the priests that it would come to pass that *at that very time*, the east would renew its strength and they that should go forth from Judaea should be rulers of the world."[51] Even the Roman Emperor Nero was advised by one or two of his court astrologers that it was prudent for him to move his seat of empire to Jerusalem because that city was then destined to become the capital of the world.[52]

All of these widespread beliefs were based on the prophecies of Daniel. Since Jewish people lived in all areas of the Roman and Parthian worlds,[53] their national aspirations would have been well known. Even among the Magi themselves there were the traditional teachings of Zoroaster (who influenced Magian doctrine in the time of Herod). Zoroaster, an early religious leader and teacher in the region where the Magi had their origin, taught that at sometime in the future there would arise a king who would raise the dead and transform the world into a kingdom of peace and security. Interestingly, the Zoroastrian traditions associated with this prophesied king said this king would come forth from the stock of Abraham.[54]

These beliefs among the peoples of nearer Asia and in the Roman Empire are a simple fact of history. Whether people wish to believe them is another matter. The job of the historian is not to give judgments on the validity or non-validity of these early

Chapter 2 - Who Were the Wise Men?

prophetic or traditional teachings of the Jews, Romans or Magi. Historians should simply state what the ancient people believed and that is what I am trying to do in this book. But one thing for certain, it is not possible to comprehend the history of the first century unless people today are aware of these beliefs that motivated the social, religious and political actions of those early peoples. All nations were then affected in a most profound way by astrological/prophetic teachings. This is simple historical fact and most scholars today accept this without argument.

These early prophetic convictions of the Jews, Romans and Magi were important to those who lived in the first century. And the use of astrological interpretations in evaluating the historical events of the time was at an all time high. So, when the Magi who were professional astrologers saw what they considered to be the "star" of a Jewish king, it was a certain sign to them to go to Jerusalem with gifts to present to that newborn king.

The Jews and the Magi

Most Jews admired the Magi of the east. This was not only because of their former association with the prophet Daniel, but also because they were not idolaters. Though the Magi believed that the power of the deity was manifested in the natural elements of fire, water, air and earth, these Gentile priests did not set up material images in recognition of him. They were, in one way of looking at it, Gentiles who were leaning toward monotheistic belief.[55]

Jews in the first century respected the Magi. The Jewish philosopher by the name of Philo who lived in Alexandria, Egypt during the time of Jesus spoke of the Magi with warm praise. Philo said they were men who gave themselves to the study of the laws of nature and that they contemplated on the divine perfections. To Philo they were worthy of being counselors of kings.[56]

The main occupation of the Magi was their interpretation of

things they considered divine. They principally dealt with the evaluation of dreams, visions and astronomical signs. Astrological interpretation was of special importance to them. The temple of Belus in what remained of the city of Babylon was in their care.[57] In particular, they were advisors to kings and princes and they were especially consulted regarding the destinies of kings.[58] The Parthian kings of the east had them as their advisors and they were the ones who performed the ceremonies at their coronations.[59] The Roman authors Cicero and Plutarch inform us that the Magi were the ones who instructed kings and princes in the east. Except in rare circumstances, only royalty were allowed to be initiated into their secret teachings and understandings.[60]

This is one reason why the Magi must have felt it proper to tell Herod the details of their interpretation concerning the "star" that they had been following. Though Herod would have had his own court astrologers, he must have paid particular attention to what the respected Magian professionals from the east had to say about a newborn Jewish king. Their interpretations were especially sought out by prominent people because of the Magian influence in the royal courts of the east. In fact, the Magi were in such high regard in Parthia that some even became kings.[61] Even the Magi who came to Jesus were also considered as being "princes" or "kings" in some early accounts.[62] But when the Magi came to Jerusalem, they arrived to do homage to the new Jewish king and to give gifts to him. In the next century, Tiridates of the order of the Magi did the same thing when he visited the emperor Nero. It is no wonder that the arrival of such Magi caused great interest to Herod and those at Jerusalem.

The Gifts of the Magi

It is interesting that the treasures brought by the Magi (gold, frankincense and myrrh) were the major gifts mentioned in the Greek translation of Isaiah 60:6 that foreign kings would one day bring to Israel's messianic ruler. The tradition that there were only

Chapter 2 - Who Were the Wise Men?

three Magi stems from the assumption that each gave one gift to Jesus. No one knows how many Magi there were who went to Jerusalem, but some traditions mention as many as twelve.[63] We have no way of knowing their exact number or how many there were in their entourage.

At any rate, these respected Magi came to Jerusalem bearing gold, frankincense and myrrh, which were the customary gifts of subject nations to their superiors.[64] The Magi, in this case, came to do obeisance to a new Jewish king. They must have realized that something more than an ordinary royal birth was awaiting them. They no doubt had in mind the prophetic beliefs among the Jews, Romans and others that a world ruler was then destined to come from the race of Abraham in the area of Palestine.

We are told in the New Testament that the main factor that brought the Magi to Jerusalem was "his star." What star or heavenly body could this have been? Though there was an interesting conjunction of Jupiter and Saturn in 7 B.C. with Mars forming a triangular aspect with those planets in early 6 B.C., the planets at that time were at least two diameters of the Moon away from one another and they could not in any way be considered as a single "star." As for the years of 5 and 4 B.C., there was nothing of astronomical importance that would have impressed anyone to journey to Jerusalem. But in 3 and 2 B.C., the whole heavens burst forth with astronomical signs and wondrous displays. It may well be, that the celestial occurrences in this latter period of time were the very ones that prompted the Magi to go to Jerusalem. Since they were astrologers, we should look in the contemporary historical records of this period for astronomical events that could be interpreted and understood within an astrological context. Let us notice what the New Testament relates on this matter.

The Magi and King Herod

In explaining to King Herod why they came to do homage to the new Jewish king, the Magi said: "We saw his star at its *rising* [or *when it rose*]." The King James Version of the New Testament suggests the Magi simply saw his star "in the east." But this rendering does not represent what the Greek signifies. It wasn't merely "in the east" that the Magi observed the star. The Gospel of Matthew says they saw it "at its *rising*." The New English Bible gives the proper translation: "We observed the *rising* of his star."

Scholars realize that the Greek words employed by Matthew to record this event were the ordinary ones then used in Greek literature to describe the regular rising of the stars or planets.[65] The plain meaning of the words suggest that the Magi had witnessed a "star" rise above the eastern horizon when they made their normal pre-dawn observations of the heavens. Later, when the Magi got to Jerusalem, they told King Herod about the *rising* of that "star." Herod and all Jerusalem were inquisitive and asked (as Vincent renders the account): "How long does the star make itself visible since its *rising* in the east?"[66] The language of Matthew shows it was an ordinary type of star that rose in the east like all normal stars.

The Magi Saw an Actual Star

There is no doubt that the New Testament is using normal astronomical terms to describe these events. The narrative is clearly showing that the Magi observed an ordinary star (or planet) ascending above the eastern horizon which they interpreted as the sign that a Jewish king was now within his nativity period. It was *one* "star" that intrigued them, though it must have been in some unusual relationship or aspect with other celestial bodies. The Magi were so impressed that they made their long, difficult journey to Jerusalem with costly gifts to present to the new king. After hearing their account, King Herod and all Jerusalem were equally persuaded that the "star" was significant.

Remember, this period of time was one when astrological interpretations made by first-class professionals were looked on as valid

Chapter 2 - Who Were the Wise Men?

scientific indications of impending events. So confident was the Roman government about such matters, that some sixty years before, the Roman Senate ordered that all boy babies must not be allowed to live in 63 B.C. when astrological and prodigious forecasts had determined a "King of the Romans" was to be born. This earlier event would have been well known to Herod and to people throughout the Roman Empire. To secure its supposed validity in the opinion of people at the time, Augustus Caesar was indeed born in that very year. Herod must have felt a great deal of uneasiness when similar prognostications were being made by the Magi about a king of the Jews who had just been born.

The World of that Time Believed Astrological Signs

Herod would have been aware of the outstanding celestial displays that had occurred from May, 3 B.C. to August, 2 B.C. His own court astrologers would certainly have given him their interpretations of these remarkable signs. But Herod wanted more information. Since the various nations and racial groups had different standards for astrological interpretations, Herod would have wanted to know the Magian version of what the signs were indicating. Some astrologers were reckoned as being better than others. Among the best in the world, as viewed by people in the first century, were the professional Chaldeans and the Magi of the east. Herod wanted to know what *their* interpretations were regarding the remarkable heavenly drama that had occurred in 3 and 2 B.C. The Magi left him in no doubt about their interpretations. They were so certain of their evaluations that they made a long journey to Jerusalem to give rich gifts to the newborn king. So important was this child to them that they even came as well to give him homage. This meant that they recognized the newborn as a personage of special significance. This is what Matthew in the New Testament related.

And indeed, like the Romans sixty years before, Herod was so convinced of the interpretations of the Magi that he killed the boy babies in and around Bethlehem to prevent this newborn "king" from being reared to adulthood. Herod was astonished by the appearance of this "star" and he was persuaded that the "Star of the Magi" was significant and important.

What was this "star" that was causing the Magi, Herod and the world to be astounded? The answer to this query can now be known, and we will understand it clearly as we continue in this book.

Chapter 3   *Was the Star a Real Star?*

The language that Matthew employed to describe the Star of the Magi strongly suggests that it was an ordinary star or planet. After all, the Magi themselves were astrologers and interested in the motions of the heavenly bodies. Since the practice of astrology was profoundly respected by most people in the time of Augustus and Herod, it has convinced many scholars that the Magi were observing a real star. This is surely what the New Testament is stating.

Probably no other star in history has been sought after more than the Star of the Magi. What star could this have been? The ingenious Kepler in the early seventeenth century suggested that it might have been a conjunction of Jupiter and Saturn appearing near some other star. In the last century, Ideler found that three conjunctions of Jupiter with Saturn in the constellation of Pisces occurred in the year 7 B.C. and there was Mars coming into their vicinity in early 6 B.C. that gave a triangular positioning of the planets to one another. It was also found that a Jewish rabbi named Abarbanel, commenting on the Book of Daniel (A.D.1437-1508), said that a conjunction of Jupiter and Saturn within Pisces had messianic meaning. It was felt by several scholars in the last century that the occurrences of 7/6 B.C. were probably the ones that inspired the Magi to go to Jerusalem.

The reason Ideler picked this early year as the likely candidate is because it was beginning to be thought among historians that Jesus could not have been born *after* 4 B.C. Though some of the prime historical sources were chronologically contradictory for the period, historians were already beginning to dogmatize that Jesus had to have been born at least 4 years (or better yet, 5 or 6 years) *before* the beginning of our common era. This is why Ideler concentrated on astronomical signs before 4 B.C.

There is, however, a major difficulty with this earlier year of 7/6 B.C. It is very early for the birth of Jesus. It is almost too early if one relies on the simple New Testament chronological statements as a guide. Accepting this earlier period also casts aside virtually all the testimony of the early scholars and historians of the Christian Church who said that Jesus was born in the period of 3 to 1 B.C.[67]

The Birth of Jesus Was After 4 B.C.

This period of 3 to 1 B.C. for the dating of Jesus' birth for the early Christian historians, however, should not be jettisoned from our thinking. It is unfair and non-professional to dismiss as unworthy of consideration the vast number of these early Christian scholars who testified that Jesus was born in the period we recognize as 3 to 1 B.C. Properly, modern scholars are now beginning to recognize those early Christian scholars had far more ancient records to consult than we do today. They were able to examine the volumes in the famous Alexandrian library (reportedly having up to 700,000 volumes), the library at Pergamus with over 200,000 volumes and the library of Caesarea on the Palestinian coast with its great numbers of historical documents. To show the extent in these libraries of historical records of important individuals, we have from a reliable source that the Alexandrian library had in their catalogue of

Chapter 3 - Was the Star a Real Star?

scrolls two million lines (at 50 lines a page this would equal 40,000 of our pages) on the life of Zoroaster alone.[68] It was Zoroaster who was the early teacher of the Magi as Moses was to the Jews. This shows that an abundance of material was available for Greek speaking peoples to read about the doctrines of Zoroaster. If the records of Zoroaster's life were found in the Alexandrian library in such quantity, what about the accounts of the other individuals who were important in the Roman Empire? There must have been vast numbers of other historical works that would have described events in Palestine and Rome within those early libraries.

This does not end the matter. Besides those libraries in the east, there were the official records at Rome, the capital of the empire itself. Records were kept at the capital like those in our Library of Congress. Those records would have been available to Christian scholars, especially after the time of Constantine. And besides government record-keeping, there were at least twenty-six other libraries in Rome that were associated with certain institutions at the capital whose scrolls could also have been examined by early Christian scholars.[69] There can be no doubt that those scholars had access to much of this literary evidence to study and to evaluate in making their historical judgments. But what do we have left of them? Only rags and tatters have come down to us.

Early Christian Historians Had Many Historical Sources Not Known to Us

Let us be plain about the early historical records which concern the time of Jesus' birth. There is not a *single one* of the Christian scholars (who was able to do research at the above libraries) who has stated that 7, 6 or even 5 B.C. was the time for Jesus' birth. Everyone of them is at odds with modern historical opinion on this particular subject. Most of the early scholars focused on the year from 3 to 2 B.C. and Dionysius Exiguus in the sixth century finally accepted a late 1 B.C. for Jesus' birth.

35

It is truly a disservice of the highest rank that no serious attention is being given to the historical beliefs of these early Christian scholars. Their historical evaluations given when Rome and the empire had functioning libraries have been dismissed out of hand and without the slightest consideration by many modern scholars. This is not only unfair, it is absurd. Forgive me for being blunt, but it is time to demand the reversal of this procedure. It is not that I want my opinion to prevail at the expense of all other historical evaluations, but it is only reasonable that all the ancient authorities be given a fair hearing in this important chronological and historical matter.

The Apathy of Modern Theologians

But what is the state of affairs today? So engraven in stone is the opinion that one has to look *before* 4 B.C. for the birth of Jesus and the celestial events that brought the Magi to Jerusalem, that few theologians have felt it is necessary to convene a forum of competent scholars even to discuss the issue. The present opinions are considered by many church leaders to be infallible. And why are some theologians so adamant today in advocating a period *before* 4 B.C.? It is because of a single section of an account by Josephus the Jewish historian which has been misinterpreted and misunderstood concerning the time of Herod's death. I will discuss this matter in a later chapter and show the simple answer to the problem.

The truth is, however, the years of 3 to 2 B.C. have far more historical credentials and spectacular astronomical displays than any immediate period before 4 B.C. When we focus on these two years, then the evidence that the Star of the Magi was a real star is overwhelming. Other years around the beginning of our era pale into insignificance compared to 3 to 2 B.C. The description of Matthew about the star does not at all fit what happened in 7 or 6 B.C. Jupiter and Saturn in their three conjunctions at that time were at least two diameters of the Moon away from each other. No one could possibly imagine them as being a single "star." As a matter of fact, there

Chapter 3 - Was the Star a Real Star?

was a similar conjunction of Jupiter and Saturn in Pisces which occurred 59 years before and it was even a closer one. If such a conjunction had messianic overtones to it from an astrological point of view, why didn't that occurrence also bring Magi to Jerusalem?

Even Abarbanel's astrological interpretation given in the fifteenth century has problems. Though the rabbi may well have been relating a general belief among Jews in his own time about the messianic significance of Jupiter and Saturn in Pisces, there is no early literature of the Jews or Gentiles that they would have interpreted it that way some 1500 years before. Indeed, there are so many uncertainties of interpretation connected with the astronomical events in 7 and 6 B.C. that even scholars today (probably most) hold little confidence that any of those celestial phenomena are the ones to which Matthew refers even though they continue to dogmatize that Jesus was born *before* 4 B.C.[70]

What Does the Bible Mean?

These difficulties have prompted scholars to offer other explanations. Some have suggested the Bible is possibly talking about a comet that cannot now be identified. This proposal is unlikely because comets were almost always interpreted as being harbingers of evil, not of good omen as the star of the Magi surely suggested. Others have thought it might be an exploding star—a nova. This theory is completely unprovable and most scholars reject the idea. After all, how can a comet or a nova "lead" Magi to Jerusalem and "stand over" Bethlehem as Matthew said the star did?

Some religious people have wanted to dismiss the account of Matthew as referring to any "star" in heaven. They believe Matthew was talking about the actions of an angel. Others say it was an outright miracle that is impossible to explain by natural laws. Of course, if Matthew were describing the actions of an angel or simply recording the results of a supernatural event, then further astronomical or historical inquiry is useless. This is the opinion that

The Star that Astonished the World

some religious folk wish to adopt. Some religious people feel afraid to look at any explanation that might be astronomical (which they often interpret to mean as "astrological"). They prefer outright miracles to anything that might be considered as natural.

Are Supernatural Explanations Correct?

The supernatural interpretations that some propose are not necessary. Such evaluations run counter to the simple descriptions given in the Gospel of Matthew. Let us recall Matthew's account in which he used words denoting astronomical terms as ordinarily understood by Greek speaking people in the first century. He said the Magi saw "his star" *rising* in the east. Would the Magi have seen an angel or some miraculous sign *rise* above the eastern horizon? This belief is hardly suitable. After all, the Magi were themselves astrologers. They were looking for celestial signs involving the Sun, Moon, planets and the stars of heaven, not miraculous events. Had the latter been the case, they simply would have told Herod that they had seen an angel or a miraculous display in the heavens and that would have been the end of the matter.

There is another problem in evaluating the star as an angel. This belief is not compatible with the narrative of Matthew and Luke. It was the custom of Matthew to state when an angel was involved in an event associated with Jesus' nativity (Matthew 1:20) or when a vision or dream was given by an angel (2:13). The same was the case with Luke. He even named the angel who gave the announcement to Mary. He called him the angel Gabriel[71] and Luke certainly did not think of Gabriel as a "star." Luke recorded that many angels were seen by the shepherds who were minding their flocks near Bethlehem. And again, he did not describe them as being "stars."

Only in highly figurative (or prophetic/poetic) language in the Bible are angels equated with stars.[72] Matthew was not giving this type of narration in his Gospel account. The terms he used to

Chapter 3 - Was the Star a Real Star?

describe the "star" were the ones that the general population used to denote ordinary "stars" or "planets" without any reference to supernatural angelic appearances.

A Supernatural Appearance?

There is yet another miraculous explanation that has been suggested for the Star of the Magi. Some theologians have imagined that the Magi simply observed an appearance of the Shekinah (the glory of God) like that which led Moses and the children of Israel out of Egypt. This was a shining light during darkness and a cloud by day.[73] Yet when the Bible mentions such visible glory, it was seen by all people in sight of it.[74] Had the Magi observed such a miraculous light, biblical examples show that others in their vicinity would also have seen it. Josephus, the Jewish historian, reported such an appearance of light over the temple just before the Passover season of A.D.66 which the people of Jerusalem observed.[75] But there is no example in the Bible or history that the Shekinah was ever seen *rising* above the eastern horizon like the Star of the Magi appeared.

Granted, some people for sentimental reasons (or to maintain private theological doctrines) wish that the "star" of Matthew could be an angel or a miraculous light in the sky. They refuse to believe that Matthew was referring to an actual "star." It is their privilege to believe such things if they wish, but the evidence in the New Testament and history profoundly suggest that the "star" was a normal heavenly body that astrologers were interpreting as the sign that a new Jewish king had been born.

The Star Was a Real Star

The Magi were basing their decisions to go to Jerusalem on the motions of the heavenly bodies. After all, that was their primary occupation. They were professional observers and interpreters of heavenly signs involving the Sun, Moon, planets and stars. This procedure is thoroughly harmonious with the teachings of the Bible about such things. In the first chapter of Genesis it says that the stellar bodies were designed to provide "signs" to those on earth.[76] For the Magi to have seen a "star" or a "planet" rise above the eastern horizon in some significant relationship to other stellar bodies would have been thoroughly in accord with the statement in Genesis 1:14. The Jewish authorities, and even King Herod, would not have found such interpretations by the Magi as being odd or anti-biblical.

The Bible and Astronomical Occurrences

The Bible actually gives much credence to astronomical signs and Herod knew this. It records a divine revelation given to the patriarch Joseph in which the twelve tribes of Israel were compared to the twelve zodiacal signs. Joseph dreamed that the Sun represented his father, the Moon (being feminine) his mother, and his eleven brothers were the other eleven constellations of the Zodiac (Joseph himself being the twelfth). "Behold, I have dreamed a dream more: and behold the sun and the moon and the eleven stars did obeisance to me."[77]

So consistent, methodical and symbolic were those motions of the heavenly bodies that King David in Psalm 19 equated the celestial bodies with the perfection of the teachings of God. David said that all of the stars, planets, Moon and Sun spoke a "language" to all people on earth. He said there was "no speech, nor language, where *their voice* is not heard. Their line [rule or motion] is gone out through all the earth, and *their words* to the end of the world."[78] David was saying that these heavenly bodies spoke symbolic teachings to people in the world. Even the apostle Paul quoted Psalm 19 and said that the heavenly bodies symbolically spoke with *their voice* or *their words* and that their sounds were heard throughout the world. "Their [the stars] sound went into all the earth, and their [the stars] words unto the ends of the world."[79] The heavenly bodies contained much symbolic teaching as far as people in the first century were concerned.

Chapter 3 - Was the Star a Real Star?

Biblical Astronomy Had Prophetic Overtones

The Old Testament contained precedents for this belief. In the Book of Job there is recorded the words of Yahweh himself [the God of the Bible]. God said that the star cluster known as the Pleiades (the Seven Sisters) *influenced* things that were occurring on earth.[80] These "Seven Sisters" may be equated with the seven "stars" of the Book of Revelation that denoted the seven angels of the seven churches (congregations). Recall that such congregations of Christians were even called "sisters."[81]

There is much teaching in the Old and New Testaments about the "influences" of the stellar bodies with affairs occurring on earth. David particularly singled out the Sun for its symbolic role in teaching. He called it a "bridegroom" (like a newly married man with a responsibility for his wife). And who is the "bridegroom" in the New Testament? It is the Messiah.[82] His coming was prognosticated as being like the *lightning* [the Sun] that comes out of the east. "For as the lightning cometh out of the east, and shineth even unto the west, so shall the coming of the Son of man be."[83] The Messiah is thus equated in a symbolic way with the Sun. This relationship should not appear strange to biblical readers. The Old Testament itself said that Yahweh was the "Sun of righteousness."[84] It was common among the early Jews to equate the Sun with Yahweh and the New Testament writers persisted with the same theme by calling Jesus the "Bridegroom" or the "Lightning [the Sun]" which shines out of the east. These astronomical comparisons were made without the slightest condemnation by the prophets or apostles.

The Book of Revelation and Astronomical Symbols

It even goes further than that. In the Book of Revelation we find four living creatures that surround the heavenly throne (see also Ezekiel 1:4-28). Scholars recognize that the faces of these creatures (like that of a lion, an eagle, a man and a bull) denote the four main seasons of the zodiacal year. These are equated with Leo the Lion,

Scorpio (an eagle with a snake in its talons), Aquarius (a man bearing water) and Taurus the Bull.[86] The tribes of Israel were positioned the same way around the tabernacle in the wilderness.[86] Leo, representing Judah, was directly east of the entrance to the temple and it was the beginning sign for the Hebrew Zodiac. The other three principal tribes were located 90 degrees from each other in a circle around the sanctuary forming a zodiacal design.

And besides that, in another section of the Book of Revelation, the apostle John saw a sign in heaven of a woman ready to give birth to a manchild who was to rule the earth with a rod of iron.[87] This woman had the Sun clothing her and the Moon under her feet. There can be no doubt that this was an astronomical symbol showing the time of Jesus' birth.[88] When the apostle John said he saw a "sign in heaven," the word "sign" in Greek is the precise word used in ordinary Greek literature to refer to a zodiacal sign.

Jews Were Interested in Astronomical Signs

These biblical matters reveal that the New Testament writers commonly identified prophetical events on earth with symbolic comparisons found in the heavenly bodies and their motions. Jews in general were also doing the same thing in the first century. Note this comment by Professor Charlesworth concerning new discoveries that show this.

> "Jewish interest in astrology and the zodiac is at least so early as Jesus of Nazareth. This new insight is shown by the early date of the Jewish Sibylline Oracles, especially 5:512-531, and the discovery among the Dead Sea Scrolls of two Jewish astrological documents, one called 4QCryptic (formerly 4Q186) and the other still unnamed and unpublished."[89]

While this is certainly true, Jewish interpretation differed from ordinary Gentile methods in reading the signs. The Jews normally stated that God was in charge of the stellar bodies and that their influences were a manifestation of God's power (his prognostications in order to teach mankind) and not some spiritual manifesta-

Chapter 3 - Was the Star a Real Star?

tions emanating solely from the celestial bodies themselves. Charlesworth gives several examples of this early Jewish mode of interpretation.[90]

The Condemnation of Astrology

We must, however, be clear about one fact. The wild interpretations that many astrologers gave about these heavenly motions brought forth the wrath of the prophets. It was the *wrong* use of the symbolic meanings that the Bible condemns. The abuse of such things brought forth the anger of the biblical prophets. "Thou art wearied in the multitude of thy counsels. Let now the astrologers, the star-gazers, the monthly prognosticators, stand up, and save thee from these things that shall come upon thee."[91] The prophets were condemning the *misuse* of the signs that Genesis 1:14 was speaking about. The author of the Book of Jubilees (written about 150 B.C.) mentioned the same thing.[92] The prophets, however, would not have censured the symbolic "teaching" associated with the celestial signs themselves. The Bible drew attention to the heavenly signs and even forecast future ones.[93] Recall that the apostle Paul himself said the voice and sound of the stars spoke a symbolic language that glorified the role of the Messiah in world affairs.[94]

Astronomical Signs and History

The purpose of this book is not to plead for a recognition of the symbolic veracity of these various celestial signs. As a book of history, I am only showing what was believed in the world in the first century. I also wish to show what is contained in the Bible that may have prompted Herod to do what he did. There can be no doubt that Herod was deeply persuaded by what the Magi from the east told him about the "star." Since celestial signs were anticipated for the arrival of the messianic king who was to rule Israel and the world, Herod was anxious to find out what the Magi were interpreting about the heavenly signs that all were able to see from 3 to 2 B.C. Herod was well aware of what Moses had prophesied in Numbers

24:17. It was a prophecy involving a future star that was to arise in Israel.

> "There shall come a Star out of Jacob, and a Sceptre shall rise out of Israel."

While Herod must have had his own court astrologers to give him celestial interpretations concerning the biblical prophecies about that important "star," he also wanted the opinion of the respected Magi from the east who were recognized throughout the world as being top professionals in the field. Herod wanted to know *their* interpretations of what the spectacular stellar signs of 3 to 2 B.C. really entailed. Since Herod was a king, he was entitled to be initiated into the divine knowledge that the Magi were thought to have.

Astrological Interpretations Are Not Science

It must be remembered that astrological interpretations could differ widely from astrologer to astrologer. The Bible itself shows this. While the early Babylonian astrologers and soothsayers were not able to interpret the visions of Nebuchadnezzar, nor the Egyptian priests the dreams of Pharaoh, the Bible shows that Daniel and Joseph were able to do so. Daniel was even in charge of the "Magi, astrologers, Chaldeans and soothsayers" in Babylon.[95] Because the Magi who came to Herod originated in the east, Herod would have been aware of the differences in skills and interpretations of the various astrologers and he would have wanted to hear the opinions of these professionals from the east. After all, they might have had the correct evaluation from Herod's point of view.

In the practical way that Matthew described the whole affair concerning the Magi, it is evident that these Magian priests observed a *normal* heavenly body ascend above the eastern horizon. It may have been seen in some kind of unusual configuration or relationship with other celestial bodies within the two year peri-

Chapter 3 - Was the Star a Real Star?

od before they visited Herod. We now know that an 18 month period within the years 3 and 2 B.C. was an extraordinary one for visible astronomical occurrences. Nothing like it had happened for centuries. Since this is the very period when most early Christian scholars said Jesus was born and also the time remarkably in agreement with New Testament chronological indications, it would be prudent to focus our attention on this period. Some major points of significance will be in store for us when we do.

Chapter 4

THE REAL STAR OF BETHLEHEM

While the spectacular astronomical signs in the 18 months from May, 3 B.C. to December 2 B.C. would have caused wonderful interpretations by astrologers on behalf of Augustus and the Roman Empire, the Magi decided to go to Jerusalem with gifts to a newborn Jewish king. The Magi focused on Judaea (not Rome) at this crucial time in history.

Let us look at some of the astrological and biblical factors that may have brought the Magi to Jerusalem and then to Bethlehem. Since the New Testament says the Magi saw the "star" *rising* in the east, it would most naturally be called a "morning star." The Book of Revelation has Jesus saying of himself: "I am the root and offspring of David, *and the bright and morning star*."[96] The apostle Peter also mentioned that Jesus was symbolically associated with "*the day star*."[97]

The above verses refer to celestial bodies that were well known and recognized in the first century and they inspired symbolic messianic interpretation by early Christians. There were several prophecies in Isaiah which generally were interpreted as referring

Chapter 4 - The Real Star of Bethlehem

to the Messiah. One has definite astronomical overtones to it. Isaiah said: "The Gentiles shall come to thy *light*, and kings to the brightness of thy *rising*."[98] This prophecy could easily refer to the rising of some star. It would be particularly appropriate to a "morning" or "day" star. Luke, in his Gospel, referring to the celestial symbolism of Isaiah 60:3 spoke of God as being "the *daybreak* [the rising] from on high that hath visited us, to give *light* to them that sit in darkness."[99]

Astronomy and the New Testament

These references reveal that celestial bodies were symbolically important to the New Testament writers. We know that the generality of the world was then engrossed with such symbolic concepts. The *rising* of a star or planet just before sunrise was particularly significant in interpreting events relating to important people. And Luke in his Gospel refers to Jesus as a star which will bring great *light* to all the world.

With this in mind, let us recall from our first chapter that on the morning of August 12, 3 B.C. (about an hour and twenty minutes before sunrise), Jupiter rose as a morning star in conjunction with Venus. How would astrologers or Magi have interpreted such a union? Let us look at some of the generally accepted beliefs of astrologers who lived in the time of Augustus and Herod.

Jupiter was known astrologically as the Father of the Gods. The planet Jupiter symbolized this deity. And in early August, 2 B.C. Jupiter had just left its vicinity near the Sun and conjoined with Venus. This could have been an indication of a coming birth. "Jupiter often was associated with the birth of kings and therefore called the King planet."[100] And here was the King planet in conjunction with Venus. To the Chaldeans and the Magi, Venus was Ishtar, the Mother, the Goddess of Fertility. Thus Jupiter (the Father) was now in conjunction with Venus (the Mother). Could this have signified to astrologers that the birth of a new king was imminent?

The Star that Astonished the World

This conjunction could have been a favorable sign because these two planets were known by astrologers as the Greater and the Lesser Good Fortunes of all the planets. And note this: While this conjunction was occurring, the Sun (the Supreme Father), the Moon (considered a Mother), and Mercury (the Messenger of the Gods) were located in the single constellation of Leo, the Lion. Christians called Jesus "the Lion of the tribe of Judah, the Root of David."[101] These primary bodies clustering in Leo while Jupiter and Venus were now in close union may reflect biblical significance. Note Olcott's remarks about the sign of Leo:

> "The Lion was the symbol of the Tribe of Judah, and the constellation appears in the Hebrew zodiac.... The association of Leo with Judah arose from the fact that Leo was Judah's natal sign. In the Bible there are frequent allusions to this connection between Leo and the tribe of Judah. Thus we read: 'Judah is the Lion's whelp,' and again, 'The Lion of the tribe of Judah.'"[102]

The interesting astral relationships which occurred in the pre-dawn of August 12, 3 B.C. could well have signified to astrologers that some important royal event was soon to happen in the Jewish nation.

Grand Astronomical Displays

Another interesting celestial occasion occurred in the heavens twenty days later. Mercury (the Messenger of the Gods) left its position with the Sun (the Supreme Father) and positioned itself in close conjunction with Venus. This took place when the Sun had just entered the constellation of Virgo (the Virgin). Mercury (the Messenger) and Venus were then in the constellation of Leo (the Lion) and Jupiter (the King planet) was just then entering Leo. All these astral signs echo clear biblical themes. God was called "the Sun of righteousness" in Malachi 4:2, and in the New Testament he is called God the Father. Christians believed that God's son was to be born of a virgin, to be a descendent of Judah (Leo, the Lion), and destined to be introduced by a Messenger (John the Baptist).

Chapter 4 - The Real Star of Bethlehem

"As it is written in the prophets, Behold, I send my messenger before thy face, which shall prepare thy way before thee."[103]

Were these celestial relationships a signal to the Magi that some royal birth was soon to occur among the Jews? This was not all that happened in the year 3/2 B.C. Following these initial planetary conjunctions, Jupiter then moved on (as we have shown in chapter one) to unite with the star Regulus on September 14, 3 B.C. Indeed, it joined with Regulus on three different occasions within that astronomical year.

Signalling the Birth of a King

These three unions could have been of great consequence to astrologers. Regulus was known as "the King." The Romans referred to it as "Rex," which means "King" in Latin. In Arabia the star was known as the "Kingly One." The Greeks called it the "King Star." Of all the stars in the heavens, Regulus was universally associated by the ancient astrologers with the attributes of greatness and power. It is located practically on the ecliptic (the path which the Sun takes in traversing the heavens). It was thought that this position made it of special importance to the Sun. According to astrologers the Sun *ruled* the heavens. Thus, the major star closest to the ecliptic of the "*ruling*" Sun was Regulus. This close relationship to the Sun made Regulus a "royal star," the one most associated with the conception or birth of kings. It was the star denoting rulership.

With this in mind, we should recall the prophecy of Balaam recorded by Moses. He spoke about a "star" to rise in Israel that would be connected with rulership or dominion. "A *star* shall come out of Jacob and a *sceptre* [ruling rod] shall rise out of Israel."[104] The arrangement of the verses in the prophecy shows that the "star" is connected with a "sceptre." This suggests that the "star" would symbolically represent "dominion." This is made clear in the following verse of the prophecy. "Out of Jacob shall come he that shall have *dominion*."[105] This is why the "sceptre" is associated with the "star." It was the tribe of Judah (Leo, the Lion) that was prophesied to possess this sceptre in Israel. "Judah is a lion's whelp... he couched as a lion... the *sceptre* shall not depart from Judah until Shiloh come."[106] Since the Bible talks of the "star," a "sceptre," and Judah (the Lion, Leo), the only star in the heavens that fits this combination of factors mentioned by Balaam is the star Regulus (the King star).

The Use of Biblical Astronomy in Prophetic Themes

In biblical symbolism, Regulus is the Star of the Messiah. It is located directly between the feet of the Lion in the constellation of Leo. Moses even prophesied that Judah (the Lion) would have a "lawgiver from [ruling staff] *between* his feet until Shiloh come."[107] Alfred Jeremias back in 1911 showed that this prophecy referred to the star Regulus (the star of rulership).[108] This was also shown by Roger W. Sinnott in his article in *Sky and Telescope*.[109]

There can hardly be a doubt that this determination of Sinnott and Jeremias is correct. It has always been known that the major star Regulus, which was situated practically on the ecliptic of the Sun, was between the Lion's paws. Indeed, Regulus was (and still is) positioned precisely where the prophecy placed it: "between the feet" of Leo (the Lion). Note the following diagram.

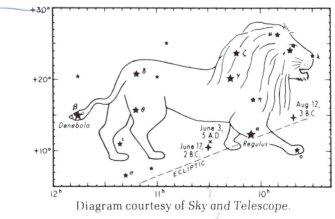

Diagram courtesy of *Sky and Telescope*.

Chapter 4 - The Real Star of Bethlehem

Leo was the constellation assigned to Judah. When it is realized that Regulus was recognized by the early Jews as the Star of the Messiah, we can then symbolically apply some significant astronomical occurrences in the year 3 to 2 B.C. that involved Regulus and the planet Jupiter.

The King Planet and the King Star

Let us now look at the interesting heavenly relationships that developed between Jupiter (the King planet) and Regulus (the King star) in the year 3/2 B.C. There were three conjunctions in which both heavenly bodies seemed to be centering on each other (over an eight month period). It was as if Jupiter were homing in on Regulus, using it as an axis and directing earthly attention to it. This could have easily signified to astrologers that some royal event was to occur. While the Magi must have considered all three as having real importance, note especially the first of the three conjunctions of Jupiter and Regulus on September 14, 3 B.C.

Here was Jupiter (the King planet), which had just united with Venus (the Mother) on August 12, 3 B.C., now joining itself with the King star Regulus (the star of the Jewish Messiah) in the zodiacal sign of Leo (the constellation of Judah), while the Sun (the Supreme Father or Ruler) was then located in Virgo (the Virgin). All of these features are reminiscent of biblical themes associated with the birth and personage of the Jewish Messiah. Recall that the Messiah was prophesied to be born of a virgin and to be the king of Judah. King Herod must have wondered about this initial display of Jupiter with Regulus.

Then note what happened. The second conjunction of Jupiter and Regulus occurred on February 17, 2 B.C. Amazingly, the Moon came to be positioned at that exact time between Jupiter and Regulus. At about 5 a.m., looking at the western horizon, an observer would have seen the Moon directly between Jupiter and Regulus. The Moon would have been occulting (covering up) the star Regulus with the lower fifth of the Moon's diameter. Then, on May 8/9, 2 B.C. (82 days later) the same conjunction occurred again. This time, however, the Moon occulted Regulus by the top one fifth of its diameter. The last conjunction would not have been seen in Palestine since the Moon was already below the horizon in the west, yet astronomers such as the Magi would have known what was happening.

These three conjunctions of Jupiter with Regulus would have shown Jupiter making a type of "crowning effect" over the star Regulus. It was like the King planet was placing a "crown" (like a circular diadem) over the King star (the Star of the Messiah). And importantly, all of this occurred within the constellation of Leo (the Lion), the zodiacal sign of Judah.

More Spectacular Signs

These were not all the signs of 3/2 B.C. After the planet's three separate conjunctions with Regulus, Jupiter then continued its westward journey (as observers would have viewed it on earth). On June 17, 2 B.C., it had its spectacularly rare reunion with Venus which we mentioned in the first chapter. The two planets were then a mere .01 degree from one another and they would have appeared to people on earth like a single "double-star" which only the sharpest eyes would have been able to separate. Let us see what this may have meant to the Magi.

Venus (now in its double role as a Mother because the planet was now an evening star) had just extended itself as far east as possible to encounter Jupiter (the King planet) which was moving west in a direct path to meet her. What occurred was a splendid planetary conjunction visible west of Babylon. Besides that, this beautiful conjunction again happened while the planets were in the constellation of Leo (Judah) and at the exact time of the Full Moon. So close were the two planets that they would have appeared very much like one gigantic star in a "marriage union" with each other.

Chapter 4 - The Real Star of Bethlehem

Furthermore, the Magi (who would have been in Mesopotamia) would have witnessed this planetary union appearing on the western horizon *precisely in the direction of Judaea*. This celestial occurrence prompted Isaac Asimov to ask the question: "Is the fact that the unusual 'star' was seen in the direction of Judaea enough to make them think of a Messiah?"[110]

This heavenly scene could well have produced an interest in the Magi to look toward Jerusalem and *not* to the celebrations in Rome for the arrival of the messianic king of the world. It could have been interpreted that these two planets, which introduced the prophesied king in their symbolic way when they were both morning stars some ten months before, were now completing their introduction with an impressively rare evening star union.

What a beautiful display this last rendezvous would have made in the early evening sky west of Babylon. But about an hour later, the planets would have appeared even closer to observers in Palestine. There had been nothing like this brilliant conjunction for centuries nor would there be again for many generations. While the earlier conjunction of Jupiter and Venus on August 12, 3 B.C. occurred in the closing degrees of the constellation of Cancer, this reunion some ten months later took place just beyond the zero line for astrological reckoning in the constellation of Leo the Lion.[111] It could well have symbolized to the Magi the *closing* of one era, and the beginning of another.

The Impressive Signs of 3/2 B.C.

The astronomical displays were not over for that significant year. On August 27, 2 B.C. (72 days after the spectacular Jupiter/Venus reunion), there occurred the extremely close conjunction of Jupiter with Mars (the planet of war), while Venus and Mercury homed in on them in an unusual massing of four planets. Jupiter was located at 142.6 degrees; Mars 142.64; Venus 141.67; and Mercury 143.71. Such closeness in the pre-dawn skies would have given astrologers much to talk about, especially when the other events of the year were connected with it.

Look at this massing of the planets. All the primary planets (except Saturn) were now clustering near one another in the constellation of Leo (Judah), while the Moon was just then entering Leo. The Sun, however, *at that very time* was entering the sign of Virgo (the Virgin). These indications once again could show remarkable prophetic themes mentioned in the Bible that people were looking for at the time.

What might this massing of the planets have meant to the Magi? Since Jupiter, Mars, Venus and Mercury had just become new morning stars, it could well have signified that war (Mars was involved) would break out on the earth just before the dawning of the new day which the planetary signs were supposedly introducing.[112] The world was then looking for a new Golden Age to emerge. The messianic teachings of the Old Testament showed that the new age would be introduced by a war to end all wars. Perhaps astrologers interpreted that it was the king of the tribe of Judah who would bring in the new age. The Roman poet Virgil, a few years before in his *Fourth Eclogue*, had given a prophetic teaching that such a Golden Age was destined to come to earth.

One thing is certain. The year 3/2 B.C. was replete with visible astronomical events. Since Genesis 1:14 says that the heavenly bodies were accounted for signs, perhaps these unusual relationships were interpreted by the Magi as indicating the birth of the Jewish Messiah into the world.

The Outcome of these Astronomical Signs

Let us now look at some interesting biblical teaching which could suggest that what I am saying is true. It has long been recognized that the Magi arrived in Jerusalem some time after Jesus was born.[113] He had already been circumcised and presented in the temple forty days after birth.[114] When the Magi arrived, the parents of

Jesus were then living in a house (not a stable).[115] Jesus was also being called a *paidion* [ordinarily, child or toddler], not a *brephos* [infant]. One cannot press the meaning of these two terms too far, but there were ordinary differences between them that most contexts would acknowledge as showing distinction. After the Magi presented their gifts, they returned home by a different route. In response to this subterfuge, Herod slew the male children in and around Bethlehem who were two years of age and younger.[116]

Since it was often difficult for astrologers to interpret whether heavenly signs were indicating events associated with conception or birth, Herod no doubt maneuvered his strategy against the newborn child by taking both possibilities into account. He killed the children up to two years of age so he could include those both conceived and born within that period. Whatever the case, all these indications show that the Magi must have arrived in Bethlehem to present their gifts several months after the birth of Jesus.

This leads us to the final suggestion that could help us identify the "Star of Bethlehem." The stellar body that played the most prominent role in the extraordinary year of 3/2 B.C. and the planet which figured in almost every celestial relationship was Jupiter. It could well be that Jupiter was "his star" that the Magi followed to Jerusalem, and finally to Bethlehem.

The Proper Star of Bethlehem

Let us observe some factors that could go a long way in showing this. Recall that the account in the New Testament said the Magian astrologers saw the star *rising* above the eastern horizon. And in August 12, 3 B.C., Jupiter rose as a morning star which soon came into conjunction with Venus. That started Jupiter off on a journey in which six conjunctions with other planets and the star Regulus took place. The final planetary union was the massing of the planets which occurred with Mars, Venus and Mercury on August 27, 2 B.C.

The Star that Astonished the World

But there was one more spectacular astronomical display that involved the planet Jupiter at the end of 2 B.C. The planet soon left its "massing" with the other three planets and continued in its apparent motion westward each morning as viewed by the Magi at their regular pre-dawn observations. If the Magi began their own journey toward Jerusalem near this time, this apparent westward motion of Jupiter each day could have indicated to the Magi to proceed in the same westward direction toward Jerusalem. They could have been "following" Jupiter in the example it was setting. The Bible says the star "went ahead of them."[117] The text could well mean that the Magi let Jupiter lead them in this symbolic fashion. I will give more on this in a moment.

Then note what took place. Upon reaching Jerusalem the Magi were told to look toward Bethlehem for the newborn king. This happened when the New Testament says the "star" came to a *definite* halt in the heavens.[118] It stopped its motion of leading the Magi and "stood over where the young child was."[119] In a word, the celestial body became stationary.

Let us now note one point carefully. The text does NOT say the star stood over the house. Some have imagined that this is what Matthew meant. This assumption is totally unwarranted. Such presumption is reading into the text what is not there. What the New Testament states is that the star became *stationary*. But who ever heard of a star becoming *stationary* in the heavens?

The Star Stood Still

It is this description of the star standing still that has caused many interpreters to characterize the whole episode in Matthew as either fictitious or a miraculous event. Most people find it difficult to imagine a normal heavenly body having the capability of stopping its movement over a small village in Palestine. At first thought, a person might agree that such a thing appears impossible. But maybe the account is not as ridiculous as it may seem. In truth,

… there is not the slightest difficulty for such a thing to happen.

The truth is, Matthew was simply describing a celestial phenomenon in popular language that all astronomers and persons acquainted with basic planetary motions would have been fully aware. Planets do come to a "stop" at prescribed times in their heavenly motions. This happens at the time for a planet's retrogression and progression. It may be that Matthew was simply showing that Jupiter had become *stationary* in its motions through the fixed stars at the time it reached its zenith over Bethlehem.

The theologian F. Steinmetzer, back in 1912, wrote an article stating his belief that Matthew was referring to one of these normal "stationary" positions of the planets.[120] Indeed, Steinmetzer suggested that the planet that suited Matthew's account the best was Jupiter. This is true.

Jupiter Does Stop in the Heavens

How is it that Jupiter can come to a stopped position in the heavens? Look at the diagram on page 58. Jupiter becomes "stationary" at its times for retrogression and progression. When we look at Jupiter we see the planet normally moving eastward each evening through the fixed stars. This apparent movement is called "proper motion." The earth, however, is moving in its orbit around the Sun faster than that of Jupiter. When the earth reaches point *A*, an observer would see Jupiter nearly along the same line as the earth's own orbital movement. When the earth is traveling more or less in a direct line toward Jupiter, the planet will continue to show "proper motion." But when earth reaches position *B*, it is no longer heading toward Jupiter. The faster velocity of the earth as it makes its turn to *B* and beyond, causes the apparent motion of Jupiter to slow down. This continues until the earth reaches *C*. At that point the speed of the earth in relation to Jupiter is the same as Jupiter's. That is when Jupiter appears to become stationary within the background of the fixed stars. As the earth progresses from *C* to *D*, it has greater relative speed than Jupiter and this causes Jupiter to retrogress. The planet reverses its motion and travels westward through the stars. At *D*, however, the speed of the earth and Jupiter are again matched (relative to each other) and Jupiter stops its reverse motion. When *D* is passed, Jupiter returns to "proper motion." This is what happened when Jupiter came in contact with the star Regulus on three different occasions in the late part of 3 and the early part of 2 B.C. The diagram below shows how this occurs.

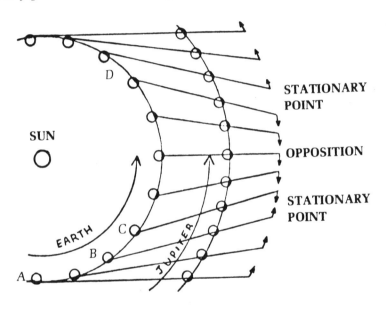

Let us now look at what happened at the end of 2 B.C. Jupiter arrived at its ordinary time for retrogression and it became *stationary* among the stars. But this time something unusual happened. In 2 B.C. as viewed from Jerusalem, Jupiter came to its normal *stationary* position directly over Bethlehem on December 25th. That's right! Just before dawn (the regular time the Magi would have begun their normal observations of the heavens), Jupiter came to a "stopped" position on December 25th directly over Bethlehem as witnessed from Jerusalem. Not only that, the planet assumed its *stationary* position while in the middle of the constellation of Virgo, *the Virgin*. What a remarkable circumstance this was.

Jupiter Stopped Within the Sign of Virgo the Virgin

We are told in the New Testament that Jesus was born of a virgin. And precisely on December 25, 2 B.C., Jupiter "stopped" in the abdomen region of Virgo, *the Virgin* (in the middle of the constellation). This position was right where a woman carries a child in pregnancy. On that day the "King planet" stopped its lateral motion through the stars and remained *stationary* for about six days. During those days it did not move longitudinally more than one fortieth of the Moon's diameter from its December 25th position. To an observer on earth it appeared completely *stationary* in the midst of Virgo. This would have appeared significant to astrologers. They looked on the Winter Solstice period as the beginning of the new Sun. This period signified to many Gentile astrologers as the time for showing the birth of the Sun. It was celebrated in most areas of the world as the nativity of the "Ruler" of the heavens. And the "King planet" (Jupiter) was now *stationary* in the central region of Virgo, *the Virgin*.

Be this as it may, how was it possible for Jupiter to be stationary over the *village* of Bethlehem at that time? There is not the slightest problem for it to do so. The Bible says the Magi saw the star come to a stop while they were in Jerusalem. And on December 25, 2 B.C., at the ordinary time for the Magi's pre-dawn observations, Jupiter would have been seen in meridian position (directly over Bethlehem) at an elevation of 68 degrees above the southern horizon. This precise position would show the planet shining directly down on Bethlehem while it was stationary among the stars. What a remarkable coincidence this was. And though this period has nothing to do with the actual birth of Jesus, as we will show later in this book, it may have been the time when the Magi presented their gifts to Jesus. This could be a reason why people in the later Christian Church said that December 25 was a day associated with

The Star that Astonished the World

the Magi presenting their costly and royal gifts to the newborn Jesus.

The Star Led the Magi to Jesus

While all this is true, there is nevertheless a problem to reckon with. Matthew said the star *"went before them."* Since the Magi were then in Jerusalem when this was stated, and because Bethlehem is located five miles south, how could Jupiter (or any planet or star) appear to move from north to south leading the Magi to Bethlehem? Does this mean that the whole story must be reckoned as fictitious or miraculous after all? Not really. A careful reading of Matthew may make the matter clear. Weymouth translates the passage: "The star they had seen *when it rose* **led them** on until it reached and stood over the place where the babe was" (emphasis mine).

This verse has interesting and revealing information in it when read closely. It helps to show that the Magi had been following the star from the time it rose which they saw at their homes in the east, and they continued to follow it until they reached Jerusalem. The church father Chrysostom also understood Matthew in the same way. "For on their way as far as Palestine it [the star] appeared leading them, but after they set foot within Jerusalem, it hid itself: then again, when they left Herod, having told him on what account they came, and were on the point of departing, it showed itself again."[121]

There are other indications in the text of Matthew which show this may be the intended meaning. One should look very carefully at the text because it has some interesting points associated with it. In regard to this, the authors of *The Expositor's Greek Testament* ask the question: "Is the meaning that they had seen the star only at its rising, finding their way to Jerusalem without its guidance, and that again it appeared leading them to Bethlehem? Against this is verse 7, which implies *continuous* visibility.... It was their celestial guide appearing again [after they left Herod]: *it kept going before them* [imperfect] all the way till, arriving at Bethlehem, it took up its position right over the spot where the child was [comments in brackets mine]."[122]

The use of the imperfect tense in verse 9 shows that the star was constantly leading them, while verse 7 suggests it was a *continually appearing* star. The star seems temporarily to have been obscured while the Magi visited Herod at his palace (clouds may have then covered it or it may have been below the horizon when they visited the king). Upon leaving the palace, however, they once again saw their celestial guide. It had led them westward to Jerusalem, but now it came to be in a meridian position over Bethlehem. It was *stationary* among the stars and shining down directly over Bethlehem as viewed from Jerusalem on December 25th. It was now pointing out the exact geographical location of the newborn king.

Jupiter and the Solstice of 2 B.C.

Interestingly, while Jupiter was in its "standing still" position over Bethlehem, the Sun was also "standing still." All know that December 25 is in the usual period of the Winter Solstice. The word "*solstice*" means "Sun stands still." These stationary coincidences of Jupiter and the Sun are quite related, and would surely have appeared significant to astrologers at the time. Cumont has the following evaluation:

> "General observance required that on the 25th of December the birth of the 'new Sun' should be celebrated, when after the winter solstice, the days began to lengthen and the invincible star triumphed again over darkness."[123]

Recall that even Luke said at the beginning of his Gospel that "the *dayspring* from on high hath visited us, *to give light to them that sit in darkness.*"[124] The Magi, being astrologers, would no doubt have wanted to give gifts to the "newborn Sun," and in Malachi the God of Israel is called "the *Sun* of Righteousness."[125]

They would have supposed that the child in their midst was the one destined to usher in the new Golden Age that most were then expecting.

Professor Eliade, whom many consider to have been the foremost authority on the past and present religious customs of people, has shown that the ancients looked on the dawning of each New Year (the Solstice period) as symbolic of the inauguration of a new age.[126] The Magi would have been aware of these well-known beliefs. Here they were, after making their long journey with expensive gifts to give to the newborn king, now discovering from their point of view that the Sun (the Supreme Father) was "standing still" in the heavens while Jupiter (the King planet) was also "standing still." These features could perfectly fit Matthew's account.

The Interpretation of the Magi

Thus, the Magi being Gentiles would have approached this astronomical relationship from their own religious point of view. Almost all non-Jewish societies placed great emphasis on the occasion of the re-birth of the "Sun God" at each Winter Solstice and they had many religious celebrations to accompany it. Jews, however, would not have viewed this season of the year in that fashion. Most Jews at the time abhorred these Gentile religious festivals at the Winter Solstice or any other seasons of the year. They could point to the prophet Jeremiah who commanded the Jews never to adhere to Gentile religious customs involving the various solstice or equinox seasons of the year.[127] The Jews considered these to be Gentile practices.

The Jews in Jerusalem would have looked on these astronomical signs in 3/2 B.C. very differently. In fact, December 25th in 2 B.C. was not a time of solstice celebrations to the Jews. Remarkably, however, it was a period for great festivity throughout the whole of the Jewish nation. It happened to be the precise time

Chapter 4 - The Real Star of Bethlehem

for their feast of Hanukkah (sometimes spelled Chanukkah). This was a feast of the Jews held near the beginning of winter and it is mentioned in the New Testament as "the Feast of Dedication."[128] The start of the eight days celebration can sometimes occur as early as November 28th or as late as December 27th on our solar calendar. The Jewish months can vary at times as much as a month out of phase with the solar calendar that we use today. But in the year 2 B.C., it is evident that Hanukkah began on December 23rd. The Magi would have given their gifts to the newborn babe on the third day of the Jewish festival. This would have been an interesting and symbolic time to present their gifts to whom they considered to be the messianic king that the Jewish nation was then expecting to appear. This was because Hanukkah was a time for gift giving.

The Magi and the Jewish Feast of Hanukkah

This feast of Hanukkah was not ordained in the Old Testament but it was held in high esteem by all Jews. It took on a secular and religious importance that was second only to the Passover season.[129] It commemorated the time in 164 B.C. when the temple had been cleansed of Gentile idols placed there by Antiochus Epiphanes. The temple had been desolate of its holiness for three years, but in the Jewish month of Kislev, on the 25th day of the month, the temple services were once again established by the Maccabees. That particular day and the seven days that followed were reckoned as days of celebration for the Jewish triumph over what they considered to be paganism and heathen idolatry. The Jewish symbolism associated with these days is the very antithesis of what the Gentile nations were emphasizing at their Winter Solstice celebrations, which probably included the symbolic beliefs that the Magi themselves adhered to in their role as priests.

Hanukkah was considered a festival of Dedication (or rather, of Re-dedication) of the temple and Jewish people to the God of Abraham and Moses. For this reason it became known as a "festival of renewal." From the middle of the second century B.C.

63

onward, the Jews regularly assembled each year at that time in the temple or their synagogues. They carried branches of trees and palms in their hands, singing psalms to God for the great salvation which they considered they had been given.[130] They looked on Hanukkah as a second feast of Tabernacles which symbolized the redemption of the Jews and the entire world to God. No fast or mourning because of any calamity or bereavement was permitted to be initiated during those eight days. It was a time of festivity and celebration. The temple, synagogues and all houses in the nation were lighted both within and without by many lamps and torches during the whole period. Josephus, for this reason, called the festival "the Feast of Lamps."

The Whole Jewish Nation Was in Celebration

The Magi would then have witnessed the entire Jewish nation in a holiday spirit. As though they were taking part in the celebrations, these eastern priests would have given their gifts to the young child [or toddler] in Bethlehem on the third day of this Jewish festival. This was a time when the Jewish people were in a happy mood with the whole landscape around Jerusalem and Bethlehem being illuminated with an abundance of lights. Interestingly, it was this precise period when it was customary for the Jewish people to give gifts to their children.[131] From the Jewish point of view, there would have been no better time for the Magi to present their gifts to a Jewish child than at this period of Hanukkah. This was the traditional time for "gift-giving."

The Jews, however, would not have been honoring the season as devoted to the renewal of the Sun God. It would have been just the opposite for them. To the Jews it was their time to celebrate their triumph over the idolatry of the Gentiles and the renewal of their lives to the God of Abraham and Moses. It is interesting that a permanent removal of idolatry from the world was prophesied in the Old Testament to take place at the advent of the Messiah. The dedication of the Messiah to the world at the "Feast of Dedication"

Chapter 4 - The Real Star of Bethlehem

may well have seemed an appropriate time for such a messianic christening to the Jews in the first century.

There can be little doubt that the symbolic emphasis of the Jews regarding these astronomical and calendar matters in 3/2 B.C. would have been far different from those of the Magi who were Gentile priests. Though this is true, it must be understood that the Jews would have been impressed as were the Gentiles at what was happening in the heavens in that spectacular astronomical year. They were well aware of the positive statement in Genesis 1:14 about the legitimacy of heavenly signs. We now know by recent literary discoveries that the Jews in the first century were very concerned with interpretations involving the motions of the celestial bodies. It is certain that many Jews would have been looking for heavenly signs that would have introduced the Messiah that they were then expecting to appear on earth.

The Magi Gave their Gifts at Hanukkah

What we find in this unique calendar circumstance is that the Jews were seeing Jesus as the Messiah by having the Magi give their gifts in the midst of their celebration of Hanukkah, while the heathen peoples in the world were seeing the Magi represent them at the time of their Winter Solstice celebrations. It is interesting that these festival occasions occurred in combination to one another in that year. Jewish and pagan celebrations combined for that year.

Of course, the astrological interpretations made in this book may or may not be in conformity with those of the Magi. Only the Magi themselves can best answer what prompted them to go to Jerusalem. The Jews observing the Magi giving their gifts to the child at Bethlehem may have (or may not have) interpreted any symbolic associations in a messianic sense by the Magi's action, even though the event happened in the midst of Hanukkah. Let's face it, none of us was there at the time to justify dogmatism on these matters. Astrological interpretation is a very subjective art and even the astrologers today are not sure how the ancients viewed all the the astronomical signs. Regardless of these uncertainties, the celestial phenomena of the year 3/2 B.C. did in fact take place.

Major Conjunctions
3 and 2 B.C.

Date	Time	Objects	Separation
19 May, 3 B.C.	22:47	Mercury-Saturn	0.67° = 40'
12 June, 3 B.C.	16:06	Venus-Saturn	0.12° = 7'
12 Aug., 3 B.C.	5:20	Venus-Jupiter	0.07° = 4.3'
31 Aug., 3 B.C.	21:03	Mercury-Venus	0.36° = 22'
14 Sep., 3 B.C.	5:05	Jupiter-Regulus	0.33° = 20'
17 Feb., 2 B.C.	15:15	Jupiter-Regulus	0.85° = 51'
8 May, 2 B.C.	16:10	Jupiter-Regulus	0.72° = 43'
17 June, 2 B.C.	17:53	Jupiter-Venus	0.01° = 0.5'
26 Aug., 2 B.C.	15:15	Mars-Jupiter	0.10° = 7'

Dates and times are expressed in Universal Time. Add $2^h 58^m$ to convert to Babylon local time. The northernmost planet is listed first. Angular separations are expressed in degrees and arcminutes (1 arcminute equals 1/60th of a degree). The resolving power of the human eye is about 3 arcminutes. I calculated the conjunctions in this booklet using Bretagnon and Simon's *Planetary Programs and Tables from -4000 to +2800* along with a program for Apple II computers (written by Peter Scott for the Griffith Observatory) that calculates angular separations and times of closest approach from a list of positions. Roger Sinnott of *Sky and Telescope* made more elaborate calculations for the June 17 event and found that, at their closest at 8:51 p.m. Babylon time, the two planets were 15° above the western horizon. Using the *Long Ephemeris Tape*, the most accurate ephemeris available, DeYoung and Hilton at the U. S. Naval Observatory found that the centers of the two planets came to within 25 arcseconds of each other as seen from the center of the earth. The major uncertainty in the Jupiter-Regulus conjunctions is in the position of Regulus in 3-2 B.C. Errors in the proper motion of Regulus could shift its position by as much as 1/8th degree and the times of the corresponding conjunctions by up to a day.

Used with permission of Griffith Observatory

Chapter 5

THE TIME OF JESUS' BIRTH

The suggestion was made in the last chapter that the Magi presented their gifts to Jesus on December 25, 2 B.C. This was not, however, the time of his birth. When the Magi arrived, Joseph and Mary were no longer with Jesus in a stable. They were now residing in a house (Matthew 2:11). Jesus had been circumcised (Luke 2:21) and dedicated at the temple some forty days after his birth (Luke 2:22-24). He was then being called a *paidion* (toddler) and no longer a *brephos* (infant). When the Magi arrived, Jesus was already walking and was able to speak a few words as most normal children would be able to do when several months old. Soon after the Magi left, Herod killed the male children in and around Bethlehem who were two years of age or younger (Matthew 2:16). This does not mean Jesus was exactly two years old at the time. The fact that all children two years and under were slain shows that Herod was taking every possible interpretation of the Magi into account for the time of Jesus' birth.

Since it was not clear in astrological interpretation whether the appearance of a star or planet signified the conception or the birth

The Star that Astonished the World

of a baby, Herod decided to kill the children born within a two year period in order to cover both possibilities. When all these evidences are considered, it shows that Jesus was certainly a few months old when the Magi presented their gifts.

There is biblical information which could go a long way in helping us understand the general time period for Jesus' birth. Luke gave more chronological data regarding the birth and ministry of Jesus than any other biblical writer. In doing this, Luke began his story with John the Baptist. He gave some chronological indications as to the time of John's conception and birth. Though his statements are general ones, they are plain enough to indicate the approximate time of John's birth, and consequently that of Jesus himself. This chronological information is found in Luke's first chapter.

Note what Luke said. "There was in the days of Herod, the king of Judaea, a certain priest named Zechariah, of the course Abijah and his wife was of the daughters of Aaron, and her name was Elizabeth" (Luke 1:5).

This verse tells us something about the parents of John the Baptist. Zechariah was a priest whose duty it was, on certain occasions, to offer the national sacrifices in the temple at Jerusalem. While he was accomplishing his assigned requirements, Luke said an angel came to him and told him that his wife Elizabeth was going to bear a child. Zechariah could hardly believe what he was told because Elizabeth was beyond the age of childbearing. The angel understood his reason for disbelief, so Zechariah was struck dumb to prove the certainty of what was prophesied. When Zechariah came out of the inner temple, the people perceived that he had seen a vision and were amazed that he was unable to speak. They realized that something significant had been pointed out to Zechariah.

Luke tells us that all this happened while Zechariah "executed the priest's office before God in the order of his course" (Luke 1:8).

Chapter 5 - The Time of Jesus' Birth

He was performing his priestly duties "according to the custom of the priest's office" (Luke 1:9). Zechariah's course was that of Abijah (KJV: *Abia*) (Luke 1:5). What was this course, and when did it serve?

The Twenty-Four Priestly Courses

There were twenty-four priestly courses that administered the services in the temple. These are enumerated in First Chronicles 24. Each course had a title associated with it. These were the names of the leaders who headed each course in the time of David. Samuel and David were the persons responsible for establishing the twenty-four courses of priests (I Chronicles 9:22). Originally, in the time of Moses, the priesthood was confined only to Aaron and his immediate sons. But by the time of Samuel and David, that family had grown to such proportions that they could not all officiate together at one time in the temple. That is why Samuel and David divided the priests into twenty-four separate groups—which were called "orders" or "courses." The course in which Zechariah served was the eighth—that of Abijah (I Chronicles 24:10). Josephus, the Jewish historian, was also a priest and he mentioned that he was a member of the first course called that of Jehoiarib.[132]

The original twenty-four priestly families established by David performed their services in the temple until the sanctuary was destroyed by the Babylonians in the sixth century B.C. When the Jews returned to Palestine, they rebuilt the temple, but they discovered that representatives of only four courses of the original twenty-four were still accounted for (Ezra 2:36-39). Something had to be done to restore the twenty-four courses to their ordained service in the temple as commanded by David. Under the authority of Ezra, the remaining four were divided back into the former number. Thus, a new set of twenty-four courses commenced their administrations in the temple. And though these family courses were different from the ones established by David, it was decided that each course was to retain the name of the family which headed each course back in David's time. The re-establishment of these twenty-four courses was accepted as proper by the New Testament authorities, because John the Baptist's father was reckoned to be of this *new* arrangement. The twenty-four elders mentioned in the Book of Revelation also reflected this *new* arrangement.

The Twenty-Four Courses Were Calendar Indications

These twenty-four courses were ordered by Samuel and David (and later by Ezra the priest) to serve once a week in the temple services at two different times each year. The first family of priests commenced their administrations at noon on a Sabbath (Saturday) and they were relieved of duty the following Sabbath at noon. The Bible said they "were to come in on the sabbath," and to serve until they "were to go out on the sabbath" (II Chronicles 23:8; II Kings 11:5). The second course then began its service in the second week; the third course the third week, etc.

Since each course administered for one week, it follows that there was a twenty-four week period for each of the courses to have its chance of serving. This occupied a span of about six months. When this was accomplished, the series started all over again. In a period of forty-eight weeks, each course would have served for two weeks—with each session being separated from the other by about six months. There are just over fifty-two weeks in each Solar Year. The Jewish calendar, on the other hand, is a Lunar-Solar one. In ordinary years it only has about fifty-one weeks. At particular intervals the Jewish authorities had to add an extra month of thirty days to keep it in season with the motions of the Sun. In a nineteen-year period, seven extra months were usually added. But, as said before, all normal years with the Jews had about fifty-one weeks. The priests served in their courses for forty-eight of those weeks. This means that there were three weeks in the year which were not reckoned in the accounting. What happened with those three weeks? David provided the answer back in his day.

Chapter 5 - The Time of Jesus' Birth

The Courses Served Together at the Three Festival Seasons

Since there were three major holy seasons on the Jewish calendar (Passover, Pentecost and Tabernacles), and since at those times there were great crowds at Jerusalem, David ordained that all twenty-four courses were to serve together for the week of Passover, the week when Pentecost occurred, and the week of Tabernacles. "For all the priests that were present [at Tabernacles] did not then wait by course" (II Chronicles 5:11). At Tabernacles (and also Passover and Pentecost) the priestly courses were suspended—they "did *not* then wait by course." In actual fact, all the courses of priests served together during those three holy seasons. But in all other normal weeks, the various courses were doing their assigned work at the temple. In the case of Zechariah (the father of John the Baptist), Luke said he was officiating in his regular office (the eighth course, or the *eighth week*) when the angel said his wife Elizabeth was to have a child.

This is a chronological clue. Luke meant it that way. He was showing his readers the general time of year that Zechariah was serving. We know that Zechariah was not serving at a festival period because the priests "did *not* then wait by course." Also it was either in the first half of the year when the course of Abijah served, or it was during the second half. Let us look at this course of Abijah, because we can know the approximate times when it served in the temple.

The Chronology of the Twenty-four Courses

It is perfectly reasonable that the priestly courses started their serving with the Springtime month of Nisan—the first month of the Jewish ecclesiastical year. This was the customary time ordained in the Bible when priests began their administrations (Exodus 40:1-38). David arranged the twenty-four courses of the priests to coincide with the time when each of the twelve tribes of Israel had their representatives helping in the temple service. Each of the twelve tribes administered a whole month. They "came in and went out month by month throughout all the months of the year...the first course for the first month" (I Chronicles 27:1,2). The first month for temple services was Nisan. The first month-long course of the twelve tribes started at the beginning of that Springtime month. This must also have been the first month for the priests.

The twenty-four priestly courses, however, lasted only for one week (from Sabbath to Sabbath). Their courses started with the Sabbath just before the beginning of Nisan in order for the priests to be on duty to perform their regular ceremonials on Nisan One. The same procedure was also followed for their second yearly tenure commencing six months later on Tishri One. There is even in the New Testament a reference to this second yearly tenure which commenced six months after the first. In Luke 6:1 in some manuscripts we read what appears to be a strange statement (at least it is strange to some scholars). It says that the Sabbath day on which Jesus excused his disciples for picking grain was the "second-first" Sabbath. Many manuscripts and in the writings of several early fathers of Christendom, they state this event was performed on the "second-first Sabbath." This must be a true reading of the original text and its supposed oddity is what helps to explain its meaning. What in the world was the "second-first Sabbath"? The answer is easy to determine. The truth is, the phrase was a regular calendar indication that all Jews in the time of the temple understood.

The answer is plain. Luke in using the phrase "second-first Sabbath" was simply following the regular order of the twenty-four courses of the priests because this chronological indication was a reference to their *second cycle* beginning with Tishri One and the disciples picked the grain on the *first* weekly Sabbath of that *second yearly tenure*. The next weekly Sabbath would have been called the *second-second Sabbath*. Of course, during the week of Tabernacles all the twenty-four priests would have attended to the temple ceremonies together, but the next weekly Sabbath after Tabernacles, the routine would have continued and that weekly

Chapter 5 - The Time of Jesus' Birth

Sabbath would have been called the *second-third Sabbath*, the next Sabbath after that would have been the *second-fourth Sabbath*, etc. until the priests reached the *"second-twenty-fourth Sabbath."* After that, the priests re-started the cycle once again with the first weekly Sabbath associated with the first day of Nisan of the next year. They would have called that first Sabbath the *"first-first Sabbath,"* the second would have been the *"first-second Sabbath,"* etc. However, when weekly Sabbaths occurred *inside* the festival weeks of Passover, Pentecost and Tabernacles, those intervening Sabbaths (which were not counted in the two cycles each year) were called the *"between Sabbaths,"* and Luke even refers to one of those which occurred during the week of Pentecost. Note Acts 13:42 where the phrase "the *next* Sabbath" as found in the King James Version, really states from the Greek, "the *between* Sabbath." This means that Luke in the New Testament was well aware of the twenty-four priestly courses and he knew the specifics concerning the weekly Sabbaths in which the twenty-four priestly courses changed their weekly tenures two times a year (separated by a six month period). These indications by Luke are calendar references and they give us important clues to help us understand some New Testament chronological facts.

Before we look at the chronological indications of the priestly courses to determine the time of the year John the Baptist was born (and consequently the nativity period for Jesus), let us find the proper year for Jesus' birth. We can then know what year to apply the chronological clues within the cycle of priestly courses for the month of John the Baptist's birth, and also that of Jesus. The year for the birth of Jesus is not difficult to determine if we allow all of the biblical and historical information to be used in our appraisal. What was the precise year of Jesus' birth?

Was Jesus Born in 3 or 2 B.C.?

If the simple chronological statements of Luke are accepted, the nativity of Jesus must be placed in 3 or 2 B.C. The historical evidences I have presented in this book support this conclusion. However, there is a problem that is not solved by Luke's narrative alone. He said that Jesus began his ministry in Tiberius' 15th year when he was "*about* 30 years of age." I will show in a moment what Luke meant by the phrase *about* 30 years of age. But for now, let us note that Luke does not inform us whether Jesus was "about 30" near the beginning, the middle or near the end of Tiberius 15. Further, we are not told whether it was the Roman method of reckoning Tiberius' 15th year, or that which people in Judaea and Syria were accustomed to which antedated the reign of kings and emperors to Tishri One of the previous year.

In spite of this, it will not be difficult to determine that Luke was using the ordinary method of dating Tiberius' 15th year as was common among easterners in the Empire.[133] This is an important thing to understand in identifying the Star of Bethlehem. This is because we must know the year in which Jesus was born to see if the celestial pageantry of 3 to 2 B.C. will fit the chronological indications in the New Testament. Indeed, it does fit remarkably well. The method of reckoning the 15th year of Tiberius is an interesting one, but very understandable and consistent. It simply means that in the eastern part of the Empire, the whole of the year in which Tiberius became emperor of Rome (August 19, 14 A.D.) is awarded to Tiberius as his first year. It means that New Year's day for the beginning of that year, begins the first year of Tiberius. This would have been on Tishri One (the first day of Tishri) in the year in which Tiberius came to rulership. Thus, the whole first year was from Tishri One in A.D.13 to Tishri One in A.D.14. Consequently, Tiberius' 15th year would have been from Tishri One in A.D.27 to Tishri One in A.D.28. I will have more information showing this matter in a later chapter.

Jesus Was Born in the Year 3 B.C.

If Jesus was about 30 years old near the commencement of the emperor's 15th year (as reckoned by people in the east), then his

Chapter 5 - The Time of Jesus' Birth

birth was in 3 B.C. Recall that Luke tells us that Jesus was born at the time of a Roman census or enrollment. If we can determine the period of that registration, this will help to pinpoint the year of the nativity. This is where the new historical information offered in this book becomes essential. We now know that an Empire-wide citizen registration took place for the award of the *Pater Patriae* upon Augustus in early 2 B.C.[134] This was the census Luke meant. I will give a full account of this registration (a census) in a further chapter of this book titled "The Census of Quirinius." But let me very briefly rehearse some of the evidence that shows when the census mentioned in the New Testament took place.

The Census of Quirinius

This registration took place in 3 B.C. Lewin points out that Augustus was already being called the *Pater Patriae* on one or two inscriptions by 3 B.C.,[135] and in late 3 B.C. he was offered the title by a deputation of people who met him at Antium[136] though he refused it until the Senate bestowed it upon him on February 5, 2 B.C. (the Day of Concord). This is good evidence that "all the Roman people" must have started to give him this most prestigious title sometime in 3 B.C. And interestingly, our historical reconstruction as shown in this book shows that an oath of obedience to Augustus was demanded of all people in Judaea in 3 B.C.[137] This oath would have been required of Joseph and Mary. More than that, a Paphlagonian inscription shows that an oath of obedience was required of all Roman citizens and non-citizens in exactly the same year, in 3 B.C. Moses of Khorene, the early Armenian historian, quoted sources which related that the census mentioned by Luke was also administered by Roman agents in Armenia (a neighbor country to Paphlagonia) in 3 B.C. and the wording of Moses of Khorene about the event was very similar to that of the Paphlagonian inscription. Orosius in the fifth century also said that in 3 B.C. an oath/census was commanded of all nations at the time Augustus was honored as "the first of all men"—an appropriate description of the title *Pater Patriae*. Remarkably, Orosius said this was the Empire-wide census mentioned by Luke in his Gospel.

This information strongly suggests that the census which brought Joseph and Mary to Bethlehem was conducted in the Summer or early Autumn of 3 B.C. A census by the Romans would hardly have been ordered in very early Spring or late Autumn—and certainly not in Winter when the rainy season was in evidence. Ramsay expressed confidence that the normal time for Roman censuses was from August to October.[138] Thus, the latter part of 3 B.C. makes sense.

The Birth of John the Baptist

Let us now return to consider the chronology of the priestly courses. This will help us arrive at a general period for the birth of John, and also of Jesus because John was born about six months before Jesus (Luke 1:36). This would indicate that the conception of John as well as that of Jesus was most probably in 4 B.C. Luke mentioned that Zechariah was serving at his regular time of administration during the week when the eighth course of Abijah served. This course had duty two times each year, once in late Spring and again in late Autumn. Look at the Spring session.

We must find out when the first day of Nisan occurred in 4 B.C. This is not a simple task in some years. Since the calendar of the Jews in the first century was dependent upon the state of the crops around Jerusalem (in order that certain ritualistic duties could then be performed regarding the first fruits), it was necessary for the priests to observe the ripeness of the barley before they would allow any ecclesiastical year to begin. If twelve lunar months had passed from the beginning of the previous year, it was the normal custom to start the next year with the thirteenth month—which, of course, would have been reckoned as Nisan, the first month of the new year. But if the barley was not yet ripe enough, the priests often postponed the start of the year for one month.

March 28 sundown – 29 sundown

Chapter 5 - The Time of Jesus' Birth

Thankfully, in 4 B.C. this agricultural requirement is no problem. The month of Nisan began on March 29. That is always late enough in the year to allow no quibbling over the state of the crops.[139] This date was also Nisan 1 on the Babylonian calendar. However, a "new moon was visible at Jerusalem thirty-seven minutes before it was visible at Babylon and therefore upon occasion the new month could begin a day earlier in Jerusalem."[140] In the year 4 B.C. this factor was a definite possibility. But in this reckoning, I will follow the date given by Parker and Dubberstein (the noted authorities regarding the calendars of the Babylonians and the Jews in this period). Yet even if Nisan 1 were a day earlier in Jerusalem it is of no consequence to our present question. Recall, also, that when we say Nisan 1 was March 29, it must be understood that the day actually commenced the previous evening at sundown on March 28 because all Jewish days start at sundown.

To illustrate how this information can help us arrive at the approximate time of John the Baptist's birth, let us understand that the first of Nisan in 4 B.C. was March 29. The priestly courses began their administrations on the Sabbath near the first of Nisan.[141] And while there was a belief among some of the Dead Sea sects that the duties of the first course started on Nisan 12,[142] the people of Qumran were out of the mainstream of Jewish thought. This reference need not be taken as reflecting normal Jewish practice. But even if it were, there would be only a two-week discrepancy, and this is not enough to seriously upset the general chronological indications associated with the course of Abijah to which we are referring.[143] The main Jewish custom, however, had the first priestly course commencing its duty on the Sabbath before Nisan 1. The Sabbath just prior to March 29 was March 24. This indicates that the week of service for the course of Jehoiarib (the first course) was from Sabbath noon, March 24 to Sabbath noon, March 31. The second course began March 31 and served to April 7. The third course started April 7 (but its week was interrupted by the period of Passover when all priests officiated together). This caused the third

77

course not to end its administration until the Sabbath after Passover, April 21. Then the weekly courses started once again in their regular order of service.

The Eighth Course of Abijah

The period for the eighth course of Abijah would have been from May 19 to May 26. If it were in this Springtime administration when the angelic messenger came to Zechariah about his wife having a child, then we have a chronological hint of the period for John the Baptist's conception—because it must have happened immediately after that time. Indeed, because Zechariah was struck dumb during his administration, he was disqualified at once from exercising the priest's office (Leviticus 21:16-23). He no doubt left very soon for home. Thus, somewhere near May 26 to June 1, Elizabeth must have conceived. The human gestation period is about 280 days—nine months and ten days. This shows the birth of John the Baptist near March 10, 3 B.C.

The Birth of Jesus

Let us now look at the birth of Jesus. From what we have observed about the approximate time of John's birth, it should be easy to compute that of Jesus. Luke said that Jesus was conceived sometime in the sixth month of Elizabeth's pregnancy (Luke 1:26,36). Five full months had passed and Elizabeth was then in her sixth month. Since John the Baptist was probably born some time around March 10, 3 B.C., Jesus' birth would be near September in 3 B.C. We will soon see from other astronomical data that this is the only year that will satisfy all the facts.

It must be admitted that it is impossible to arrive at an exact birthday for either John or Jesus based on the priestly courses, yet the information provided by Luke helps us to pick the approximate periods with some confidence. Two or three weeks each way would be the outside limit.

Chapter 5 - The Time of Jesus' Birth

There is, however, a possibility that Luke was referring to Zechariah's late Autumn session in the temple instead of the Springtime one. If so, we would have a six-month displacement for the time of John's and Jesus' births. John would then have been born near the middle of September and Jesus would have been born early the following March. Yet, there are reasons for not accepting this. Luke said that Jesus was born at a time when his parents went to Bethlehem in response to Caesar's command for a census. Ramsay showed that considerable confidence can be placed in the belief that the general time of the year for the start of a census was from August to October.[144] The September period for Jesus' birth we are suggesting fits this well. There are also other reasons.

A late Summer or early Autumn date for Jesus' birth has also been suggested because Luke said the shepherds were tending their flocks at night at his nativity (Luke 2:8). Many have believed this precludes a wintertime birth (either early Winter on December 25th or a late Winter in early March) because it would have been too cold for the flocks to be out in the open at that time. But this evidence is very problematic. In exceptionally cold Winters this may have been the case, but in mild Winters sheep are often out of doors in Palestine all night.[145] Since no one knows what kind of weather there was in Palestine the year of Jesus birth (either severe or mild), this factor can be of no chronological value.

Some have thought that Jesus was born at the period of the Jewish Feast of Tabernacles because John in his Gospel said that he "tabernacled [Greek] among us" (John 1:14). Tabernacles in the year 3 B.C. was from September 26 to October 3 B.C. But Jesus's birth at this time is not possible. Actually, there is clear proof that Jesus' birth could not have been at any of the three holy periods of Passover, Pentecost or Tabernacles. These were times when all Jewish men were required by biblical law to be in Jerusalem (Deuteronomy 16:6,11,16). Yet Luke tells us that during the time of Jesus' nativity "everyone went into his own city" (Luke 2:3).

Besides, the Romans would *not* have selected the three primary festival seasons for a census when most of the Jews in Palestine were required to be in Jerusalem. The reason there was no room at the inn was not because the people were crowding into the Jerusalem area for ceremonial purposes, but, as Luke tells us, they were there to be registered for the census. Also, since our new history shows that the census and the oath of allegiance to Augustus (for his award of the *Pater Patriae*) were one and the same, it then makes sense that even Mary who was in biblical law able to bear a king of the Jews would also be expected to swear that she and her offspring would remain loyal to the existing government. And this census no doubt occurred in the latter part of 3 B.C. (as I will show in detail), not in the late Winter or early Spring of 3 B.C.

There is another reason for placing Jesus' birth in September, and it is a powerful one. This is because the New Testament itself gives a precise chronological sign that identifies the exact day Jesus was born (and within a period of an hour and a half on that day). It is now time to look at this New Testament indication.

An Exact Date Can Be Picked

There are only three places in the New Testament that record events connected with the birth of Jesus. They are in Matthew's Gospel, Luke's Gospel and chapter twelve of the Book of Revelation. This latter book has some information about Jesus' birth that should be considered, though it must be admitted that all data in the Book of Revelation are highly symbolic. Yet the figurative nature of the book may contain the very clue we need to precisely date the birth of Jesus.

People of the first century were very prone to use astronomical signs as having bearing on historical and religious events. They were especially important regarding the births of eminent people, and kings in particular. Because of this, the section about Jesus' birth in the Book of Revelation may have been significantly relat-

Chapter 5 - The Time of Jesus' Birth

ed to particular heavenly signs that Jesus had formerly told his disciples to be aware of (Luke 21:11). Let us look at Revelation 12:1-5. It gives us precise indications as to the hour and the day that Jesus was born. This section should be read carefully.

> "And there was a great wonder [sign] in heaven; a woman clothed with the sun, and the moon under her feet, and upon her head a crown of twelve stars: and she being with child cried, travailing in birth, and pained to be delivered. And there appeared another wonder [sign] in heaven; and behold a great red dragon, having seven heads and ten horns, and seven crowns upon his head. And his tail drew the third part of the stars of heaven, and did cast them to the earth: and the dragon stood before the woman which was ready to be delivered, for to devour her child as soon as it was born. And she brought forth a man child, who was to rule all nations with a rod of iron."

The scene just described is symbolic. Certainly, this could hardly be a description of the virgin Mary. This "woman" had the heavens associated with her—the Sun, Moon and the Twelve Stars. John said that the display was a wonder (a sign) and that it was "in heaven." What did he mean by the phrase "in heaven"?

The Bible speaks of three "heavens." The first is that in which the birds fly and all weather phenomena occur (Jeremiah 4:25; I Kings 18:45). The second is that of the Sun, Moon, planets and stars (Genesis 1:17). The third heaven is that where God lives (II Corinthians 12:2). Which of these heavens is meant? People of the first century would have had no difficulty in interpreting the proper "heaven" that was intended by the apostle John. The Sun, Moon, and stars are not located in our atmosphere where the birds and the clouds exist. They are also not found in the heaven where God has his abode because we are told by John himself that the Sun or Moon are not needed in that region (Revelation 21:23). The only "heaven" that is reasonable is that where the Sun, Moon and the Twelve Stars are located. The Book of Genesis revealed that the celestial bodies were made by God to give signs (Genesis 1:14). Jewish opinion included among these "signs" the astronomical associations between the Sun, Moon, planets, stars and constellations.[146] There can hardly be a doubt that such astronomical "signs" as these are referred to in the Book of Revelation.[147] With these points in mind, we may have some interesting clues that will provide us with the exact time of Jesus' birth.

Astronomy and the Birth of Jesus

The essential factor in interpreting the symbol of Revelation 12:1-5 is the identification of the woman. What is John signifying by mentioning her? This much is certain: The woman in the first three verses is featured as being *in heaven* and both the Sun and the Moon are in association with her. After the dragon casts down a third of the stars of heaven (Revelation 12:4), the woman is then found on earth (verses 6 and 14). But the important factor is the birth of the man-child and the Woman's relationship with the heavenly signs while she is symbolically in heaven (the first three verses of Revelation 12 shows the Sun clothing her, the Moon under her feet and the Twelve Stars on her head).

The "birth" of the Messiah is associated with this heavenly spectacle. Since some noted heavenly bodies are a part of the picture, it could well be that John intended the woman to represent a constellation that the two primary luminaries transverse, and that she was a part of the zodiacal system which gives headship to the signs (the Twelve Stars were a "crown" upon her head). Recall that interpreting astronomical signs dominated the thinking of most people in the first century, whether the people were Jews or Gentiles. Indeed, the word "sign" used by the author of the Book of Revelation to describe this celestial display was the same one used by the ancients to denote the zodiacal constellations.[148]

This is made clearer when one looks closely at the text. Since the Sun and Moon are amidst or in line with the body of this woman, she could be, in a symbolic way, a constellation located within the normal paths of the Sun and Moon. The only sign of a woman

Chapter 5 - The Time of Jesus' Birth

which exists along the ecliptic (the track of the Sun in its journey through the stars) is that of Virgo the Virgin. She occupies, in body form, a space of about 50 degrees along the ecliptic. The head of the woman actually bridges some 10 degrees into the previous sign of Leo and her feet overlap about 10 degrees into the following sign of Libra, the Scales. In the period of Jesus' birth, the Sun entered in its annual course through the heavens into the head position of the woman about August 13, and exited from her feet about October 2. But the apostle John saw the scene when the Sun was "clothing" or "adorning" the woman. This surely indicates that the position of the Sun in the vision was located somewhere mid-bodied to the woman, between the neck and the knees. The Sun could hardly be said to clothe her if it were situated in her face or near her feet.

The Sun Clothed the Woman

The only time in the year that the Sun could be in a position to "clothe" the celestial woman called Virgo (that is, to be mid-bodied to her, in the region where a pregnant woman carries a child) is when the Sun is located between about 150 and 170 degrees along the ecliptic. This "clothing" of the woman by the Sun occurs for a 20-day period each year. This 20 degree spread could indicate the general time when Jesus was born. In 3 B.C., the Sun would have entered this celestial region about August 27 and exited from it about September 15. If John in the Book of Revelation is associating the birth of Jesus with the period when the Sun was mid-bodied to this woman called Virgo (and this is no doubt what he means), then Jesus would have to be born within that 20-day period. From the point of view of the Magi who were astrologers, this would have been the only logical sign under which the Jewish Messiah might be born, especially if he were to be born of a virgin. Even today, astrologers recognize that the sign of Virgo is the one which has reference to a messianic world ruler to be born from a virgin.[149]

This heavenly woman called Virgo is normally depicted as a virgin holding in her right hand a green branch and in her left hand a sprig of grain. In the Hebrew Zodiac, she at first (in the time of David) denoted Ruth who was gleaning in the fields of Boaz. She then later became the Virgin when the prophecy of Isaiah 7:14 was given in the time of King Hezekiah and the prophet Isaiah. This Virgin held in her left hand a sprig of grain. This was precisely where the bright star called Spica is found. Indeed, the chief star of the constellation Virgo is Spica. Bullinger, in his book "The Witness of the Stars" (pp. 29-34), said that the word "Spica" has, through the Arabic, the meaning "the branch" and that it symbolically refers to Jesus who was prophetically called "the Branch" in Zechariah 3:8 and 6:12. And Bullinger (and Seiss in his book "The Gospel in the Stars") maintain that this sign of Virgo designates the heavenly witness for the birth of the Messiah (Jesus). They say that Virgo should actually begin the zodiacal signs which give the story of the Messiah. This may be. The apostle John may have given the same indication as far as the first full sign of the zodiac is concerned. He depicted the woman of Revelation as having a crown of Twelve Stars on her head.

This could well show that the woman (Virgo) is the constellation of headship for all the twelve signs. The "head" position of Virgo is actually located within the last ten degrees of Leo. It was in this very region where the story of the career of the Messiah would begin that Bullinger and Seiss were referring to. Thus, the story of Jesus and his mission on earth, as related by these heavenly symbols, should logically begin with his birth from a virgin and conclude with him being crowned king in the final sign of Leo the Lion (with its chief star being Regulus—the King star). This is no doubt what the apostle John was trying to show through the symbols found in Revelation Twelve.

The birth of this child in Revelation Twelve (whom John identified with Jesus) should have occurred while the Sun was "clothing" the woman, when the Sun was mid-bodied to Virgo. This period of

Chapter 5 - The Time of Jesus' Birth

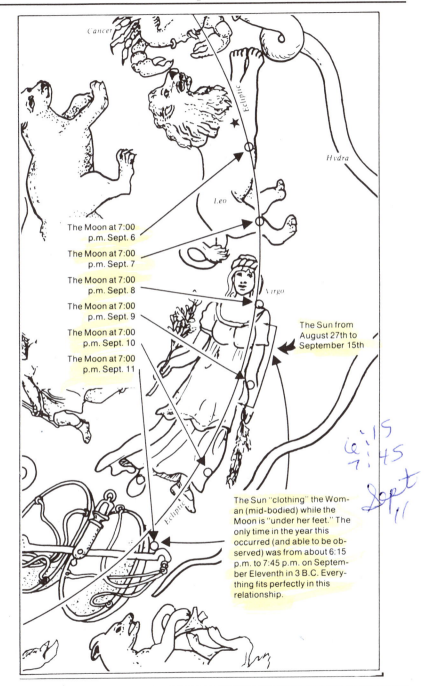

85

The Star that Astonished the World

time in 3 B.C. covered 20 days (August 27 to September 15). If Jesus were born within that 20-day period, it would fit most remarkably with the testimony of Luke (relative to the birth of John the Baptist and the eighth course of Abijah). Indeed, the chronological indications associated with the priestly course of Abijah place Jesus' birth exactly within this period. But there is a way to arrive at a much closer time for Jesus' birth than a simple 20-day period. The position of the Moon in John's vision actually pinpoints the nativity to within a day — to within a period of an hour and a half (within 90 minutes) on that day. This may appear an absurd assessment on the surface, but it is quite possible.

The key is the Moon. The apostle said it was located "*under* her feet." What does the word "under" signify in this case? Does it mean the woman of the vision was standing on the Moon when John observed it or does it mean her feet were positioned slightly above the Moon? John does not tell us. This, however, is not of major consequence in using the location of the Moon to answer our question because it would only involve the difference of a degree or two. The Moon travels about 12 degrees a day in its course through the heavens. This motion of one or two degrees by the Moon represents on earth only a period of two to four hours. This difference is no problem in determining the time of Jesus' birth. What is vital, however, is that this shows the Moon as a New Moon.

The Precise Position of the Moon is Important

Now note this point. Since the feet of Virgo the Virgin represent the last 7 degrees of the constellation (in the time of Jesus this would have been between about 180 and 187 degrees along the ecliptic), the Moon has to be positioned somewhere under that 7 degree arc to satisfy the description of Revelation Twelve. But the Moon also has to be in that exact location when the Sun is mid-bodied to Virgo. In the year 3 B.C., these two factors came to precise agreement for about an hour and a half, as observed from Palestine or Patmos, in the twilight period of September 11th. The relation-

Chapter 5 - The Time of Jesus' Birth

ship began about 6:15 p.m. (sunset), and lasted until around 7:45 p.m. (moonset). This is the only day in the whole year that the astronomical phenomenon described in the twelfth chapter of Revelation could take place.

This also shows one other important point. The Moon was in crescent phase. It was a New Moon day, the start of a new lunar month. (See plates one and two on pages 88 and 89 which show early depictions of the celestial scene of Revelation 12:1-3 and how the Moon is shown to be in its crescent phase.)

Modern Man and Astronomical Motions

While ordinary people in modern times who are not professional astronomers have little knowledge of the solar, lunar, planetary and stellar motions, the people from the first century up to the Industrial Revolution were well accustomed to them. Even people of little education were generally knowledgeable of the main motions of the astronomical bodies—even more than most college educated people today. When anyone of early times read Revelation 12:1-3, an astronomical relationship was realized at once. There was no doubt that a New Moon display was being shown to them. And when the woman of the sign was interpreted as Virgo the Virgin, and with the Sun mid-bodied to the Virgin, they clearly saw a New Moon day occurring sometime in late Summer.

The apostle John said this heavenly relationship occurred at the time of Jesus' birth. And in 3 B.C. this exact combination of celestial factors happened just after sunset only on one day of the year. It was on September 11th. It could not have occurred at any other time of the year. Indeed, even one day before — on September 10 — the Moon would have been located above the Virgin's feet with the crescent not visible, while one day farther — on September 12 — the Moon had moved too far beyond the feet of the Virgin, at least 25 diameters of the Moon east of her feet. Thus, only one day applies. That day was just after sunset on September 11th.

Chapter 5 - The Time of Jesus' Birth

The Exact Day of Jesus' Birth

The apostle John is actually presenting to his readers something of significance in a symbolic way. Revelation 12:1-3 certainly shows a New Moon day that could only be observed from earth just after sunset and the day was September 11th. This matter fits well with Luke's description of the birth of Jesus in Bethlehem. Recall that "there were in the same country shepherds abiding in the field, keeping watch over the flock by night...and the angel said...unto you is born this day [which began at sundown] in the city of David a Savior, which is Christ the Lord" (Luke 2:8-11). Jesus was born in early evening, and Revelation 12 shows it was a New Moon day.

What New Moon could this have been? The answer is most amazing. It is almost too amazing! September 11, 3 B.C. was Tishri One on the Jewish calendar. To Jewish people this would have been a very profound occasion indeed. Tishri One is none other than the Jewish New Year's day (*Rosh ha-Shanah*, or as the Bible calls it, The Day of Trumpets—Leviticus 23:23-26). It was an important annual holy day of the Jews (but not one of the three annual festivals that required all Palestinian Jews to be in Jerusalem).

What a significant day for the appearance of the Messiah to arrive on earth from the Jewish point of view. And remarkably, no other day of the year could astronomically fit Revelation 12:1-3. The apostle John is certainly showing forth an astronomical sign which answers precisely with the Jewish New Year Day. John would surely have realized the significance of this astronomical scene that he was describing.

In the next chapter I will show the symbolic and religious meaning of this New Year's day as interpreted by the Jews (and consequently by the apostles and early Christians) as it relates to the Messiah and his kingship. The information may provide a better understanding why the early apostles of the first century, and many Jews and Gentiles, so quickly came to accept Jesus as the Messiah.

Chapter 5 - The Time of Jesus' Birth

Whatever the case, the historical evidence supports the nativity of Jesus in 3 B.C., at the beginning of a Roman census, and (if we use the astronomical indications of the Book of Revelation) his birth would have occurred just after sundown on September 11th, on *Rosh ha-Shanah*, the Day of Trumpets—the Jewish New Year Day for governmental affairs. There could hardly have been a better day in the ecclesiastical calendar of the Jews to introduce the Messiah to the world from a Jewish point of view and this is no doubt what the apostle John was clearly intending to show by the sign that he recorded in Revelation Twelve.

Chapter 6

THE BIRTH OF JESUS AND THE DAY OF TRUMPETS

The historical evidence I have presented in this book shows that Jesus was born in the year 3 B.C. It appears most probable that a late Summer birth in 3 B.C. has the best credentials. I need not rehearse my reasons for this, but they are very strong. Indeed, the evidence from the priestly courses alone suggests that a September nativity is the most likely. This is a pretty close approximation that most scholars would probably accept as reasonable. But now, we come to the nitty-gritty! To propose an early evening birth on September 11, 3 B.C. appears almost impossible to believe. To get that close to his time of birth might at first seem to be fanciful.

The fact is, however, I can state without a shadow of a doubt, that the celestial scene as described by the apostle John in Revelation 12:1-5, if viewed astronomically, would center precisely on a New Moon date within mid-September, and that in 3 B.C. that exact celestial phenomenon would have occurred in the early evening of September 11th. I can also state with assurance that sundown on September 11th, 3 B.C. was also the beginning of the Jewish New Year (*Rosh ha-Shanah* — The Day of Trumpets).

Chapter 6 - The Birth of Jesus and the Day of Trumpets

Even if the apostle John were only giving the symbolic time for Jesus' nativity, and not the actual, we are provided with a great deal of insight on how early Christians interpreted significant periods of time on the holy calendar of Israel. If Jesus were actually born on *Rosh ha-Shanah* (the Day of Trumpets) in 3 B.C., a most impressive astronomical panorama of events burst forth on the scene that would have awed and astonished most Jewish people who lived at the time. Truly, this is not an exaggeration.

The Importance of the Day of Trumpets

Look at the celestial events that occurred around that *Rosh ha-Shanah* date of September 11th in 3 B.C. Exactly one month before (on August 12) the world would have witnessed the close conjunction of Jupiter (reckoned astrologically as the Father) and Venus (the Mother) when they were only .07 degrees from one another when they appeared as morning stars on the eastern horizon. This was a very close union. But then, nineteen days later (August 31), Venus came to within .36 degrees of Mercury in a very similar astronomical display. Then, on September 11th, the New Moon occurred which represented the Jewish New Year. This happened when Jupiter (the King planet) was then approaching Regulus (the King star). And, on September 14th, Jupiter and Regulus came to their first of three conjunctions in this extraordinary year. And then, over an eight month period, Jupiter made its "crowning effect" over the King star Regulus. There could hardly have been a better astronomical testimony to the birth of the new messianic king from the Jewish point of view. Why? Because everyone of these celestial occurrences I have mentioned happened with the Sun or planets being positioned within the constellation of Leo the Lion (the constellation of Judah—from whence the Messiah was destined to emerge) or in Virgo the Virgin. The apostle John may have seen importance in these extraordinary occurrences when he symbolically showed that Jesus was born at the New Moon of Tishri, the Day of Trumpets (Revelation 12:1-3).

What we now need to do is to rehearse some of the typical and figurative features of the biblical accounts associated with this particular day. They may well reveal why John and early Christians looked on Jesus as the Christ and the king of the universe. The Day of Trumpets was a special day that symbolically showed this rule.

Jesus Was Born on the Day of Trumpets

If one can realize that the New Testament shows Jesus born on the Day of Trumpets (the first day of Tishri—the start of the Jewish civil year) an impressive amount of symbolic features emerge on the biblical and prophetic scenes. Before the period of the Exodus in the time of Moses, this was the day that began the biblical year. It also looks like this was the day when people were advanced one year of life—no matter at what month of the year they were actually born. Notice that the patriarch Noah became 600 years of age "in the first month [Tishri], the first day of the month [later to be called the Day of Trumpets]" (Genesis 8:13). That was the very day when "Noah removed the covering of the ark, and looked, and, behold, the face of the ground was dry" (v. 13). This was not only Noah's official birthday, it became a new birth after the Flood for the earth as well. There is more. Even the first day of creation mentioned in Genesis 1:1-5 could be reckoned as being this very day. The early Jews discussed whether the actual creation took place in Spring or in Autumn. But since the Autumn commenced all biblical years before the Exodus (Exodus 12:2), and since all the fruit was then on the trees ready for Adam and Eve to eat (Genesis 1:29; 2:9,16,17), it suggests that the month of Tishri was the creation month, beginning near the Autumn. If so, then the first day of creation mentioned in Genesis was also the first of Tishri (at least, Moses no doubt intended to give that impression). This means that not only was this the birthday of the new earth in Noah's day and what was later to become the Day of Trumpets on the Mosaic calendar, but it was also the day which ushered in the original creation of the heavens and the earth.

Chapter 6 - The Birth of Jesus and the Day of Trumpets

As shown before, among the Jews this day was called *Rosh ha-Shanah* (the Feast of the New Year). The majority belief of Jewish elders (which still dominates the services of the synagogues) was that the Day of Trumpets was the memorial day that commemorated the beginning of the world. Authorized opinion prevailed that the first of Tishri was the first day of Genesis 1:1-5. It "came to be regarded as the birthday of the world."[150] It was even more than an anniversary of the physical creation. The Jewish historian Theodor H. Gaster states: "Judaism regards New Year's Day not merely as an anniversary of creation—but more importantly—as a renewal of it. This is when the world is reborn."[151] Gaster's insight is so germane to the interpretation of the significance of biblical festivals that I will be referring to his research several times in my following references.

When Was the "Last Trump"?

The matter does not stop there. Each of the Jewish months was officially introduced by the blowing of trumpets (Numbers 10:10). Since the festival year in which all the Mosaic festivals were found was seven months long, the last month (Tishri) was the last month for a festival trumpet. This is one of the reasons that the day was called "the Day of Trumpets." The last trump in the seven months' series was always sounded on this New Moon day. This made it the final trumpets' day (Leviticus 23:24; Numbers 29:1).

This was the exact day that many of the ancient kings and rulers of Judah reckoned as their inauguration day of rule. This procedure was followed consistently in the time of Solomon, Jeremiah, and Ezra.[152] The Day of Trumpets was also acknowledged as the time for counting the years of their kingly rule. Indeed, it was customary that the final ceremony in the coronation of kings was the blowing of trumpets. For Solomon: "Blow ye the trumpet, and say, God save king Solomon" (I Kings 1:34). For Jehu: "And [they] blew with trumpets, saying, Jehu is king" (II Kings 9:13). At the enthronement of Jehoash: "The people of the land rejoiced, and blew with trumpets" (II Kings 11:11).

There could well be a reflection of this symbolic feature in the New Testament. The Day of Trumpets was the time for the start of the seventh month (since the time of Moses) and the time for the "last trump" for introducing festival months. Note that in the Book of Revelation, we have the record of a heavenly angel who will blow the seventh and last trumpet blast. And recall what happens at the exact time this "last trump" is sounded. "And the seventh angel sounded [blew the *last trump*]; and there were great voices in heaven, saying, the kingdoms of this world are become the kingdoms of our Lord and of his Christ; and he shall reign forever" (Revelation 11:15). In New Testament parlance this shows the time of the coronation of Jesus, and it happens at the seventh (or last) trump in the Book of Revelation—the Day of Trumpets.

Further Significance of the Day of Trumpets

The early Jews also recognized that the Day of Trumpets was a memorial day for considering those who had died. It was not a simple type of "Memorial Day" that we moderns are accustomed to. Gaster said it was a symbolic time when "the dead return to rejoin their descendants at the beginning of the year."[153] Such a day was a time when Israel would rally to the call of God for the inauguration of God's kingdom on earth. Gaster also states this was the time that became "a symbol of the Last Trump."[154] Since the apostle Paul was Jewish, it is possible that his reference to the "Last Trump" and the resurrection from the dead was also connected with the same biblical theme. The "Last Trump" of the early Jews was when the dead were remembered. And to Paul the "Last Trump" was the time for Jesus' second advent and the resurrection of the dead (I Corinthians 15:52; I Thessalonians 4:16).

Truly, the Day of Trumpets' theme is that of kingship. There may even be a reference to this in the elevation of the patriarch Joseph to kingship on this New Moon day which began the month of Tishri. Notice that he had been in a dungeon for "two full years" (Genesis 41:1). It was not simply a two year period which Moses

Chapter 6 - The Birth of Jesus and the Day of Trumpets

was intending, but the passage *of two full years*. The implication is that the story of Joseph's rise to kingship happened on a New Year's Day. This is manifest in Psalm 81 — a New Year's psalm commemorating Joseph's royal enthronement (Genesis 41:40). As with Jesus, in Revelation 11:15, the kingdoms of the world became Joseph's on the day intended for coronations—the day that later became the Day of Trumpets. Of course, Pharaoh retained top leadership, but as the New Testament shows, God the Father still maintains supreme rule over Jesus even when Jesus is prophesied to rule the kingdoms of this world.

The Crowning of Kings

As we have shown from the Bible, the blowing of trumpets was the sign that kings could then begin to rule (I Kings 1:34; II Kings 9:13; 11:11). Jewish authorities long acknowledged this royal import to the Day of Trumpets. Gaster states: "The Sovereignty of God is a dominant theme of the occasion [and] it is one of the cardinal features of New Year's Day."[155] The main issue that prevailed in the significance of the day was the triumph of God as a king over all the forces of evil. The symbolic motif of the Day of Trumpets, as Gaster shows, was God "continually fighting His way to the Kingdom, continually asserting His dominion, and continually enthroning Himself as sovereign of creation. At New Year when the world was annually reborn that sovereignty was evinced anew."[156]

The theological thrust of the early Jews within their synagogue services for the Day of Trumpets was the fact that God rules over all and that he is the King of kings. On Trumpets it was common to quote Zechariah 14:16. "The king, the Lord of hosts." Indeed, some scholars have suggested that psalms which begin "Yahweh is become king [or 'The Lord reigns']" (Psalm 93, 97) were originally designed for recitation at the New Year festival."[157] Recent study is showing this to be true. It is postulated by many scholars that in Israel, Yahweh was crowned annually at the "New Year feast of

Yahweh." The scholar Mowinckel has argued that the "enthronement psalms" (Psalms 47, 93, 96-99) in which Yahweh reigns were a part of the liturgy of the ancient synagogues.[158] There is no doubt that this is true. This was also the very day when Jesus was born.

Jesus as the King of Kings

The central theme of the Day of Trumpets is clearly that of enthronement of the great King of kings. This was the general understanding of the day in early Judaism and it certainly is that of the New Testament. In Revelation 11:15, recall that the seventh angel sounds his "last trump" and the kingdoms of this world become those of Jesus. This happens at a time when a woman is seen in heaven with twelve stars around her head and the Sun mid-bodied to her, with the Moon under her feet. This is clearly a New Moon scene for the Day of Trumpets. And note: Prof. Thorley who reviewed the first edition of my work has shown that there are exactly twelve stars surrounding the head of Virgo as we see them from earth. And indeed there are. If one will look at Norton's Star Atlas, twelve visible stars will be seen around Virgo's head. They are (according to astronomical terminology): (1) Pi, (2) Nu, (3) Beta (near the ecliptic), (4) Sigma, (5) Chi, (6) Iota — these six stars form the southern hemisphere around the head of Virgo. Then there are (7) Theta, (8) Star 60, (9) Delta, (10) Star 93, (11) Beta (the 2nd magnitude star) and (12) Omicron—these last six form the northern hemisphere around the head of Virgo. All these stars are visible ones that could have been witnessed by observers on earth.

Thus, the description of the apostle John describes a perfectly normal heavenly scene that could be recognized by all people. Here was Virgo with twelve stars around her head, while the Sun was in uterine position and the Moon under her feet. And again, the only time this could have occurred in 3 B.C. was on the Day of Trumpets. This is when the "king of kings" was born.

Another explanation of the Twelve Stars around the head of

Chapter 6 - The Birth of Jesus and the Day of Trumpets

Virgo is that it represents the headship position (the "head" of Virgo is situated in the last ten degrees of Leo) for the beginning of the story found within the Twelve Constellations as reckoned in the biblical Zodiac. In the biblical Zodiac, the tribe of Judah (the Lion, or Leo) was situated around the Tabernacle directly east of its entrance. This meant that half of the tribe of Judah was south and the other half north of the east/west line from the Holy of Holies through the court of Israel and then eastward through the camp of Israel (in this case, Judah) to encounter the altar outside the camp where the Red Heifer was burnt to ashes. This means, unlike some Gentile reckonings which started their zodiacal story with the zero line between Cancer and Leo (that is, at the very commencement of Leo), the biblical Zodiac that Drs. Bullinger and Seiss were talking about began with the 15th degree of Leo (of Judah). This signifies that the first constellation to be met with in this celestial story would have been the "head" of Virgo the Virgin which occupied the last ten degrees of Leo. So, John began his story at this point.

The Significance of Being Born on New Year's Day

The Day of Trumpets in the biblical and Jewish calendars is New Year's Day for commercial and royal reckonings (just as we have January the first on our Roman calendar as the start of our New Year). This New Year's Day signified a time of "new beginnings" to all those in Israel who accepted the teachings of the Bible. As a matter of fact, the Jews over the centuries have held to the belief that the Day of Trumpets was a cardinal date in the history of Adam (our first parent). It was the very day when Adam and Eve came to the recognition of whether to obey God or to defy him (see *The Complete Artscroll Machzor*, p.xvi). But that was not all that occurred on that day. No day in the year could be reckoned as being of more esteemed value and symbolic influence than *Rosh Ha-Shanah*. That day is important for the birth of the Messiah in several ways that are very profound in Jewish symbolism.

The Star that Astonished the World

The book "The Complete Artscroll Machzor" gives some chronological details that the early Jewish theologians and scholars worked out from indications in the Old Testament to show when important individuals were born or major events happened in association with their lives. And what an array of significant things occurred on the Day of Trumpets and the month of Tishri. The book gives a summary of accounts found in the Jewish Talmud (*Rosh Ha-Shanah* 10b-11a).

Note what the Machzor states about this particular Day of Trumpets. The quotes are interesting and of value. "The Patriarchs Abraham and Jacob were born on *Rosh Ha-Shanah*. Abraham was a new beginning for mankind after its [mankind's] failure to realize the promise of Adam and Noah. Jacob was a new beginning for the Jewish people, for it was with him that Jews advanced from the status of individuals to that of a united family on the threshold of nationhood" (p.xvi, italics and bracketed word mine).

The Machzor does not stop with Abraham and Jacob. Look at the following quote: "On *Rosh Ha-Shanah* God remembered three barren women, the Matriarchs Sarah and Rachel, and Hannah the mother of the prophet Samuel and decreed that they would give birth. Not only was *Rosh Ha-Shanah* a turning point in the lives of these great and worthy women, *but the births of their children were momentous events for all Jewry*, because they were the historic figures Isaac, Joseph, and Samuel" (*ibid*. italics mine). If the Jewish people would realize that the New Testament in the Book of Revelation (chapter 12:1-5) also places the birth of Jesus on the very same Day of Trumpets, they might begin to understand just how important Jesus is in a Jewish sense as well as to the world. The New Testament states that he is the Messiah. He shares many similarities with the births of Abraham, Jacob, Isaac, Joseph and Samuel. People should begin to realize the significant coincidences of the birthdays of these prominent men as understood by the Jewish people. And standing out above them all, is the teaching of the apostle John that *Rosh Ha-Shanah* is also the birthday of Jesus.

Chapter 6 - The Birth of Jesus and the Day of Trumpets

More Significance of the Day of Trumpets

Jewish chronological evaluations show other important events associated with the Day of Trumpets (*Rosh Ha-Shanah*). The Machzor continues: "On *Rosh Ha-Shanah*, Joseph was freed from an Egyptian prison after twelve years of incarceration. He became viceroy of Egypt, provider to the world during the years of famine, and the leader of Jacob's family. God's plan called for Joseph to set in motion the years of exile and enslavement that were the necessary preparation for Israel's freedom, nationhood, and emergence in a blaze of miracles to accept the Torah and march to the Land of Israel" (*ibid.*). This shows *Rosh ha-Shanah* as a day of freedom.

There is more on the theme of freedom. The Machzor continues: "On *Rosh Ha-Shanah*, the Jewish people in Egypt stopped their slave labor [they began their time of liberty and freedom], while they waited for the Ten Plagues to play themselves out so that Moses could lead them to freedom" (*ibid.*, words in brackets mine).

The Final Festivals of Israel

As I have stated, this day at the beginning of the month of Tishri was the day when the seventh trump (or the last trump) was sounded to introduce the final month when the festivals of God ordained at the time of Moses would be held. This last trump is mentioned by the apostle Paul as heralding the events associated with the Second Advent of Christ back to this earth (I Corinthians 15:52 and I Thessalonians 4:16,17). This last or final trump is also mentioned by the apostle John in Revelation 11:15 as the warning sound that the Kingdom of God will soon be coming to earth. And soon after, the seven angels of the Book of Revelation will bring on the seven last plagues (in the same fashion as the Jewish analyzers of chronology saw that from the same day of *Rosh Ha-Shanah* the Ten Plagues were sent forth on Egypt in the time of Moses).

What is certain is the fact that the Book of Revelation (with its teaching that Jesus was born on the Day of Trumpets) is giving us in a symbolic way the time for the nativity of Jesus whom Christians considered to be the king of the world. He was prophesied to lead all people into a time of freedom and profound peace. This is the central reason why the apostle John in Revelation 12:1-5 shows that the birth of Jesus occurred within the first few minutes (the twilight period) of the Day of Trumpets that works out to be September 11th in 3 B.C.

Chapter 7

THAT DARK DECADE IN HISTORY

It is evident that the chronological indications in the Bible clearly point to 3 B.C. for the nativity of Jesus. While this is the case for the Bible, what about the secular records which have come down to us from ancient times? Do they also support this time as the proper period for Jesus's birth? The answer is, YES. Though one thing must be kept in mind about the secular records that describe this period. Historians are well aware that they are very obscure. In fact, the decade in which Jesus was born is one of the least documented that we have for the entire period of the Roman Empire.

It is well known among classical historians who specialize in the early period of the Roman Empire, that the decade from 6 B.C. to A.D. 4 is one of the most nebulous in the history of Rome. It is a common lament among Roman historians that this ten year period (one of the most important in the history of western civilization) bristles with many historical and chronological difficulties because of garbled or imperfect records that have come down to us.

Professor Timothy Barnes rightly states that "the years of

[handwritten: least amt of records —]

Tiberius' retirement from public life are one of the most *obscure* decades in the history of the Roman Empire" (emphasis mine).[159] Sir Ronald Syme echoed the same sentiment when he spoke about "the hazards inherent in the *obscure* decade 6 B.C.—A.D. 4" (emphasis mine).[160] If there was ever a "dark decade" in the history of Rome, it is this one. And sadly, this lack of information occurs at the very time the historian who specializes in the time of Augustus Caesar and the birth of Jesus needs it most. A great deal of confusion emerges within and among the historical records, and this is no exaggeration.

It would be appropriate to note the sad difficulties that classical historians encounter regarding this ten year period. One of the problems involves the records of Velleius Paterculus who covers this period of time. The fact is, Velleius was deficient in giving information from 6 B.C. to A.D. 4. Note the remarks of Sir Ronald Syme. "The name Velleius brings up the multiple inadequacies of the ancient sources for the decade during which Tiberius was absent from political life at Rome. By what he says and by what he suppresses, by lavish laudation and dishonest distraction, this writer puts Tiberius on exhibit as the unique general, the indispensable '*custos vinderque imperii*,' the predestined successor to Caesar Augustus."[161]

The Difficulties With Secular Records

The inadequacies of Velleius are not the only illustration of the sad state of affairs in understanding the history and chronology of this decade. Other ancient authors are also lacking. Syme continues: "Chance conspires with design to the same sad effect. There are gaps in the text of Cassius Dio between 6 B.C. and A.D. 4. In three places two *folia* are missing from the manuscript. Hence notable transactions are truncated, garbled, or lost to knowledge. It is hardly possible to work out a satisfactory narrative. Mere paraphrase or amalgamation is not enough. Investigation of *this obscure decade* calls for various resources, and rational conjecture cannot be dispensed with." (emphasis mine)[162]

Chapter 7 - That Dark Decade in History

What are some of the problems with Cassius Dio? The manuscripts that contain his writings give historical information for the years 70 B.C. to A.D. 71 (a 140 year period), but he leaves out the years 4 and 3 B.C. and we only have part of what happened in 2 B.C. In actual fact, from 10 B.C. onward his work is probably an abridgement of an eleventh century scholar because we have quotes from Cassius Dio in other works that do not occur in the abridgement from 10 B.C. onward.[163] Worse yet, the abridgement itself is clearly defective because it has Cassius mentioning that Gaius assumed the toga of manhood in 5 B.C. and then makes the chronological absurdity that Lucius, his brother, received the same thing "after the lapse of a year"—in 4 B.C. We know from the writings of Augustus himself that Lucius received the *toga virilis* in 2 B.C.[164]

The imperfect state of the historical records regarding the decade in which Jesus was born ought to evoke caution among some theologians in their interpretation of chronological and historical matters at this time. It is certainly no time to be expressing dogmatism on chronological questions, but strangely (and sadly) this is the very time that dogmatism is expressed. Caution is normally thrown to the wind in most encyclopaedias and historical works regarding the time of Jesus' nativity. It is usually assumed without the slightest question or tinge of doubt that Jesus was born *before* 4 B.C. This appraisal (looked on as an "infallible" judgment by most modern theologians) is in full contradiction to the writings of the early Christian scholars who say that Jesus was born *after* 4 B.C.[165]

But why do modern theologians insist on a year *before* 4 B.C. (as early as 5, 6, 7 and now as early as 12 B.C. is even suggested) for the birth of Jesus? The common belief centers on some remarks made by Josephus regarding the death of King Herod. He mentions that there was an eclipse of the Moon not long before the death of Herod. There was such an eclipse in March 13, 4 B.C. This is the Lunar Eclipse that most scholars select as the one associated with the death of Herod. Still, there were other lunar eclipses near that same time, and these must be considered too. The remarks of Josephus about a lunar eclipse are important, but they must be interpreted within the framework of a proper understanding of the history of the time. The records of Josephus are even vital, but they must be examined and applied prudently or else confusion will continue to reign concerning the time of Jesus' birth.

The Anomalies of Josephus

One must be very careful in evaluating the records of Josephus. He is not an easy author to understand in matters dealing with chronology. At times he seems consistent in what he relates and at other times he is absurdly inconsistent. As a matter of fact, for certain periods he avoids giving chronological details at the very time the historian needs them most. For example, the main years of Archelaus, the successor of King Herod, are glossed over with one or two general statements and the period from A.D. 6 to the time of Pilate (A.D. 26) is practically blank. For some strange reason, the twenty year period just prior to the ministry of Jesus is glossed over as not being of necessary worth to report and this applies to both of the major works of Josephus. The lacunae were a deliberate glossing over by Josephus, probably for political reasons.

There are also anomalies in Josephus' treatment of Herod's reign. In the first years of Herod's kingship, he buttressed his history with known and reliable chronological eras of time. He equated Herod's seventh year with the year following the Battle of Actium. Josephus also gave reference to the Olympiads (a reasonably known international chronological benchmark). Josephus continued giving such exact dates until Herod's twenty-eighth year (a few years before the birth of Jesus).[166] But from then on, for some unexplained reason, Josephus stopped giving chronological indications which would link the latter years of Herod's reign with known historical eras. He did not resume his normal international cross-references until the tenth year of Archelaus (son of Herod) in A.D.

Chapter 7 - That Dark Decade in History

6. From then until the Jewish War of A.D. 66 to 73 his chronological references are sensible.

Why did Josephus abandon internationally recognized chronological references from 9 B.C. to A.D. 6? No one knows. But this very period of time is when Roman historians are sadly saddled with deficient chronological evidence for what was happening in the Roman Empire. Some of the most important events in Palestinian and Roman history were occurring during that period of sixteen years. But for all those years, not one historical event mentioned by Josephus is cross-referenced to the Olympiads, the Battle of Actium, the years of the Roman consuls, or to the year of Caesar's reign.

These and other factors have caused historians to suspect the motives of Josephus in his writings of history. The German scholar Stauffer has summed up some of the problems in accepting Josephus without a critical eye.

> "The past fifty years of research on the work of Josephus have taught us to be severely critical of his method and presentation. Josephus had an ax to grind. His historical journalism was intended as a self-defense and self-aggrandizement. He wrote to glorify his people and to eulogize the Roman Emperor. He was an ardent sympathizer with the pro-Roman collaborationists among the Jews and an opponent of all the anti-Roman and anti-Herodian partisans of the Palestinian resistance movement. Crucial parts of Josephus' historical works, moreover, were casually patched together from older sources of uneven value: consequently they were replete with gaps and contradictions, are muddled and misleading. This is particularly true of his remarks on Augustus, Herod, Quirinius, and the census. Of course, Josephus remains an invaluable source: but he is not to be read uncritically."[167]

Long ago, Edersheim in his valuable analysis of Josephus in *The Dictionary of Christian Biography* (A.D. 1882), recorded a panoply of contradictions from one part of Josephus to another. "Discrepancies are not wanting between statements in *Antiquities* and others in the *Jewish War*, and even mistakes in regard to plain biblical facts." This is especially true in chronological matters.[168]

The Star that Astonished the World

There Are Chronological Errors in Josephus

There can be no doubt of Josephus' chronological errors. As one example out of many, note his appraisal of the first year of Cyrus the Great. In the *War*[169] he said the year was what is recognized today as 570 B.C. But in one part of his *Antiquities*[170] he said it was 578 B.C. and in another[171] he said it was 586 B.C. In reality, most historians today feel the year was actually 538 B.C. Not only was Josephus inconsistent in his own references, he was wrong in all of them.

One might excuse Josephus for mistaking chronological matters some six centuries before his time, but it should be expected that he would fare better in periods much nearer his own lifetime. Yet at the very time of Herod (during whose reign Jesus was born), Corbishley, some fifty years ago, shows that the writings of Josephus contain much evidence of a deeper corruption than many seem to suspect. Everyone who has gone into the subject at all is aware that there are obvious blunders in the chronology of Josephus, but no successful attempt to remedy them appears to have been made.[172] A few examples can be given.

Josephus made the statement that Herod's government over Galilee began when he was "very young"—when he was "fifteen years of age."[173] Hardly anyone today accepts this statement of Josephus as accurate. Some even want to correct the text to read "twenty-five." However, Professor Marcus, who helped translate the Loeb edition of Josephus, relates that "fifteen" is certainly the genuine reading. Josephus must have said "fifteen" otherwise, how could Herod be described as "very young"? There is not the slightest textual authority for changing the "fifteen" to "twenty-five." Still, Josephus was wrong. Herod was certainly in his "twenties" when he became governor of Galilee or else he could hardly have been nearly seventy years old (as Josephus later attests) at his death.

This does not end Josephus' chronological anomalies. He tells

Chapter 7 - That Dark Decade in History

us that Herod's appointment as king was in the 184th Olympiad which was inaccurate by a few months with his next reference which said it took place when Calvinus and Pollio were consuls (40 B.C.). However, a close inspection of what Josephus stated, and comparing it with other Roman records, we find that Herod was actually made king in the Spring of 38 B.C. (not in 40 B.C.). That is not all. Cassius Dio said Herod captured Jerusalem in 38 B.C.,[174] while some scholars think Josephus identified its capitulation with the year of 37 B.C. in the first part of a sentence and in the latter part of the same sentence Josephus indicates it was in 36 B.C.[175] These contradictions have given modern historians considerable difficulty in arriving at chronological exactitudes from Josephus.[176]

Even Standard Dating Systems Josephus Does Not Seem to Understand

Josephus appears not to have understood how to date events in Palestine with the Olympiad dating system because he was notoriously in error in several places when he attempted to utilize it.[177] But there are other problems with Josephus' chronological statements. Relative to Herod's death, the modern historians Vermes and Millar feel "that Josephus reckons one year too many" which would put his death in 3 B.C. But if the year 36 B.C. was the year that Herod captured Jerusalem as some historians believe (and the cycle of Sabbatical Years as shown in history certainly reveal this to be the year), Herod's last year would have been from 2 to 1 B.C. And this is the truth.

Indeed, in *Antiquities*, XIV.490 Josephus said the Hasmonean reign ended after a rule of 126 years, but it was actually a reign of 128 years if one reckons 164 B.C. as the start of Maccabean rule. In *Antiquities*,[178] he stated that Hyrcanus was 81 years old at his death, but historians clearly realize that Hyrcanus was in his early 70's when he was killed. In *Antiquities*, XV.181 he related that the interval between Pompey's restoration of Hyrcanus to power and the time of Antigonus' usurpation was more than 40 years, but that span of time was actually only about 23 years. In *Antiquities*, XV.231 he said that Mariamme was executed late in 29 B.C., but in his *War*, I.442 he said it was in 34 B.C.

There is even more confusion in the works of Josephus at the very period where we need accurate chronological information. In two places Josephus wrote that Archelaus, Herod's successor, reigned 10 years,[178] but in another place he said 9 years.[179] He also recorded that Archelaus married Galphyra, wife of King Juba of Mauritania, after Juba died,[180] but he was clearly in error. It is well known that Juba was alive about 20 years after Archelaus married Galphyra.

These chronological inconsistencies should cause modern historians to tread cautiously when they come to evaluate what Josephus recorded. But they go merrily on their way of dogmatism when it comes to Josephus' statements concerning the number of years for Herod's reign. The truth is, Josephus himself (when he was not an eyewitness to historical events and relying on the statements of earlier historians) did not always understand the actual chronological facts. He often gave two or even three different dates for certain events in his different works, and sometimes all his indications do not accord with the modern chronological tables.

Josephus Leaves Out Important Persons

One thing for certain, Josephus was a very subjective writer. With his own words he admitted that the writing of his autobiography was to assure his Roman benefactors that he was thoroughly pro-Roman in every respect.[181] His loyalty to Rome went so far that he identified the prophesied Messiah of the Old Testament as being Vespasian, the Roman Emperor.[182]

And another point. It has amazed Jewish scholars that Josephus said not one word about the most important rabbi from the close of the Old Testament period until modern times—Hillel the First. This rabbi was most prominent in Jewish affairs and he lived at the exact

Chapter 7 - That Dark Decade in History

time of Josephus' silence on chronological matters. Josephus full well knew of Hillel's prestige. Indeed, he mentioned that Simon (one of Hillel's descendants) was of very distinguished stock.[183] And distinguished he was! The Hillel that Josephus refused to write about was no less than the originator of rabbinic Judaism which has become the mainstream of Judaic thought ever since. He was reputed to have been in charge of the Sanhedrin (the Jewish Supreme Court). He was so important that later Jews considered him to be equal to Ezra the reputed canonizer of the Old Testament itself. Hardly anyone was more important to Judaic theology from the time of King Herod until modern times, but if we had only the writings of Josephus to go on, no one would know that Hillel existed. Such an avoidance has to be looked on as an attempt on the part of Josephus to avoid comment—because of biased opinions. This may be the reason why he recorded so little about Jesus and his times.

The truth is, Josephus may have tried to give a reasonable appraisal of certain historical events, but it is what *he left out* (or gave no chronological indications about) that gives us of modern times our problems in understanding what was actually happening at this crucial period of time. There were good reasons for Josephus to adopt his subjective approach. To be frank, he was interested in keeping the top part of his anatomy attached to its nether parts.

To stay alive, Josephus had to watch very carefully what he wrote. Had he been too plain, not only would he have been in jeopardy of losing his life, but his historical works would have gone up in smoke as well. He must have felt it prudent to judiciously avoid giving comment on certain crucial periods (and especially to the mention of some key individuals) because the political climate in Rome did not warrant plain speaking. One could hardly blame him.

Worse Yet, the Manuscripts of Josephus Have Been Edited

Though it is generally accepted that Josephus did write about Jesus of Nazareth in his *Antiquities* XVIII.63,64, it is felt by many scholars that there has been some alterations in the text to give a favorable account of Jesus as being the Christ. The notes in the Loeb edition of Josephus give the pros and cons of the issue in a fair and concise manner. What this section does indicate is the fact that there have been editings in the text of Josephus by later individuals and one must be careful in accepting all of the statements of Josephus (especially those involving chronological matters where numerical indications are in the text). The fact is, there are manuscripts of Josephus which show variations in the number of years in which important rulers lived and reigned. One of the most important of these vagaries is in regard to the death of Philip, the son of Herod. Josephus said he ruled for thirty-seven years.[184] But note this. The earliest copies of the manuscripts of Josephus show him dying in the twenty-second year of Tiberius. Since Tiberius' twenty-second year was A.D.36, this shows that Philip began his reign in 1 B.C. (at the very time I am showing in this book that his father Herod died). With modern manuscripts of Josephus copied since the year 1700 A.D., it is common to erroneously read the "twentieth year," not the older and proper "twenty-second."

In order to confirm what the various manuscripts of Josephus do in fact state on this matter, David W. Beyer of San Diego, California made a survey of all the major manuscripts of Josephus in the British Museum (plus referring to others in the libraries in Europe) and found that before 1700 A.D., twenty-seven of the manuscripts in the British Museum have the "twenty-second" rather than the "twenty," while only three have the "twenty." But note this. When one consults manuscripts produced before 1544 A.D. (some twenty-five manuscripts), *all of them* have the number "twenty-two." Beyer has come to the conclusion that the number "twenty-two" is the correct figure that Josephus wrote. Only in the year 1544 A.D. did the spurious "twenty" begin to come into vogue.[185] There is no doubt that the number "twenty-two" is what Josephus wrote. Indeed, Beyer methodically has reconstructed the manuscript history of these two different numbers regarding

Chapter 7 - That Dark Decade in History

Philip's death as shown in the manuscripts of Josephus (and to his credit, he has done it in a most reasonable way).

So important is Beyer's work on this matter in giving the real manuscript evidence for the "twenty-second" year of Tiberius for Philip's death, that Professor John Dominic Crossan asked that Beyer present his research (titled: "Josephus Re-examined: Unraveling the Twenty-Second Year of Tiberius") at the Historical Jesus Section of the SBL meeting in Philadelphia in November, 1995. Beyer is to be congratulated for presenting a survey of the manuscripts of Josephus on this matter. The survey was long overdue, but Mr. Beyer has now accomplished the job for the scholarly world. What this early manuscript evidence of Josephus shows is the fact that Herod did die in 1 B.C. and that Philip his son commenced his reign at the death of Herod in 1 B.C. That is precisely what the historical records show that I have been presenting in this book. I am thankful to Mr. Beyer for his painstaking research into the manuscripts which show this fact.

The Editing of Later Scribes Gives Problems to Interpreting Josephus

These difficulties that I have been showing, reveal that one must be careful in accepting historical data (especially those items involving chronology) that we find in the present manuscripts of Josephus. Every statement of Josephus must be critically evaluated. This is because there is no doubt that there have been tamperings with the texts of Josephus by later scribes who have wanted to "improve" the statements of Josephus in matters that disagree with their own theories. This does not mean that the writings of Josephus should be abandoned, but it does show that one must weigh his historical and chronological statements that have come down to us in the manuscripts with a great deal of caution. They must be counter-checked with other sources. We must realize that Josephus has given us a great deal of valuable information, but his statements must be judiciously tested for their veracity. Josephus is especially

113

good when he records what he saw as an *eyewitness*. His account of the Jewish/ Roman War of 66 to 70 A.D. is an excellent and forthright account of the events and most historians give him credit for being reasonably objective. But when it comes to historical events *before* he was born, he then becomes much less reliable. Even what we find in the manuscripts may not be what Josephus actually wrote. This could account for his many inconsistencies.

Josephus Presents Several Difficulties at Particular Periods

The period we are discussing in this book is one of those difficult times in understanding chronological matters. One must exercise caution in the reading of Josephus—especially in chronological affairs from about 9 B.C. to A.D. 6. We do not know why Josephus in that period neglected to give cross-references to internationally recognized eras of time, but he was negligent! And this is precisely where our problem lies. Not only are the records from Roman historians very deficient at this period of time (it was when *that* dark decade was in effect), but Josephus himself fails us too when it comes to precise chronological indications. It is no wonder historians are confused regarding the time of Jesus' birth.

Early Christian Historians

In the first and third chapters of this book, attention was drawn to the historical opinions of early Christian scholars who lived from the second to the sixth centuries. I showed that the majority placed the birth of Jesus in a period that we now recognize as 3 to 2 B.C.—and this is indeed the very period in which he was born.

This is important testimony and it should be seriously considered by modern historians. In spite of this, we do not want to give the impression that the early Christian scholars were always correct. This is because some say Jesus was born in 3 B.C., others in 2 B.C. and even 1 B.C. Even they are inconsistent in their precise datings as to the exact year. Yet, importantly, they are all *consistent* in showing that Jesus was certainly born *after* 4 B.C., and *not before*

Chapter 7 - That Dark Decade in History

4 B.C. that scholars dogmatize about today. This is a significant point and it is of utmost importance in discovering the time of Jesus' birth.

One, however, might ask why the early Christian scholars were not in unanimity in regard to the year of Jesus' birth (though all knew it occurred *after* 4 B.C.)? This is not difficult to explain. The records they had to consult were written at different times and in different places in the Roman Empire. Besides the application of internationally used chronological indicators such as Olympiads, the Battle of Actium, the consuls of Rome, etc., many ancient historians simply gave dates according to the years of certain kings. Some kings reckoned their years from the day they took office, others from the year they were crowned (and there were numerous ways of doing this). Other dating systems involved the eras of cities or states and these often differed among various peoples who lived at the same time over the Roman Empire.

In other words, chronological indications of early historians (and often when faithfully recorded) were scarcely understood by later scholars who lived in other areas of the world who did not use their time-reckoning systems. It is entirely conceivable why the early Christian historians might be as much as one, two or even three years off in reckoning the time of Jesus' birth. Even Josephus was in error in the same way for the time of Herod when he used such Gentile dating systems.

The Chaotic Conclusions of Modern Scholars

What is the present state of affairs in sorting out the problems involving the understanding of the time of Jesus' nativity? Things now have gone from bad to worse. Sheer bedlam presently reigns among modern scholars who specialize in these chronological matters. The wide differences of opinions of scholars are so askew from one another that the variety of their theories becomes almost laughable when their conclusions are compared with one another.

Indeed, it would be laughable if the subject were not so serious. Look at the confusion that now exists in the scholarly world about the year of Jesus' birth.

In a book titled *Chronos, Kairos, Christos* published in 1989 by the prestigious firm of Eisenbrauns as a *Festschrift* in honor of one of the finest chronologists of our day, Professor Jack Finegan, the two editors (Dr. Jerry Vardaman and Dr. Edwin M. Yamauchi) included articles of research from some of the top scholars today in the field of chronology regarding the time for Jesus' nativity. Both Vardaman and Yamauchi must be congratulated for having the courage to publish the various articles (almost all of them contradictory to one another in many of their essential factors). The disunity of opinion among the scholars, as shown in this book, is so wide in their evaluation of the historical sources that the only reasonable word to describe this state of scholarly affairs is *"chaos."* Confusion presently reigns among the scholars. The laity need to know about this *chaos* that now prevails in the professional research now being conducted The above book does the job of showing this *chaos* (and one should be thankful for its candor).

Look at what we find. In this single book, one scholar argues that Jesus was born sometime between August to October of 12 B.C. and that he was crucified at the Passover in A.D. 21. Another using different research as his basis of evaluation also accepted the 12 B.C. birth for Jesus, but he felt the records show Jesus' crucifixion was in A.D. 36. Another thinks Jesus was born in January of 7 B.C. and that the Magi visited him (while he was a young toddler and standing by his father and mother) on November 12, 7 B.C. Another suggests Jesus was born in late 5 B.C. and his crucifixion was in A.D. 33. My research is also contained in this book. I show my reasons for believing that Jesus was born in 3 B.C. and crucified in A.D. 30.

Now remember, all of the diverse conclusions from the top

Chapter 7 - That Dark Decade in History

scholars from various universities *occur in one book*! This ought to show the state of confusion that presently exists on the whole issue. The attempt that I am presently making in this book is to bring a reasonable amount of pragmatism and common sense to the chaos that now reigns among scholars. Indeed, I believe that this book you are now reading does that very thing. My contention is that the lunar eclipse that Josephus said was associated with Herod's death was that of 10 January, 1 B.C. (and not the earlier eclipse of 13 March, 4 B.C.). There are other modern historians who feel the same way, notably W.E. Filmer, Ormund Edwards and especially the important work of the classical scholar Dr. Paul Keresztes in his two volume work written in 1989 titled *Imperial Rome and the Christians*. This latter work provides some outstanding research throughout its pages. It shows the reasonableness of accepting the basic premises on the death of Herod in 1 B.C. that I am advocating in this book.

And we are not the only ones who have understood the historical records in this fashion. Scaliger, as early as the sixteenth century, was very decisive in stating that Herod's death was associated with the eclipse of 10 January, 1 B.C. He was supported by the German historian, Calvisius, who recorded nearly 300 eclipses as chronological benchmarks for reckoning historical events of the past. In the last century the English scholars William Galloway, H. Bosanquet and C.R. Conder also affirmed that the 10 January, 1 B.C. eclipse was the proper one. This belief was also maintained by Professors Caspari and Reiss of Germany in their chronological studies.

In the next chapter we will find that Josephus, in spite of his chronological errors, provides eyewitness information from Nicolas of Damascus which can prove the time of Herod's death. And that time has to be in January, 1 B.C. This will place Jesus' nativity in 3 or 2 B.C. Astronomy is the key to understand Josephus. When we apply the rules of astronomy with history, we will find that the *dark decade* in Roman history which has caused so much confusion to scholars, becomes full of light and understanding.

Chapter 8

ASTRONOMY AND THE DEATH OF KING HEROD

In the face of the historical evidence against it, the majority of theologians have up to now placed the birth of Jesus before the Spring of 4 B.C. They have insisted on this early date because of a reference in Josephus that King Herod died not long after an eclipse of the Moon and before a Springtime Passover of the Jews. This eclipse has become an important chronological benchmark in reckoning the year of Herod's death.

Eclipses are powerful astronomical indicators to show the precise times when events happened in history. Even those that happened 2000 years ago can be calculated to within a few minutes of their occurrence, and if one can pick the proper lunar eclipse that Josephus referred to, then further historical inquiry is considered unnecessary because "astronomy" has settled the chronological issue.

Those theologians who have adopted this astronomical principle for solving chronological questions are absolutely correct. There is no arguing with eclipses. They are solid and unchallenged witnesses to support the truth of early historical records. And when astronomers in the last century told theologians that an eclipse of the Moon occurred during the evening of March 13, 4 B.C. (and that it could be seen in Palestine), *this* eclipse is the one that theologians have accepted as the one referred to by Josephus. They have particularly preferred this eclipse because Josephus also said Herod died *before* a Springtime Passover. Since March 13, 4 B.C. was just one month *before* the Passover, they have felt justified in placing all the historical events associated with Herod's death and his funeral within that *twenty-nine day* period. The truth is, however, it is completely illogical to squeeze the events mentioned by Josephus into that short period of time. By selecting the wrong eclipse, modern scholars have been forced to tighten considerably the historical events into an abnormally compressed space of only *twenty-nine days*.

Eclipse records are very important, but they must be interpreted correctly regarding the chronological period in which they occur. Over a ten year period, several lunar eclipses are capable of being observed in most areas of the world. Two or three can even occur in one year. This relative frequency of lunar eclipses can be a problem in identifying the ones mentioned by the ancient historians if the early historians gave no details about the time of night, the day of the week, the calendar date on which they happened, or whether the eclipses were full or partial. With the eclipse of Josephus, none of these factors is evident. Josephus gave the single clue that a Springtime Passover was celebrated not long after the eclipse. This would appear a reasonable hint that the eclipse happened sometime in the early or late winter.

It is the mention of this Passover that has prompted most theologians up to now to select the eclipse of March 13, 4 B.C. as the one that seems to meet the historical circumstances. But this is not possible. A close examination of the records provided by Josephus unearth formidable problems in accepting this eclipse. Using common sense, plus the application of a general understanding of the

Chapter 8 - Astronomy and the Death of King Herod

Jewish social and religious customs in the first century, will allow anyone to select the proper eclipse. In no way can it be the one of March 13, 4 B.C.

Let us look at the lunar eclipses that were observable in Palestine during the general time for the nativity of Jesus. From 7 to early 1 B.C. there were four lunar eclipses. It is one of these four eclipses to which Josephus has reference regarding the time of the death of Herod. Let us look at them carefully. The following table shows when they happened. For reference, see *Solar and Lunar Eclipses of the Ancient Near East,* by M. Kudlek and E. Mickler (1971).

7 B.C. = No eclipses
6 B.C. = No eclipses
5 B.C. = March 23. Total eclipse. Central at 8:30 pm
(elapsed time between eclipse and Passover: twenty-nine days).
5 B.C. = September 15. Total eclipse. Central at 10:30 pm
(elapsed time between eclipse and Passover: seven months).
4 B.C. = March 13. Partial eclipse. Central at 2:20 am
(elapsed time between eclipse and Passover: twenty-nine days).
3 B.C. = No eclipses
2 B.C. = No eclipses
1 B.C. = January 10. Total eclipse. Central at 1:00 am
(elapsed time between eclipse and Passover: twelve and a half weeks).

Which was the eclipse that was associated with Herod's death? Most theologians have picked the one that occurred on March 13, 4 B.C., but they are clearly three years too early. They have thrown to the wind the testimonies of the majority of the early fathers of the Christian Church who placed the birth of Jesus from 3 to 1 B.C. If those early fathers would have been consulted and given a reasonable amount of credibility which they deserve, then Herod's death would have been sought for somewhere around 1 B.C., not three years earlier as is commonly done today.

We now have, however, new historical documentation quite independent of the early Christian fathers or Josephus showing that Herod died in early 1 B.C. The later chapters of this book will demonstrate what those historical documents state and what the new archaeological discoveries have shown to prove this. This evidence, along with that given by Josephus, will provide a great deal of weight to show that the eclipse mentioned by Josephus *was not* that of March 13, 4 B.C. The proper eclipse had to have been that of January 10, 1 B.C. This gives us a veritable key to open the door of understanding for this *obscure* period of time.

All of this new evidence when considered together can pinpoint the eclipse of January 10, 1 B.C. as the *proper* eclipse associated with the death of King Herod. When this is realized, not only will the history of Palestine become much clearer in understanding, but that "dark decade" in Roman history from 6 B.C. to A.D.4 will also take on a great deal of illumination. Historical events which have been confusing and which appear contradictory to historians of the early part of the Roman Empire, will become harmonious and consistent. So much depends upon selecting the *proper* eclipse mentioned by Josephus. Let us now look at the evidence from Josephus himself (which is actually the eyewitness account of Nicolas of Damascus whom Josephus quotes). His records will prove that the eclipse of March 13, 4 B.C. (now almost universally accepted as correct) is *not* the proper one.

The Sickness, Death and Funeral of Herod

What the modern historian needs to do is to catalogue the events that occurred from the day of the lunar eclipse until Herod died, then add on the time that elapsed for his funeral and burial, and then count the period from Herod's burial to the Springtime Passover which found Archelaus (the son of Herod) reigning in Jerusalem. The events are well recorded by Josephus. True, Josephus does not give in his writings the exact number of days from the lunar eclipse to the next Passover, but this interval of time can be generally deter-

Chapter 8 - *Astronomy and the Death of King Herod*

mined without difficulty. Note the sequence of events recorded by Josephus that shows this.

The day before the lunar eclipse two prominent Jewish rabbis were burnt alive at the command of Herod for tearing down a golden eagle which he had erected over the eastern gate of the temple: "and on that very night there was an eclipse of the moon."[186] The morning after the eclipse, Josephus said Herod's illness became worse (he had been sick some two or three months). People began to say that the intensification of Herod's affliction was a result of the rabbis' deaths.[187] One has to allow two or three days after the eclipse for Herod's physical deterioration to become noticeable. His physicians then tried "one remedy after another."[188] For *several* remedies to be practiced on Herod in order to cure him occupied at least four or five days—a remedy for each day. The elapsed time for these events would reasonably occupy (at a bare minimum): *one week*.

Those various remedies performed on Herod, however, did not improve his condition. The physicians then recommended that he leave Jericho which was then his temporary residence and retreat to the mineral baths at Callirrhoe. These baths were located on the Dead Sea about 25 miles southeast of Jericho. Herod heeded their advice. Since he was very ill and getting worse—it would have taken at least a day for him to have been carefully transported to the baths—probably longer. He then began a period of treatment using the mineral waters. The therapy certainly took two or three days to give the chemicals in the waters a chance to work. But the use of the baths gave Herod no sign of improving his condition. He then ordered his attendants to carry him back to Jericho. The elapsed time for these events associated with taking Herod to the baths of Callirrhoe and returning to Jericho would have occupied at least *one week* (the interval of time would now be *two weeks away* from the eclipse).

Once back at his palace in Jericho, Herod devised a monstrous

123

The Star that Astonished the World

plan. Since he knew his death was not far off, and realizing that most of the Jewish people had a vehement hatred of him, he decided on a scheme which would have the whole nation in mourning at the time of his death. He had many prominent Jewish elders from *all areas of his kingdom* assemble at Jericho. Without the elders realizing his intention, Herod's plot was to place them in custody, then on the day of his death, they were to be executed. This would guarantee in his warped reasoning that all the Jewish nation would go into a state of mourning.

This heinous plan was put into action. Messengers were sent from Jericho to all parts of Herod's realm bearing orders for the elders of the cities and villages to appear at Jericho on pain of death for their refusal.[189] Since the northern cities of Herod's kingdom were at least 130 miles away, a period of 3 days for the couriers to reach the elders, a day or so for them to prepare for the trip, and then 3 or 4 days for the elders to reach Jericho would occupy, at the very least, a week's time. Josephus said these municipal elders with other Jewish dignitaries finally arrived at Jericho and were locked up in the hippodrome (the race-track area). The elapsed time for this assemblage of elders was at the very least one week (the interval of time now being *three weeks away* from the eclipse).

Josephus then said that after this, letters came from Augustus in Rome giving Herod permission to kill his son Antipater. The king had him executed immediately and Herod died 5 days later.[190] Herod's survivors then determined that the elders imprisoned in the hippodrome were not to be killed. They were released and many were allowed to return home. The elapsed time for these events would reasonably occupy *5 to 7 days* (now almost *four weeks away* from the eclipse).

The Funeral of Herod

Josephus said that Herod ordered his funeral to be the grandest ever bestowed on a king.[191] And Archelaus carried out his father's

Chapter 8 - Astronomy and the Death of King Herod

wish.[192] The preparations for such a funeral would have taken some time. Josephus shows that the arrangements for the official procession were begun only after Herod died.[193] In no way was it possible for a royal funeral to be arranged in a single day. Indeed, several days would have been needed before the procession from Jericho toward Jerusalem could commence. The final burial place of Herod was to be at the Herodian about 8 miles south of Jerusalem.

It surely took a few days to prepare for the procession in order for it to proceed. This must be the case because we are told that all the royal ornaments were brought to Jericho for the procession.[194] The "crown jewels" and other regalia would have been kept under guard in the palace at Jerusalem and it surely would have taken 2 or 3 days to procure them. Even the abundance of spices to treat the body along the way and at the tomb (*e.g.* Luke 23:56 and 24:1) which required 500 domestics of Herod to carry no doubt took some time to collect and prepare (*e.g.* Pliny, XII,41). To keep the body in reasonable condition until the funeral and burial ceremonies were over, the body had to be prepared in a way to prevent putrefaction.

Josephus showed that those having royal dignity were embalmed, and in Palestine this was done with honey.[195] For the time it took the funeral procession to journey from Jericho to Jerusalem and then to the Herodian, Herod's body had to be prepared to prevent the senses of those attending the funeral solemnities to suffer the consequences of being near an unburied and unembalmed corpse. King Herod's body, however, was properly embalmed for the trip to the Herodian. Placing the body in honey was one way to prevent putrefaction—and the 500 domestics carrying spices also had their duties assigned to preserve a proper dignity for the king. This took time to accomplish, but there were other reasons why the funeral cortege could not have started on the day following Herod's death.

Josephus said the "whole army" was represented in the procession.[196] For military commanders of the armed forces located throughout the realm to be summoned to Jericho and to give them time to arrive would have taken several days, at least a *week* and probably longer. There was little pre-arrangements for a massive funeral procession that Josephus said took place since Herod at first believed he could find a cure of his sickness while at his winter home in Jericho. But elite units of the army were not the only ones summoned to Jericho for the procession. It would also have taken some time for the relatives of Herod and other political and religious leaders of the realm (as well as representatives of neighboring nations) to arrive for the procession. These military commanders and other political luminaries gathering at Jericho would have taken a week or so. We are now about *five weeks away* from the eclipse.

Once all the official dignitaries were assembled for the procession, the funeral cortege then moved toward the Herodian in stages. Notice what Josephus said quoting the eyewitness account of Nicolas of Damascus.

> "The body was carried upon a golden bier, embroidered with very precious stones of great variety, and it was covered over with purple, as was the body itself: he had a diadem upon his head, and above it a crown of gold; he had also a sceptre in his right hand. About the bier were his sons and his numerous relations; next to these the soldiers, distinguished according to their several countries and denominations; and they were put in the following order: first of all went his guards, then the band of Thracians, after them the Germans, next the band of Galatians, every one in their habiliments of war; and behind these marched the whole army, in the same manner as they used to go out to war, and as they used to be put in array by their muster-masters and centurions; these were followed by five hundred of his domestics, carrying spices."[197]

Nothing of such grandeur was given to the funerals of ordinary people. They were usually buried within a day and that was the end of the matter. But with kings it was different. An elaborate procession was designed by Archelaus (at the behest of Herod himself) for

Chapter 8 - Astronomy and the Death of King Herod

the grandest kind of funeral that any man had ever had. It was majestic indeed.

The procession set out toward Jerusalem and the Herodian in stately style. The mourners went 8 stades (exactly one Roman mile) toward the Herodian.[198] Plutarch in his account of Caius Gracchus tells us how 8 stades was the distance selected to be reckoned as one Roman mile on the imperial highways (Langhorne, 582). The distance of 8 stades became a standard that all followed in judging distance on the Roman roads. So, Josephus tells us that while all of the military personnel in the funeral procession were fully dressed for war, they did not rush to the burial site. They walked in a slow funeral cadence in a military style called an "eight stades" march, at single mile intervals.

This military type of mourning march was slow. The army marched a mile a day. Many scholars recognize this fact (*e.g.* Professor Wikgren of the University of Chicago who helped translate Josephus for the Loeb edition relates this as the meaning of Josephus, and he is correct). Josephus, who himself had been a military man simply stated that the military cadence of the army was in the "eight stades" mode of military march—a solemn, mournful, funeral march. Indeed, since Herod planned his own funeral ceremonies and since the Jews were accustomed to a thirty day mourning time called a *Sheloshim*, Herod simply ordered that the procession to Jerusalem (for a brief lying in state) and then to the Herodian for burial would occupy the whole of that required thirty day mourning period.

A Slow Funeral March

It had to be a slow journey for other reasons. Since it was customary for biers in royal funeral processions to be carried on the shoulders of the king's relatives or important state officials, the journey took considerable time. Transporting the bier by a wheeled vehicle was out of the question. Even good roads at the time were normally paved with cobblestone and ordinary ones were simple dirt tracks with uneven pavements. With the axles of ancient wagons bolted solidly to their frames and not having the convenience of springs to soften the jolts, transporting the king by wagon would have shaken the body into quite an unceremonial condition. This would have jeopardized even the preservation of the delicately embalmed state of the body. To prevent such an undignified condition, it was essential for the close relatives and state officials *to carry the bier*. It was customary to place horizontal poles at convenient locations under the coffin and then place those supports on the shoulders of the pallbearers.

With this being the case, the procession was only able to proceed to the Herodian in military "eight stades'" fashion, a Roman mile a day. There was another reason for this. Funerals were accounted as sacred ceremonies which were conducted in accordance to strict religious laws. They were holy occasions and people had to act accordingly. Both Moses and Joshua were told to take off their shoes because they were standing on holy ground (Exodus 3:5; Joshua 5:15), and in funeral ceremonies it was demanded that people in the procession go *barefoot* (Ezekiel 24:17; *e.g.* II Samuel 15:30; Jeremiah 13:22). Going unshod at such times was a general custom adopted by most ancient nations as well as the Jews. The *Encyclopaedia of Religion and Ethics* has the following account to show this prevailing custom among the various peoples of the world at this time in history.

> "The women in the procession through the town mourning Demeter *went unshod*, and so did the Locrian virgins in approaching the altar of Athene. In drought a procession and ritual was intended to propitiate the gods by this token of humiliation and sorrow. Many other instances of this are known. In actual mourning rites *going barefoot* was used by both Greeks and Romans; e.g. Suetonius describes how the young nobles who removed the ashes of Augustus from the pyre *were barefoot*. Bion describes Aphrodite wailing for Adonis *as barefoot*, and Autonoe was *unshod* at the death of Actaion. It was also a token of distraction,

Chapter 8 - Astronomy and the Death of King Herod

as when the Roman vestals fled from Rome with sacred utensils. *Among the Hebrews to go barefoot was also a sign of mourning*" (emphasis mine).[199]

With people in the stately procession *having to go **barefoot*** for 25 miles, it can easily be understood why they proceeded by stages (about a mile a day to the Herodian). This has to be the case because the barefoot carriers of the bier being relatives of Herod or dignitaries of the realm were not accustomed to going barefoot. With their tender feet they could not have gone much further in a day carrying the heavy weight of the bier. This would mean that the funeral procession from Jericho to the Herodian lasted about 25 days, but this does not take into account a period of lying in state at the capital of the nation. Such a ceremonial procedure was normal for kings and high government officials. The Romans usually had their dignitaries lie in state for seven days. Herod must have had a similar period (or nearly so) at his capital city of Jerusalem. It would have been entirely out of character to have denied the king such recognition.

The Army of Herod Governed the Funeral March

Some people, on the other hand, have thought that Josephus meant that only the army went a mile from Jericho with the cortege and then they dispersed to their areas of duty throughout the realm.[200] In no way could this be the meaning of Josephus. Such a departure of the army would have left the expensive royal items in jeopardy of seizure. Without the army, the Jewish people, who despised Herod with extreme passion, could well have heaped abuse on the corpse and stripped the bier of all its treasures and honor. Even the life of the new king Archelaus who accompanied the body of his father to its destination could well have been placed in jeopardy. Indeed, it is really inconceivable that the royal troops and servants did not attend the procession all the way to the Herodian. Such a thing would have been entirely out of character with the funeral of any king, let alone one with the immense egotism of Herod. And remember, Josephus said it was Herod himself who planned the entire funeral ceremonies. We can rest assured that it was no fly-by-night affair. It was planned to be grand and impressive. This is why it was necessary for the army, in stately and regimented style, to accompany the bier of the king from Jericho, to the capital at Jerusalem and then to his final resting place at the Herodian. Everything must have been done with complete grandeur and majesty.

To give stateliness to the procession, Josephus shows it journeyed from Jericho by stages—proceeding about a mile a day in the direction of the Herodian which was about 25 miles away. This means the procession would have lasted *four weeks* (because the cortege would not have travelled on the three Sabbath days). If the king, however, lay in state in the vicinity of Jerusalem for a period of time, additional days would have to be given to the interval. Since to reach the Herodian from Jericho in this fashion took at least four weeks (which was designed by Herod to occupy the whole of the required thirty day mourning period known as the *Sheloshim*), then Herod was buried *eight weeks* away from the eclipse if we allow the bear minimum of time for these things to be accomplished.

Royal Funeral Marches Went by Stages

For royal funeral processions to proceed by stages, with each stage being a daily stopping of the procession, is well attested for this period. When Herod's benefactor, the emperor Augustus, died at Nola in southern Italy, his body was conveyed over the 120 miles to Rome *by stages*.[201] Starting from Nola, senators from the various communities along the route carried the body of Augustus by night from one town to the next until it reached the outskirts of Rome. During the day the bier rested in the town hall or principal temple of each halting place. When the body reached Bovillae just outside Rome, knights of the Empire then conveyed the body of the dead emperor to Palatine Hill inside the city. From there the final part of

Chapter 8 - Astronomy and the Death of King Herod

the procession began. The body was taken to the Forum where it lay in state (as mentioned before, lying in state for Roman leaders was usually for seven days).[202] And then, with great solemnity, the body was carried to the Campus Martius for cremation. The ashes were finally taken to the Augustan Mausoleum in the north of the city. This terminated the procession. A funerary feast was then held and a nine-day mourning period begun.[203] The whole funeral period for Augustus lasted from the 19th of August to the 11th or 12th of September. This means the solemnities lasted just over three weeks.

The funeral of Herod would no doubt have had a solemnity certainly equal to Augustus and it was probably even more grand. Herod had an excessive feeling of personal worth and he ordered his funeral to be "most splendid."[204] It was to be "a majestic funeral such as no other king ever had."[205] And we are told by Archelaus, that Herod did indeed obtain his wishes.[206] And with royal Jewish funerals the official time of mourning for the general public was thirty days (called a *Sheloshim*) and this was followed by a further seven days mourning period for the family of Herod. While the Roman time of mourning was for only nine days (with Augustus' procession and funeral rites taking just over three weeks), Herod's funeral ceremonies lasted much longer to accord with biblical and Jewish mourning customs.

Royal Funerals Involve Much Preparations

One thing for certain, royal funerals took time to accomplish. This is the case even today. Witness the funeral ceremonies a few years back associated with Emperor Hirohito of Japan. It took about *a month and a half* for all the funeral protocol (both religious and secular) to be accomplished. Hirohito's funeral rites occupied slightly more time to celebrate than even those of Herod, and they were about twice as long as those of Augustus. Recall that it took a lot of time for heads of state and other dignitaries from around the world to attend the final funeral ceremonies of Hirohito.

Something similar to this would have taken place with the funeral of Herod. When Herod's younger brother Pheroras died, Herod himself "prepared him for burial and brought him to Jerusalem, where he provided a burial place and ordered a solemn mourning for him."[207] And later, when Herod's son Philip died, "his body was carried to the tomb that he himself had built before he died and there was a costly funeral."[208] These ancient solemnities are not practiced in modern Jewish customs. The funeral and mourning services of Prime Minister Rabin (who was recently assassinated) occupied only seven days, but ancient funerals were much longer.

A Thirty Day Mourning Period

Let us look at the important mourning periods which accompanied Herod's funeral rites. These necessary religious ceremonies show that just over a *four week* period elapsed from the death of Herod until he was finally buried at the Herodian. Note the periods of public and private mourning. This point is a very significant factor in determining the interval of time between Herod's death and his burial. The fact is, there were *two types* of mourning periods that were accomplished at the death of a king or someone who was of national prestige. As mentioned before, the first was a public mourning period of thirty days begun immediately *after the death* of an important person (Numbers 20:29; Deuteronomy 34:8). There was also a further seven day mourning period for the close relatives which took place *after the burial* (Numbers 19:14). It was possible for the separate *public* and the *private* mourning periods among the Jews to overlap one another either completely or partially depending on when the burial itself took place. But it is highly unlikely that they overlapped in Herod's case.

There is such an example in the Bible itself of the various ceremonies associated with the death of a prominent person. We need to look at the mourning periods involved in the wake of this person's death, and also the procession that accompanied the person to his final resting place. The biblical example is that of Jacob, the

Chapter 8 - Astronomy and the Death of King Herod

father of Joseph. Immediately at the death of Jacob in Egypt, the Egyptian embalmers took their normal forty day period to prepare the body. It was the custom in ancient Egypt for people to mourn during the period for embalming the body. Then there followed a thirty day mourning period which became the common custom among Israelites. This was known as a *Sheloshim* (*thirty days*) which became the official mourning period for all people honoring any dignitary. Then Joseph arranged a magnificent procession of all the top people in Egypt and Israel with "chariots and horsemen: and it was a very great company" (Genesis 50:9). Jacob's regal procession went all the way to the border of Palestine. Then was accomplished a further *seven days* of mourning (verse 10). Thus, in this example (which Herod would have been well aware of and would have wanted to emulate), the *Sheloshim* (*thirty days*) after the embalming was completed and the seven days after Jacob's burial, were two separate periods of mourning that did not overlap. A similar situation must have occurred with Herod's procession to Jerusalem and to the Herodian with its funerary ceremonies.

Long Mourning Periods for Dignitaries

While the public mourning period for the Romans was normally only nine days, the Jews were subjected to an extended period of time. From the time of Jacob onward, public mourning lasted *thirty days*. As I have shown, that thirty day mourning period was known as a *Sheloshim*. It was common for all dignitaries in Israel to be honored with such a period of mourning that began at the time of their deaths. Moses and Aaron were formerly honored with such a "Sheloshim" and Josephus informs us that Miriam their sister was similarly mourned.[209] And interestingly, there is absolute historical information that such a public mourning period for national figures was commonly practiced by the Jews in the first century. When the Jews in Jerusalem erroneously heard that Josephus had been killed in the line of duty (who was then commander of Jewish forces in Galilee at the beginning of the war with the Romans in A.D. 67), the people of Jerusalem immediately went into a period of public mourning for thirty days (the *Sheloshim*).[210]

If a military commander such as Josephus was given a *Sheloshim* at the announcement of death, we can be utterly assured that King Herod was given a similar *Sheloshim* by his son Archelaus and the people of Judaea when his death was announced. Indeed, we are informed by Josephus that there was a public mourning conducted throughout the realm and that the people of Judaea showed an honorable respect for the whole of the funeral ceremonies for the dead king.[211]

This is a very important indication regarding our question of the interval of time between Herod's death and the end of the public mourning which happened near the time of Herod's burial at the Herodian.[212] This fact standing alone shows there had to be just over *four weeks* between Herod's death and his burial, and this dovetails remarkably with the 28 to 30 days or so (travelling about a mile a day) for the funeral procession to reach the Herodian from Jericho.

But there is even more. Once Herod was buried, then Archelaus and the immediate family had to undergo their further seven days' *private* mourning period.[213] After those seven days, a funeral feast was then ordered by Archelaus for the people of Jerusalem. This would mean that the public mourning period (called the *Sheloshim*) and also Archelaus' private mourning period, as well as the funeral feast would have been concluded (at the bare minimum) about *nine weeks* after the eclipse of the Moon, probably a little longer.

The Passover of the Jews

Then Josephus records that other things took place in Jerusalem *before* the Springtime Passover occurred that year. After both mourning periods and the funeral feast were over, Archelaus then assumed his normal activities as the new king of Judaea. He gave audience to the people as a king. He made changes in the duties of army personnel and he conferred promotions on numerous officers.

Chapter 8 - Astronomy and the Death of King Herod

He also took time to liberate many prisoners confined by his father, and publicly heard and made decisions on a number of lawsuits occurring in the courts.[214] The hearing and judging of several lawsuits certainly took a few days to accomplish. Josephus (or rather, Nicolas of Damascus whom Josephus was quoting) said Archelaus did these official duties "and many other things"[215] between the time when all the public and private mourning periods and the funeral feast were completed and when the beginning of the Passover season took place. Sheer reason would have to allow a *minimum* of *one week* for these official duties of Archelaus to have taken place when he resumed his normal executive activities. And after all these requirements were met by Archelaus and the general population, then came the Passover.

Now for an important point. Because it is clear that Archelaus resumed his normal duties as king *before* the start of the Passover season, this proves conclusively that both the *Sheloshim* (*thirty days*) mourning period and the personal and private mourning period of seven days were fully completed before Passover. The reason this is important is because some people have imagined that the mourning periods for the dead ceased if the Passover season came on the calendar before the mourning periods were fulfilled. This is true, but in this case we find from the records of Josephus himself that the mourning periods (both of them) were entirely fulfilled *before* the Passover that year commenced. This is proof positive that there were at least *five weeks* of time between Herod's death and the start of Passover in the year that Herod died.

If one were conservative in estimating the interval of time between the lunar eclipse (which occurred just after the two rabbis were executed) and the arrival of the Springtime Passover, one has to allow (at a bare minimum) *ten weeks*. But, to be reasonable, one has to admit that a few days more would make the historical scenario fit better. It would allow for a more comfortable timetable. The interval of time was probably near *twelve weeks*.

The Importance of this Information

The above historical events can easily be seen in the records of Josephus. And importantly, they allow us to determine the exact eclipse of the Moon that Josephus was referring to. It will also help us to eliminate in a decided way the principal eclipse that almost all modern theologians have erroneously accepted as the one intended by Josephus.

For the past 200 years it has been common for the generality of theologians to accept the partial lunar eclipse on the night of March 13, 4 B.C. as the one referred to by Josephus. But they are wrong. Since lunar eclipses can only occur at Full Moon, the interval of time from the Full Moon day of March 13, 4 B.C. to the beginning of Passover in 4 B.C. (the next Full Moon day) is a period of only *twenty-nine days* on the Jewish calendar. In no way, shape or form can all the many events associated with Herod's death and funeral as recorded by Josephus be squeezed into that short *twenty-nine day* period.

This major difficulty in accepting the March 13th eclipse has been noted by the Roman historian, Professor Timothy Barnes.[216] To alleviate the problem, some scholars have suggested that the Passover to which Josephus referred was that of the next year, 3 B.C. But the Passover a year hence is far too remote for consideration. Among other things, Josephus said the people at that following Passover were still mourning for the two rabbis that Herod killed on the eve of the eclipse. This would hardly have been the case some 13 months later. Also, Josephus shows that the new king, Archelaus, went to Rome after that Passover ("in haste to depart"[217]) in order to confirm his kingship with the Roman emperor. Archelaus would not have delayed his trip a whole year. And too, Sabinus, Caesar's financial officer for Syrian affairs, met Archelaus at the port city of Caesarea as Sabinus was going to Jerusalem (Sabinus had just arrived from Rome) in order to secure to the imperial treasury the effects of the dead king. Josephus said

Chapter 8 - Astronomy and the Death of King Herod

Sabinus had been going "with haste."[218] In no conceivable way can one imagine that Sabinus waited 13 months to take charge of Herod's property.

All these events prove that the Passover after the eclipse of Josephus was the very next Passover, not one year away. But they also prove that the eclipse of March 13, 4 B.C. cannot be the one mentioned by Josephus because it is impossible to compress those historical and ritualistic requirements into a period of *twenty-nine days*!

In the next chapter I will give further information that will show the only eclipse that can possibly fit the historical scenario that Josephus recorded from the eyewitness account of Nicolas of Damascus whom he was quoting. It was that of January 10, 1 B.C. As a matter of fact, we do not need exact chronological dates given in the text of Josephus to determine the time of Herod's death. The historical context in which that lunar eclipse was mentioned is sufficient enough to give us the precise period for the death of Herod. It occurred somewhere between the eclipse of January 10, 1 B.C. and the following Springtime Passover.

When this fact is recognized by historians today, even that "dark decade" over which classical historians lament in regard to the fragmentary history of the early Empire of Rome will be greatly illuminated and made clear. Astronomy is the key to it all, and it is time to pay attention to it.

Chapter 9 — THE LUNAR ECLIPSE OF JOSEPHUS

It is not difficult to know which eclipse Josephus referred to if historians will do two things. First, they must eliminate unqualified lunar eclipses that could not be seen in Palestine from 7 B.C. to early 1 B.C. After that, the historical, archaeological and chronological evidence must be evaluated that supports the eclipse that can properly conform to the evidence provided in the records. Astronomy is the key to it all. It is a sure guide to any chronology if one has enough documentation to provide a historical environment within which the evidence of astronomy can be utilized. In the case of Josephus' eclipse, there is considerable historical and archaeological documentation to allow historians to pinpoint the precise lunar eclipse to which Josephus had reference even in that *dark decade* in Roman history.

In the last chapter it was shown how impossible it is to squeeze the events mentioned by Josephus from his lunar eclipse to the next Passover into a *twenty nine day* period that the March 13, 4 B.C. eclipse demands. There are further points that show that such an identification is contrary to reason. Let us look at a ritualistic

Chapter 9 - The Lunar Eclipse of Josephus

requirement of the Jewish people that is fatal to it.

If the March 13, 4 B.C. eclipse were the one referred to by Josephus we have with it an impossible situation concerning an event on the Jewish calendar. The day of the eclipse would have been Adar 15. In the biblical book of Esther it is recorded that the Jewish nation in the time of Ahasuerus, king of Persia, ordained the 14th and 15th days of Adar as days of resting and rejoicing. The days were known as Purim (Esther 9:26,32). Even Adar 13 was known as "the Day of Nicanor." This was a day when the Jewish nation rejoiced in honor of the overthrow of Gentile domination back in the early Maccabean period.[219] And immediately following were the two festival days of Purim. If March 13, 4 B.C. were the day of Josephus' eclipse, then it occurred on the night of Adar 15, the second high day of Purim.

Why should this be a problem? The truth is, it is a difficulty of major proportions. Josephus reported that a few days prior to the eclipse two important rabbis had encouraged some of the youth at Jerusalem to destroy a golden eagle which Herod had placed over the eastern gate of the temple. These religious leaders had interpreted the existence of this eagle as being contrary to the Law of Moses. And in broad daylight a number of young boys began to cut down the eagle.

These Jewish youths were caught in the act and about forty of them were ordered to appear before Herod and the Sanhedrin (the Supreme Court of the nation) to answer for this outrage. The two rabbis who perpetrated the plan were especially singled out for judgment. Realizing the great popularity of these two religious leaders, Herod felt it wise to move their trial to Jericho and away from the capital at Jerusalem. He, himself, was ill and since Herod's winter home was in Jericho he wanted to be in the warmer climate of the Jordan Valley to alleviate the effects of his illness.

This was accomplished. The rabbis and the young men who

assisted them were finally convicted of high criminal actions (sacrilege and sedition). While most of the young men were given milder sentences, the two rabbis were ordered to be burnt alive. Now let us take up the story as recorded by Josephus. He will bring us right up to the important eclipse of the Moon about which we have been talking.

> "They were found guilty of sacrilege against God therein. But the people, on account of Herod's barbarous temper, and for fear he should be so cruel as to inflict punishment on themselves, said, what was done, was done without their consent, and it seemed to them that the perpetrators might certainly be punished for what they had done. But with Herod, he dealt more leniently with others; but he deprived Matthias of the high priesthood partly because of this action, and made Joazar, who was Matthias' wife's brother, high priest in his stead. Now it happened, that during the time of the high priesthood of this Matthias, there was another individual made high priest for a single day, that very day which the Jews observed as a fast. The situation was this: This Matthias the high priest, on the night before that day when the fast was to be celebrated, seemed in a dream to have sexual relations with a woman; and because he could not officiate himself because of this, Joseph, the son of Ellemus, his kinsman, assisted him in that sacred office. But Herod deprived this Matthias of the high priesthood, and burnt alive the other Matthias, who had raised the sedition, with his other accomplices. And that very night there was an eclipse of the Moon."[220]

Now, what has this information to do with the significance of our eclipse, assuming it was the one of March 13, 4 B.C.? The truth is, it is devastating to it. It means that those rabbis would have been burnt alive on the Jewish day of Adar 14, the first day of the two high days of Purim. No court, unless completely illegal, would have had criminals executed and certainly not rabbis on the special day commanded in the Bible when the Jews "rested... a day of feasting and gladness" (Esther 9:17,18). The whole nation would have been in an uproar over such a procedure.

And note this important point. Josephus shows that the decision to execute the rabbis was made by the Supreme Court of the Jews. And though it appears that some of the judges—especially the high priest—were reluctant to sentence them, the court still made the decision to have it done. There can be no doubt of the legality of the whole affair. When some of the Jews just before the next Passover expressed their displeasure over the sentence and execution of the rabbis, Archelaus (Herod's son) tried to calm their outrage by reminding them that their trial had been conducted and the sentence carried out "according to law."[221] The whole affair was certainly accomplished in a legal manner. Severe punishment such as burning was sometimes interpreted as allowed in the Bible for certain types of crimes (see Leviticus 20:14; 21:9; Joshua 7:25,26). Even the burning of criminals was judged acceptable in extreme cases,[222] and the rabbis were charged with sedition and sacrilege. *But were they executed on holy days?*

Executions Were Not Performed on Holy Days

True enough, there was a belief in the second century A.D. that one who rebelled against the Court could be retained for execution in Jerusalem until one of the three festival periods.[223] Since the Jewish people who lived in Palestine were expected to be in Jerusalem at those times, the criminal could be executed in the presence of the multitudes to fulfill Deuteronomy 17:13. However, as Krauss has shown, the criminal was not executed during the festival itself but immediately before, when people were gathering in Jerusalem.[224] The Gospel of John shows this was the time when Jesus was crucified.

Purim, however, was not one of the three pilgrim festivals which required Jewish males to be in Jerusalem. Purim was a time of carnival and celebration by all people throughout the land. It celebrated the former deaths of Haman the Agagite (an Amalekite tribe of Edom) and his ten sons (Esther 3:10; 9:24), plus the deliverance of the Jews from enemies who planned their mass genocide in the Persian period. These days of Purim would have been a most unlikely time for any judicial executions among the Jews, especially on the first day of the festival itself.

No Executions on Purim

There is another reason why Herod would not have planned the executions of the popular rabbis on the high days of Purim. Such a procedure would have been counter to the biblical symbols of happiness and joy that governed that festival period. And note this: Herod who was of Edomite ancestry could easily have been linked, even in a racial way, to the Haman of old, a race that was a mixture of Edomite and Canaanite stock (Genesis 36:11,12).

What has this to do with Herod? From the Jewish point of view, very much indeed. Herod was a descendant of the Edomites. The Jews could well have made capital of the fact that Herod was kin to the ancient Amalekites through his Edomite ancestry. And now (if the eclipse of Josephus were that of March 13, 4 B.C.), Herod would have been burning alive two prominent rabbis on one of the very days Jews were celebrating their earlier victory over Haman, the Amalekite.

An ancient custom of the Jews was the burning of an effigy of Haman at the close of the Purim festival. The ceremony is mentioned in the Talmud,[225] and was condemned by the Theodosian code as being a symbolic attack on Christianity.[226] This is sufficient evidence to show that the custom was widespread among the Jews and that its observance no doubt reached back to the time of Herod and earlier. A document found in the Genizah at Cairo describes how young men among the Jews used to make a dummy of Haman and expose it on the roof top for a few days before Purim. Then, on the festival, they would build a bonfire and burn it amid great merriment and jubilation. The same custom is reported also by an eleventh century scholar as having been current in ancient times among the Jews of Babylon and Elam.[227]

If the eclipse of Josephus were on March 13, 4 B.C., then the

Chapter 9 - The Lunar Eclipse of Josephus

two rabbis were burnt to death on the first day of Purim. The Palestinian countryside must have been strewn with countless bonfires during the days of Purim with effigies of Haman being burnt on them. Are we to imagine that Herod would execute by burning two popular rabbis in the period when those "Hamans" were also being burnt? This would be similar to a foreigner now ruling the United States, a descendant of our former enemies, intensely hated by the populace, now burning two of our leading and popular senators in public view on *July Fourth*, while the Declaration of Independence was being read in all our houses of worship. The Book of Esther was then being read in all Jewish synagogues at Purim. Even Herod would have been too politically wise to attempt such an affront which all Jews would have considered a clear violation of a festival ordained of God.

Further, Herod and Haman can be symbolically associated in several ways. Both had ten sons,[228] and just as Haman had been one of the chief advisors of the Persian emperor in the fifth century B.C., Herod was one of the two top friends of Augustus, the Roman emperor of the first century B.C.[229] Besides this, many Jews considered the existing Roman Empire at the time as the government of the "earthly Edom."[230] It even became common among Jews to believe that the original Roman people were the actual descendants of Edom.[231]

Herod Would Not Execute Rabbis at Purim

Look at what this could have meant to the Jews at the time of Herod. Here was Herod, who was an Edomite,[232] having been made king of the Jews by the "earthly Edom" (Rome). This would mean that both "Edoms" were now conspiring together to rule the chosen people of God, the Jews. And note the outrage: On the very days of Purim (if the eclipse of March 13, 4 B.C. was the one of Josephus) when the Jews were celebrating their deliverance from Haman and his ten sons, the Edomite Herod (also a father of ten sons) was now burning alive two of the most holy men of the Jews at the time that bonfires were all over Judaea burning effigies of Haman. The use of type and antitype was then a common practice in prophetic interpretation by the Jews as the New Testament and other Jewish literature attest. Such a coincidence of Herod with Haman would have been extremely dangerous to Herod's political position and he would have been well aware of it.

The whole thing is unthinkable. Herod may have been without principle in regard to laws or customs when the need arose, but he was too wise a politician to risk the outcome of such an insult to the Jewish people and a festival of God while he was alive and in hopes of recovering from sickness. Given the circumstances, two or three days after Purim for the execution of the rabbis would have satisfied Herod.

Besides, Herod knew the eclipse was coming. They were easy to predict at the time.[233] He no doubt timed the execution of the rabbis to coincide with the eclipse that night. He would have told the populace that God himself would show his displeasure at what the rabbis did by darkening the Moon, and many of the superstitious might have believed him. But if the eclipse were that of March 13, 4 B.C., the Jews could have turned the tables on Herod himself. The eclipse could have been interpreted as censuring Herod's killing of two righteous rabbis during Purim and thereby desecrating the sanctity of the holy period. Killing the rabbis on the very days of Purim would have gained no advantage for Herod. In fact, it would have been a major political catastrophe for him to have done so.

A Further Invalidation

There is another argument against the March 13, 4 B.C. eclipse. Immediately after the Passover following Herod's death, Archelaus (Herod's designated heir) started on his journey to Rome in order to have Augustus confirm him in his kingdom. When Archelaus reached the port city of Caesarea, he was met by Sabinus on his way to Jerusalem. Sabinus was the officer in charge of financial

Chapter 9 - The Lunar Eclipse of Josephus

affairs for the province of Syria. There can be little doubt that Sabinus had just come *from Rome*. He certainly had not come from Antioch in Syria which was the provincial capital. This is made clear in the narrative of Josephus.

Note that when Archelaus heard that Sabinus was going to Jerusalem to place all of Herod's effects under imperial control, he immediately sent his trusted friend Ptolemy to Antioch "urgently soliciting" Varus who was governor of Syria to come to Caesarea in order to intervene with Sabinus.[234] Varus then left for Caesarea, "he had come in answer to the appeal made by Archelaus through Ptolemy."[235] Upon arrival, Varus persuaded Sabinus that it was not in Rome's interest for him to go up to Jerusalem at that time to perform his responsibility. Hearing the appeal of Varus convinced Sabinus that it was better to remain at Caesarea for the time being.

Varus then took the legion of soldiers (about 5000 men plus auxiliaries) which he had brought with him from Antioch and went to Jerusalem.[236] He left the troops in the capital and returned to Antioch. After Varus accomplished these matters, what did Sabinus do? "But after Archelaus had sailed for Rome and Varus had returned to Antioch, Sabinus moved on to Jerusalem and took possession of the palace."[237]

These events tell us several things. First of all, Sabinus could not have had his residence with Varus in Antioch. Had this been the case, Varus would already have known of Sabinus' authority and would have talked with him about the best manner in which to accomplish his task. But the narrative in Josephus strongly implies that Varus did not know of Sabinus' intentions until Ptolemy informed him in Antioch of what was happening in Caesarea. The truth is, Sabinus had just come by ship from Rome.

Some, however, might think that Sabinus may have been a resident of Beirut (a major city in the province of Syria), but this is an unlikely possibility. Why would the imperial financial officer for the province of Syria live in a city over 200 miles from the capital and out of reach with the daily affairs of provincial government? The evidence supports the proposition that Sabinus had come directly from Augustus in Rome to take over temporary financial affairs of Herod. Indeed, there is evidence to show that Sabinus had greater authority in this matter than Varus himself.

As soon as Archelaus sailed for Rome and Varus returned to Antioch, Sabinus went to Jerusalem and took over the command of the legion.[238] He then began to carry out the imperial administration assigned to him. This clearly shows that Sabinus had more authority over the situation than Varus, the governor of Syria. Had Sabinus not have had authority directly from Augustus in Rome, the commanders of the legion at Jerusalem would hardly have let Sabinus take over control *contrary* to the express wishes of Varus.

But Sabinus took over command of the legion and other auxiliary forces at Jerusalem. Even the Jews called the division of troops the legion of Sabinus.[239] And indeed, when war broke out over the actions of Sabinus, he commanded all the military operations.[240] This superiority of Sabinus is demonstrated in other ways. Had Sabinus been under the control of Varus, the governor of Syria would simply have sent a note with Ptolemy restraining Sabinus from going to Jerusalem. Moreover, Josephus shows that Sabinus sent reports directly to Augustus without having to submit them to Varus in Antioch for approval.[241] And when Varus finally came to Jerusalem to rescue Sabinus and the Roman troops from Jewish insurgents when war broke out in Jerusalem, Sabinus did not feel it necessary to report to Varus for his actions.[242] As a matter of fact, Sabinus managed to take 400 talents of money with him for his efforts in Jerusalem.[243]

All of this is good evidence that Sabinus was not a subsidiary of Varus in Antioch, but rather that he had come to Palestine directly *from Rome* with imperial authority to take the financial affairs of Herod's kingdom in hand.

Since this is the case, look at the impossible situation that this places with the eclipse of March 13, 4 B.C. Since Herod must have died about two weeks or so after the eclipse, this would put his death about April 1st. The next event was Passover which lasted from April 11 to 17 in 4 B.C. Josephus informs us that Archelaus was on his way to Caesarea before the Passover had ended. This means that Archelaus got to the port city about April 17th. And just before he was to sail to Rome, he found Sabinus sailing into Caesarea. Now for the problem: How was it possible for the knowledge of Herod's death to have gotten to Rome (1700 sea miles away), for Sabinus to have discussed the situation with Augustus, which he must have done, and then for him to have sailed to Palestine (another journey of 1700 miles), and finally meet Archelaus in Caesarea *all within a sixteen or twenty day period?* Impossible! This point as well shows that the March 13, 4 B.C. eclipse cannot be the one of Josephus.

The Eclipse of March 23, 5 B.C.

Could all of the above events have occurred one year earlier, in 5 B.C.? After all, there was an eclipse of the Moon on March 23, 5 B.C. This springtime eclipse, however, cannot be the one associated with Herod's death. There were still only *twenty nine days* between this eclipse and the next Passover. All of the impossible situations which the March 13, 4 B.C. eclipse encounters are precisely the same with this eclipse. And besides, early 5 B.C. for the death of Herod plays havoc with all the chronological indications of Josephus and Roman records regarding the period of Herod's death. Why even modern scholars have to add an extra year to Herod's reign of 34 years from Antigonus' death (reckoning only two or three days of Nisan in 4 B.C. as a whole year) to make any reasonable sense out of their calculations. An early 5 B.C. date would cause utter chaos in the records of Josephus.

The Eclipse of September 15, 5 B.C.

Several scholars have seen the absurdities in accepting either the

March 13 eclipse of 4 B.C. or that of March 23 in 5 B.C. Because of this, it has been suggested that the eclipse of September 15, 5 B.C. is a better eclipse for consideration.[244] But there are major difficulties associated with this eclipse as well. Look at it for a moment.

Scholars recognize that Josephus reckoned the years of Herod's reign from the Jewish springtime month of Nisan to the next Nisan. In order to make any sense whatever out of Josephus' statements that Herod reigned 37 years from the time he was proclaimed king by the Romans and 34 years from the death of Antigonus (his immediate predecessor), they have put Herod's death in the first two or three days of Nisan in 4 B.C. and they reckon the whole year (from Nisan 4 B.C. to Nisan 3 B.C.) to the reign of Herod.[245] But if one puts Herod's death back in late 5 B.C., then the year lengths of Herod's reign as mentioned by Josephus become altogether garbled and in no way do they make any sense to the historian. Indeed, the September 15, 5 B.C. eclipse is impossible for other reasons.

If the eclipse of Josephus were that of September 15, 5 B.C., then seven months would have passed before the next Passover. Seven months are far too long for the intervening events to have taken place. Note this point. Herod was in Jericho when the eclipse near his death occurred. The city is a furnace in late summer. It is situated just over 800 feet (c. 240 meters) below sea level and its mid-September temperatures are very high. Why would Herod who was uncomfortably ill at the time, subject himself to such oppressive conditions in the Jordan Valley when the pleasant environment of Jerusalem was so near? It might be added, however, that if the eclipse were in the depth of Winter, one could easily understand Herod's wish to be in Jericho. This point alone renders the September 15th eclipse as an improbable one for consideration.

Yet there is another factor that certainly overthrows it. Josephus said that on the very night of the eclipse the high priest Matthias was deposed from office by Herod. This Matthias had a pontificate

Chapter 9 - The Lunar Eclipse of Josephus

of about nine or ten months. This is proved by Jeremias.[246] The proof centers primarily on the fact that Josephus (or rather, Nicolas of Damascus who was an eyewitness to the events) said that Matthias had been appointed to the high priesthood when the scheme of Antipater to kill his father (Herod) was first discovered. Josephus records that there was a seven month span from that time until Antipater returned from Rome to Jerusalem for trial.[247] Within three days after Antipater got back to Jerusalem, Herod dispatched messengers to Rome asking Augustus' approval to have Antipater executed. The couriers would have taken no longer than three months to go to Rome and return. But a few days before news came back from Augustus that Antipater could be executed, the eclipse occurred. Notice what these facts mean.

Matthias the high priest was deposed on the night of the eclipse. So, by adding the seven months between the discovery of Antipater's plot (when Matthias was promoted to the high priesthood) and Antipater's arrival back in Jerusalem, plus the two or three months for the messengers to go to Rome and return to Herod, there was a period no longer than ten months (probably closer to nine months) for Matthias' tenure as high priest.

This may seem technical and complicated, but the results of the inquiry can help us very much in showing that the September 15th eclipse could not be the one referred to by Josephus. It would involve an impossible situation regarding the high priesthood of this Matthias. Indeed, this very Matthias was a famous personality in matters dealing with the priesthood and something happened to him during his priesthood that was remembered hundreds of years afterward. What was this?

Josephus records a remarkable occurrence that happened during the time Matthias was high priest. He had a dream prior to the day of a "fast" in which he was sexually intimate with a woman. This rendered Matthias ritualistically unclean (no one could be sexually intimate even with his wife prior to conducting the sacred cere-

149

monies of the Day of Atonement). Nothing like this had happened before in the history of the priesthood.

The Sanhedrin had to make a decision about the matter. They determined that Matthias should step down from his office for one day. In the meantime a relative of his was commissioned to perform the sacred duties on that fast day. They appointed Joseph, the son of Ellemus, to stand in for Matthias. This incident was so unique in the conduct of temple ceremonies that it was talked about in the Talmud centuries later.[248] And significantly, the Talmud records that the day of Matthias' disqualification was the Day of Atonement. This was the great fast day of the Jews commanded in the Law (*cf.* Acts 27:9).

But how does any of this show that the September 15th eclipse could not be the one referred to by Josephus? It is quite simple to disqualify it. If this eclipse were the correct one, it would mean that Matthias' pontificate ended on that very night (recall that Herod dismissed Matthias on the day of the eclipse), and that his high priesthood lasted nine or ten months at most. To go backwards nine or ten months from September 15th covers a period of time in which no Day of Atonement occurred. The previous Day of Atonement would have happened at least a month or two *before* Matthias was appointed to the high priesthood. These clear facts of history are certain on this matter. This shows that the eclipse of September 15, 5 B.C. thoroughly fails as a candidate.[249]

The Only Eclipse that Meets All Factors

The eclipse of Josephus had to have been that of January 10, 1 B.C. All the events mentioned by Josephus fit quite comfortably with this eclipse, and *only* with *this* eclipse as we will soon show. There were three months from this eclipse to the next Passover. The messengers sent by Herod to Rome at the end of Antipater's trial in the previous Autumn would have arrived back in Palestine (to Herod in Jericho) in 2 or 2 and ½ months, which is very reasonable

Chapter 9 - The Lunar Eclipse of Josephus

At the death of Herod in late January, messengers immediately would have been sent to Rome to inform Caesar of Herod's death, thus permitting Sabinus to arrive from Rome just after the Passover to secure to the imperial treasury the property of Herod. Matthias would also have been available for the Day of Atonement in the previous Autumn.

In fact, everything fits beautifully in other ways. There is a Jewish document called the *Megillath Taanith* (Scroll of Fasting, though it records festival days too) which was composed, initially, not long after the destruction of Jerusalem in A.D. 70. This scroll mentions two semi-festival days during which no mourning was permitted. One is Kislev 7. The month of Kislev corresponds in most years with our December. The other commemorative day was Schebat 2. This month answers to our late January or early February. No one knows why these two days of feasting are commemorated yet they must have been days of joy ordained before the destruction of Jerusalem in A.D. 70. What did they honor?

An early Jewish commentator who probably lived in the seventh century wrote a brief remark to Kislev 7 (December 5th): "The day of Herod's death." However, M. Moise Schwab, who studied the information about the scroll very extensively, felt that it was really the second of the days, Schebat 2 (January 28th) that was the actual day commemorating Herod's death.[250] And interestingly, this latter date fits remarkably well with the January 10th eclipse of Josephus. Herod's death on this very day would have occurred 18 days after the eclipse. All the information in Josephus about Herod's activities between the eclipse and his death fit compatibility with the chronological facts.

Indeed, even the earlier date of Kislev 7 (December 5th), which the commentator associated with Herod's death, may have relevance too. Look at what could have happened on that day. This could have been the time when the two rabbis (who were later executed) provoked the young men to tear down the golden eagle from

151

the eastern portal of the temple. Such an occasion could well have inspired some commemorative date in which it was accomplished. In fact, this is the thing that Josephus reports.

The Importance of the Rabbis Who Were Executed

Those rabbis were, as Josephus states: "two of the most eloquent men among the Jews, and most celebrated interpreters of the Jewish laws, and men well beloved by the people because of the education of their youth; for all those who were studious of virtue frequented their lectures every day."[251] They urged their students to tear down the eagle which they considered idolatrous in order that "*lasting fame and commemoration*" be afforded them and their pious act. And interestingly, the reason why the *Megillath Taanith* was composed in the first place was to put aside days for "*lasting fame and commemoration*." It may well be that the day on which the golden eagle was torn down and also the day of Herod's death were recorded in the *Megillath Taanith* for commemoration because on that very day was when a cry went throughout Jerusalem that "the king was dead."[252] Though the report was false, it prompted the young men to storm the east wall of the temple and in full daylight they cut down the golden eagle. Since the Feast of Dedication was fast approaching (a festival commemorating the overthrow of idolatry in the time of the Maccabees), the two rabbis could well have incited the youths to destroy the golden eagle at that important period of time since they were teaching that it was now "a very proper time to defend the cause of God."[253]

Then what happened? The youths were rounded up and the two illustrious rabbis who had instigated the destruction of the eagle were brought before Herod. But strangely, Herod decided not to bring them to trial in Jerusalem. He had their trial transferred to Jericho. The principal reason that Herod did this was no doubt because of his ill health and he needed to be in Jericho. He then ordered that the Sanhedrin should meet together with him in that desert oasis. A quorum of the Sanhedrin followed Herod to Jericho

Chapter 9 - The Lunar Eclipse of Josephus

and the trial in which the two rabbis were condemned took place.

Now, the *Megillath Taanith* records an unknown fast day for commemoration. It was Tebeth 9 (January 6th in 1 B.C.). This could very well have been the day the rabbis were tried and sentenced. And three days later on Friday, January 9th, the rabbis were burnt alive to correspond with the lunar eclipse that was predicted for that night. Delaying their execution to the eve of the eclipse (and especially since there were no biblical festival days involved as with the March 13, 4 B.C. eclipse) would have allowed Herod to tell the superstitious that even God himself was frowning on the sacrilegious deeds of the two rabbis and that God would express his displeasure that night with an eclipse.

Herod would have died 18 days later on Schebat 2 (January 28th). As mentioned before, this date is one of the undesignated festival days of the Jews mentioned in the *Megillath Taanith* and that it points to the time of Herod's death makes good sense. Just before Herod died, he said: "I know that the Jews will celebrate my death by a festival."[254] And Schebat 2 (as well as Kislev 7 for the tearing down of the eagle and Tebeth 9 for the sentencing of the rabbis) fits the historical timetable perfectly. Also, the events that Josephus said happened between Herod's death and the next Passover can be chronologically placed in a reasonable way.

Only the Eclipse of January 10 Will Work

Recognizing that the January 10, 1 B.C. eclipse is the one mentioned by Josephus has much historical value in another way. Scholars have wondered for years why Josephus referred only to this one eclipse out of the hundreds that occurred over the generations that he covered in his histories. Why single out this one? Indeed, during the reign of Herod there were at least 32 lunar eclipses visible in Palestine (20 partial and 12 total).[255] There must have been special reasons for heralding this single eclipse associated with Herod's death. And so there were.

Other than the historical importance of Herod's death itself, it should be remembered that it was also the very day following the martyrdom of the two illustrious rabbis whom the whole nation admired and esteemed. This was an important event for commemoration to the Jewish people. But there was a national event even more disastrous than that. The occasion of the rabbi's deaths led directly to 3000 Jewish worshippers at the next Passover being slaughtered in the temple precincts.[256] This massacre, which was ordered by Archelaus (the successor to Herod) resulted in the unusual cancellation of the whole Passover services, a requirement mentioned in Numbers 9:6-14.

This was a most extraordinary event. Such a repeal of Passover services because of 3000 dead bodies being within the temple precincts was a most unique circumstance in the history of temple services. Nothing like it had ever happened before. The suspension of this most important Jewish festival in the calendar of the Jews (like our government today forbidding the celebration of Christmas this year) would long have been remembered by the generality of the Jewish people. Yet, there was another event associated with this cancellation of Passover that would equally have brought that year to special remembrance by the Jews.

This slaughter of the 3000 Jewish worshippers in the temple led directly to a major war between the Jews and the Romans that occupied the whole of the following Summer and Autumn. Josephus said that this war was no minor skirmish. It was the most significant conflict to occur in Palestine from the time of Pompey in 63 B.C. to the Roman/Jewish War of A.D. 66 to 73.[257] In order to subdue this Jewish rebellion, the Romans had to muster their three legions in Syria, plus auxiliary forces (about 20,000 armed men in all), to put down the rebellion that erupted. At the end of the war, 2,000 Jews were crucified and 30,000 sold into slavery. This was a very serious war in Palestine. And what started it? It was the death of the rabbis associated with the eclipse of the Moon near Herod's

Chapter 9 - The Lunar Eclipse of Josephus

death. This is one of the major reasons that *that* eclipse was long remembered by the Jews.

In the next chapter, it will be shown that all these important historical events could only have occurred in 1 B.C. This major Roman/Jewish War that Josephus records took place in the Summer and Autumn of 1 B.C. and it was fought as a result of Herod's death, the killing of the rabbis, and the Passover massacre. For this reason, no lunar eclipses beyond the one of 10 January, 1 B.C. need be considered as being the eclipse mentioned by Josephus. The next chapter will demonstrate why this is the case.

Chapter 10

THE WAR THAT NO ONE CAN FIND

Roman historians have expressed a great deal of uncertainty about events that happened during the period from 6 B.C. to A.D. 4. They call it that *dark decade*. To be sure, there are several records of various events which occurred at this time but they are often contradictory, not complete, or else they are heavily flavored with excessive bias and flattery. Most historians prefer to walk cautiously within the history of this period. However, the research we are providing in this book can bring much enlightenment to this time.

The key to the whole thing is to find the year in which King Herod died. Once it is realized that this happened in early 1 B.C. and not 4 B.C., an abundance of historical evidence bursts on the scene that can take away much of the ambiguities with which this period bristles. The fact is, scholars have been misplacing major events some three years too early in the history of Rome and Palestine. But once the reconstruction of the chronological events is recognized, the historical records which have come down to us begin to make perfectly good sense. As an example, there was a

Chapter 10 - The War that No One Can Find

major war that occurred within this period, but the proof of its existence has alluded historians over the years. They can't find it because they have tried to place it three years before it actually occurred. But by dating Herod's death in 1 B.C. (which is proper to do), it is now possible to find several Roman documents that mention not only that war, but other historical events of the period begin to make sense. What is that war that presently can't be found?

This is the war that Jewish scholars call *The War of Varus*. It is the war that took place in Galilee, Judaea and Idumaea just after the death of Herod which started with the massacre of the 3000 Jewish worshippers in the temple at the Passover of 1 B.C. Josephus stated that this war against the Jews which was directed by the governor of Syria, Quintilius Varus, took place in Palestine, but it has been a puzzle to historians that there appear to be no contemporary Roman accounts that would justify it as having occurred. Imagine a period in the remote future when some Iraqi documents might be found of a war in Iraq in which American, British, French and other allied forces fought against Iraq which scholars at that future time had misdated to 1988. But try as they may, no records could be found in the United States that such a war took place in that year. If, however, those future historians looked at United States' records for January and February *of 1991* (three years after 1988), they would have an abundance of records that such a war occurred.

This is the very thing that has happened to *The War of Varus* which took place in the Spring and Summer of the year following Herod's death. Jewish records make it clear that this major war occurred, but there is no Roman testimony (whether it be literature, coins, or inscriptions) that would justify such a war in 4 B.C. Let us, however, be clear. There are no records *if* we place *The War of Varus* in 4 B.C. as most scholars have done. But if the war is correctly dated *three years later* to 1 B.C., we find that there are a number of important Roman references to it. Everything makes sense in a remarkable way.

157

The War of Varus

This was a significant war. Josephus stated that for Rome to gain the victory, it involved the totality of the regular Roman military forces in the province of Syria (about 20,000 men involving three legions plus auxiliaries and allied troops). This war was located in what Rome considered to be one of the most strategic regions in the Empire. In no way could this war be called a minor skirmish. It was well recognized in Jewish circles (both ancient and modern) that it was one of the most serious military operations to occur in Palestine from the time of Pompey (63 B.C.) until the Roman/Jewish War of A.D. 66/73.[258] Such a war had national as well as international implications. About a tenth of the Empire's population was Jewish. They were scattered in most of the cities, but there were heavy concentrations of Jews in the east. Not only that, there were probably as many Jews in Parthia (Rome's arch enemy) as there were in Palestine. Any war involving Jewish revolutionaries which took three Roman legions plus auxiliaries to overcome could not have been a minor military action.

Wars involving the Jews were *not looked on* by the Romans as mere provincial affairs of little import, especially if those wars were based upon Jewish messianic expectations. This was a problem to Rome. The messianic aspect of *The War of Varus* was evident. Over 6000 Pharisees not long before the war had predicted to the house of Pheroras, the brother of Herod, that Herod's kingdom was prophesied to end and "the eunuch" would then have children.[259] This was clearly the messianic age that they were predicting to come with signs and miracles. The Pharisees were the popular leaders of the Jews and the ones most laypeople looked to with confidence. The majority of the Jewish population was then expecting a world ruling messianic king to arise on the historical scene. And indeed, Josephus tells us that after Herod's death many "kingly upstarts" emerged in Judaea and this reflects the general expectancy of the Jews that the messianic age was then imminent.

Chapter 10 - The War that No One Can Find

Rome would have been well aware of these national aspirations of the Jews. And when the revolt broke out after the 3000 Jews were massacred in the temple during Passover, and since the event had messianic overtones to it, Rome began to flex its legionary muscles to quell the uprising. Since the Jews in Parthia would have known what was going on in Judaea, and with Parthia a rival of Rome anyway, this was no time for Rome to be resting on its laurels. With the Jews in revolt, it was an indispensable time for Rome to take action and to get their armed forces to full strength. In such a situation, the security of the eastern provinces if not the Empire itself was at stake.

One of the principal reasons why Rome had earlier given Herod the kingship was to make him a bulwark against the Parthians.[260] While Herod was alive he did just that. But now, with Herod dead and his kingdom in rebellion, with the full armed forces of the Romans in Syria fighting to overcome it, and with only the client kings of Cappadocia, Pontus and Commagene protecting the frontiers with Parthia, it was no time for Rome to be discharging professionally trained legionaries from the armed services. But note this. If this *War of Varus* took place in the Summer and Autumn of 4 B.C. as scholars have felt up to now, a most unlikely state of affairs was then happening in the Roman military. We have the plain statement of Augustus himself that he had been steadily discharging many of his soldiers and giving them handsome bonuses from 7 to 2 B.C.[261] Within that six year period, there were no major wars involving Roman troops while this continual discharging of soldiers was going on. And though Augustus tells us that there was a temporary respite from the discharging in 5 B.C., from 4 B.C. on to and including 2 B.C. the demobilization of the Roman army continued unabated. Rome fought no wars from 7 to 2 B.C.

No Roman/Jewish War from 7 to 2 B.C.

Professor Syme describes the discharging of these soldiers at this period as evidence that peace and security was then found throughout the Empire. "The titulature of the ruler [Augustus] registers no fresh imperatorial salutation for many years after he was acclaimed 'imp.XIV' in 8 B.C."[262] Salutations such as these were given to the emperors when the Romans had secured victories in war. But none were given to Augustus from 8 B.C. up to and including 2 B.C. So peaceful was this period that Syme describes the third closing of the temple doors of the god Janus to this time. This was a sign that peace was then secure throughout the Empire. And with the steady demobilization of the legionaries from 7 to 2 B.C. (with the exception of 5 B.C.), it surely indicates a time of peace and harmony within the Empire.

Now for a difficulty. Scholars today who place Herod's death in early 4 B.C. are also required to place *The War of Varus* in the Summer of 4 B.C. right in the middle of this Augustan peace. They have had to do so because of their erroneous selection of the March 13, 4 B.C. eclipse of the Moon as that associated with the death of Herod. But this is nonsense and this makes the Roman records *three years out of phase* with reality. Herod actually died in January, 1 B.C. This means that *The War of Varus* took place in the Summer and Autumn of that year. Look at what this means and how sensible the historical records now become. Augustus steadily discharged his legionaries from 7 to 2 B.C., and there was peace throughout the whole Empire during that period of time. But with the Palestinian war breaking out in the Spring of 1 B.C., the demobilization of the legions had to stop. The Romans from then on mustered their armed forces and reserves for war. The same thing happened with the United States when Saddam Hussein invaded Kuwait. The United States government quit discharging military men (even lengthening the stay of those scheduled to be discharged) and called up the reserves to fight a significant war in the volatile Middle East. The similarities are most interesting.

Correctly Dating the War of Varus

The War of Varus actually broke out in Palestine in 1 B.C. And at that very time, the Roman records show that the Armenians in

Chapter 10 - The War that No One Can Find

the northeastern section of the Empire also began to stir up rebellion. While this was happening, the Parthians further east also in 1 B.C. maneuvered to take advantage of the deteriorating military situation in Rome's eastern provinces. Understanding that *The War of Varus* was in 1 B.C. can make these known activities of the Armenians and the Parthians understandable.

There was another prime reason why we can know that *The War of Varus* was in 1 B.C. When significant conflicts took place outside the official boundaries of the Empire such as the war just after Herod's death, it was customary for the emperor to be awarded an "imperial acclamation" if victory were achieved by Rome. And, as Professor Syme has noted, Roman records show that Augustus did in fact receive such an "acclamation" (his fourteenth) in 8 B.C., but not another until A.D.1. If Varus' war occurred in 4 B.C., as scholars have wanted to believe, why was there not an "acclamation" in 4 or 3 B.C.? That victory over the Jews had all the earmarks for gaining such an award for Augustus. But if that war and victory were in 1 B.C. (as actually was the case) then an "acclamation XV" in the following year of A.D. 1 becomes perfectly reasonable. Professor Barnes has made it clear that the war which gave Augustus his "acclamation XV" in A.D. 1 to 2 must have occurred sometime between June, 2 B.C. and A.D.1.[263] The dating of *The War of Varus* to the Summer of 1 B.C. fits the historical scenario perfectly. Augustus' acclamation XV was actually given to him for Varus' victory over the Jewish rebellion.

Indeed, there is far more to it than that. When the proper chronology is recognized, more historical material can be understood about Roman affairs in the eastern provinces. Let us look at the matter closely.

Roman History Can Now Make Sense

We have stated that the lunar eclipse associated with Herod's death was that of January 10, 1 B.C. Two prominent rabbis were martyred on the eve of that eclipse. A few weeks later the Passover occurred on which 3000 Jews met their deaths in the temple precincts in protest over the rabbis' executions. This led to the outbreak of war in late Spring of 1 B.C. and Varus entered the conflict in early Summer. In the meantime, Archelaus, the successor of Herod, had sailed to Rome to plead his case that Herod's kingdom should be given to him. When Augustus in Rome heard the case for and against Archelaus in late Spring, he had at his side his grandson Gaius Caesar.[264] But soon, knowledge of the new Palestinian war and the seriousness of it reached Rome. This was the time when Gaius Caesar was dispatched hurriedly to Syria "under the stress of necessity."[265] It looks like he was sent via the lower Danube region. The primary purpose of his mission was to "compose the troubles in Armenia."[266] And what a logical time for the Armenians on the northeastern frontier to start trouble. With Varus and all the legions of Syria then fighting a major war in Palestine, this left a vacuum in Roman military defense in the border areas with Parthia and in Armenia. Gaius Caesar's assignment was to speed toward Armenia through the Danube region. Why via the Danube?

The Roman historian Tacitus said that the strategic reserves of the Roman armed forces were located in Dalmatia.[267] Two extra legions were stationed in that area specifically for deployment purposes in times of national emergency. These were special troops that were trained to speed to areas of need. Another Roman historian, Dio Cassius, said that Gaius had been given the command of the Danube legions in 2 B.C. when all was peaceful.[268] And there was general peace from 7 to 2 B.C. But with the revolt in Judaea starting in the Spring of 1 B.C., followed soon with the insurrection in Armenia and the stirrings in Parthia, diligent and decisive action was then needed and Gaius journeyed east to put down these belligerent maneuvers.

When Gaius Caesar was given charge of the Danube legions in 2 B.C., the Roman historian Velleius Paterculus said he then made

Chapter 10 - The War that No One Can Find

a leisurely journey through some of the provinces under his command, but now in mid Summer of 1 B.C. he was "dispatched to Syria"[269] and "under the stress of necessity."[270] Since the Danube legions were his direct responsibility, he no doubt mustered some of the reserve forces located in that region and promptly hastened them toward Syria. It is interesting that when Varus went to war against the Jews, there were only *three* legions in Syria, but in the early years of Tiberius (a few years later) there were *four*.[271] It is very possible that one of the reserve legions was sent at Gaius' behest to buttress the three Syrian legions normally stationed in the area. This movement of troops to the eastern frontier at this time is substantiated by Professor Syme, referring to the comments of Velleius Paterculus.[272]

A strange thing then happened before Gaius reached Armenia. When he came to the island of Samos in the Aegean, he met the exiled Tiberius (the later emperor). From that encounter he made the decision to go first to Egypt and then to the northern parts of Arabia. What an odd route to take if he were supposed to be heading directly to "compose the troubles in Armenia." So why did Gaius go to Egypt and why was it necessary to be in northern Arabia in the late Summer and early Autumn of 1 B.C.? The answer comes from a first century Roman historian called Pliny. He said that Gaius went into Arabia to achieve military victories. He went to fight a war. He fought the war and obtained great fame for the victories he achieved.[273] Interestingly, Pliny said these military accomplishments of Gaius occurred north of the Gulf of Aqaba. He only "looked at" the Arabian peninsula, he did not enter it. This tells us something about the area of Gaius' battles.

Gaius' Battle Was In Palestine

This war that Gaius fought was either to the east of the Aravah (the region between the Dead Sea and the Gulf of Aqaba) or to the west of it. If east, then he would have been in conflict, most likely, with the Nabataean Arabs. Professor Bowersock, though, discounts this possibility since the Nabataeans were noted for their docility and unbellicose manner of life.[274] This evaluation is true. Even in *The War of Varus*, the Romans had to dismiss the Nabataeans as unreliable in fighting the Jewish rebels in Idumaea.[275]

It is almost certain that Gaius' victories were accomplished west of the Aravah. This region was the southern part of Herod's kingdom known as Idumaea. And remarkably, this location is the very region where the last fighting in *The War of Varus* took place. There were 10,000 Jewish insurgents in the area that had to be pacified.[276] And note this. This last bit of "mopping up" operations, as our new chronological reconstruction shows, occurred in the Autumn of 1 B.C. *This would have been the exact time* that Gaius Caesar was in the region securing those victories that brought him fame. So important was this expedition of Gaius that the celebrated King Juba of Mauritania wrote an account of it and dedicated the book to Gaius himself.[277] This war was not a minor affair.

It now looks probable that when Gaius reached Samos in the Aegean, he was told that the conflict in Palestine was about to end. His presence at the conclusion of the war could help stabilize the whole region and give Rome an "imperial" victory with himself as the heir to the Empire commanding the final military actions. So, Gaius instead of going to Armenia went first to Egypt and hurriedly continued on to Idumaea to bring the war in Palestine to an end. He then went to Jerusalem where he failed to allow the customary devotions to be given "to the Jewish God."[278] From there, he and Varus must have gone to Antioch with two of the legions while one legion was left in Judaea. He would have arrived in the provincial capital of Antioch by late 1 B.C. or at the beginning of A.D. 1. He would then have joined forces with the one or two legions he sent to Syria from the Danubian reserves. This would have given him the needed reinforcements he required for his own operations soon to occur against the Armenians. But this doesn't end the story.

Chapter 10 - The War that No One Can Find

History Now Makes Sense

There are two other historical documents which now make sense whereas before they were a puzzle to historians. There is an eyewitness account of *The War of Varus* which tells about the person who secured the victory. This Jewish writer who lived in Judaea (and wrote a work called *The Assumption of Moses*) said that the war was conducted by a "king" who had come from the west to gain the triumph.[279] The reference has normally been applied to Quintilius Varus because historians up to now have assumed the war mentioned by this Jewish writer took place in 4 B.C. This, of course, was three years before Gaius Caesar arrived on the scene in late 1 B.C. But we now know that Gaius was in this very region at the conclusion of *The War of Varus*. And much truer to the Jewish author's account, Gaius had come directly from the west to end the war and he had all the credentials to be called a "king." Varus hardly fits the account. The Roman governor was not a "king" and he came from the north, not the west! Even this reference is helpful in showing that *The War of Varus* ended in 1 B.C. and that Gaius ("a king") was there to help in the "mopping up" operations.

An Ancient Inscription Settles It

The next point is even more significant. In 1960 an inscription was found in Greece that mentioned these activities of Gaius while he was on his mission to the east. It refers to some splendid victories. Though it does not specify exactly what they were, what was written on this inscription has an important bearing on our question under discussion. The inscription states: "Gaius, the son of Augustus, who was fighting the barbarians *for the safety of all mankind*" (italics mine). So important was the conclusion of this war mentioned on the inscription that it records there were "lavish and varied spectacles, so that what took place then rivaled what had come before."[280] For festivals of victory to be held as far away as Greece that were so sumptuous (and to be continued annually) that nothing ever excelled them, surely means that some conquest of great importance was being celebrated. It must have been a prominent triumph because it was reckoned that Gaius had been fighting "for the safety of all mankind."

Even when one allows for inscriptional adulation, it is hardly possible that the inscription is referring to some minor skirmishes. The victory in some major war was being honored. But what war could this have been? Because *The War of Varus* has been misdated by scholars in the past to 4 B.C., about the only suggestion for any 1 B.C. conflict has been the possibility of Rome fighting against some nomadic Arabs wandering up from the Arabian peninsula. One wonders how a Roman victory over such intruders could be construed as being "for the safety of all mankind"? But if the inscription is telling us about *The War of Varus* in 1 B.C., the information it records makes perfectly good sense.

The inscription also states that Gaius was victorious over "barbarians." This term can be interpreted variously, but it would apply most particularly to people who lived outside the boundaries of the Roman Empire. Added to this, we have the Pisan cenotaph (another inscription) which mentions this same expedition of Gaius and it states that Gaius' victories were accomplished "beyond the Roman frontiers."[281] The region of Idumaea in 1 B.C. would fit the description precisely. The areas of Galilee, Judaea, Peraea (across the Jordan River) and Idumaea were formerly the lands controlled by Herod. Though Herod was associated politically with the Empire in close alliance, his kingdom was technically outside imperial territory. It only became provincial in A.D. 6/7 when Quirinius assumed governorship of Syria and Palestine. However, in 1 B.C. Idumaea was still "beyond the Roman frontiers" as far as the Roman government was concerned.

The War Was In Palestine

Besides this, there were other reasons to call the area of Palestine "barbarian" at that time. Rome would have considered the

Chapter 10 - The War that No One Can Find

Jewish rebels as fighting against the philosophical and political concepts within the Hellenistic principles that then dominated Roman thinking. If there were any people at the time who would naturally have been against such Roman philosophical thinking and would have been called "barbarians," it would have been the Jews of Palestine after the death of Herod. This would especially have been true because they had just fought a major war with Varus and his Roman legions. We have some modern parallels. Recall that during World War II the Americans, British and other allies were quite accustomed to call Germans and Japanese "barbarians" (and, of course, the axis powers had some uncomplimentary things to say about the allied powers). It is the nature of humans to use such terms in times of war or their immediate aftermath. Thus, it is no problem in believing that the Romans would have referred to the Jews at this time as "barbarians."

This belief is further strengthened because the inscription found in 1960 stated that Gaius had been fighting "for the safety of all mankind." The Romans must have considered their victory of great consequence. After all, as stated before, there were Jews who had messianic convictions at that time scattered throughout the Empire as well as Parthia. What if all the Jews decided to fight against Rome? This, of course, was an unlikely proposition but the potential for such a thing was always there. There was also the possibility for fifth column subversion by the Jews as well as their active aggression against the Empire which gave Rome concern. Putting an end to the resistance in Palestine must have given the Romans the feeling of having accomplished a major victory. It could have been stated that Gaius' final victories in Idumaea were "for the safety of all mankind."

Such an appraisal is reflective of Roman beliefs at this period. Tacitus, a century later, gave ordinary Roman opinion of the Jews when he said they customarily hated "all mankind."[282] Even the apostle Paul felt that Jewish social beliefs at the time were "contrary to all men."[283] Josephus records a plethora of Gentile antipathy against the Jews within this period we are discussing.[284] The emperor Claudius wrote to the people of Alexandria in A.D. 41 saying that the Jews and their opinions were "a general plague infecting the whole world."[285] We only give these references to show ordinary Roman belief about the Jewish population during the period of our discussion. If there were ever a people "out of step" with the rest of the world at that time, it was the Jews. It is well within reason that those mentioned on the inscription as being like "barbarians" that Gaius subdued "for the safety of all mankind" were the final Jewish insurgents in Idumaea who fought in *The War of Varus*.[286]

Once these historical indications are placed into proper chronological sequence (as I am showing in this book), the history of the eastern provinces becomes much more sensible. It could even be said that the basic information in the New Testament that Jesus was born before the death of Herod, coupled with the history of Josephus that Herod died not long after an eclipse of the Moon (and the eclipse was that of January 10, 1 B.C.) are the very keys that make the Roman historical records understandable.

Truly, Herod died in early 1 B.C. and *The War of Varus* took place in the Summer and Autumn of 1 B.C. with Gaius Caesar in Idumaea for the conclusion of that war. The historical records become perfectly understandable. This means that *The War of Varus* has been found within the Roman and Greek records after all. It also allows the historical statements of the New Testament concerning the nativity of Jesus to take on a new credibility. Jesus was born in 3 B.C. (within the period the majority of early Christian scholars stated) and we now find this substantiated by the records of Roman history.

Chapter 11 — *THE TWO GOVERNORSHIPS OF QUINTILIUS VARUS*

Once the eclipse of January 10, 1 B.C. is accepted as the one referred to by Josephus, it follows that Herod would have died a few days afterward (say January 28th). A little over two months later the 3000 Jews were massacred in the temple at Passover and then ensued *The War of Varus* in the late Spring and Summer of 1 B.C. This means, obviously, that Quintilius Varus was certainly governor of Syria in 1 B.C. and Josephus shows that he had taken over the governorship in the latter part of the previous Summer (2 B.C.) when Antipater the heir to King Herod had returned from Rome to Jerusalem. "At that time there happened to be in Jerusalem Quintilius Varus, who was sent to succeed Saturninus as governor of Syria."[287]

We thus have an interesting question regarding the governors of Syria at this crucial time in history. We find that Quintilius Varus was *twice* governor of Syria. Coins have been found which show that Varus was supervisor over Syria in the 25th, 26th and 27th years of the Actian Era (6 to 4 B.C.). And in the reference quoted above, Josephus states that Sentius Saturninus was governor just before

The Star that Astonished the World

Varus became governor *again* in 2 B.C. and he ruled in that capacity (this *second* time) from 2 B.C. till at least A.D. 1. So, between Varus' two governorships of Syria, Sentius Saturninus ruled from the middle of 4 B.C. to the middle part of 2 B.C.

Remarkably, the early Christian apologist Tertullian, who lived in the late second century and was by profession a lawyer and well acquainted with Roman governmental affairs, said that the census that brought Joseph and Mary to Bethlehem was conducted when Sentius Saturninus was governor of Syria. And Tertullian in his work *An Answer to the Jews*, stated that Jesus was born in a year that we now recognize as 3/2 B.C.[288] This fits precisely with our reconstruction of history during this *dark decade*. It means that Quintilius Varus was governor of Syria from 6 to 4 B.C., followed by Sentius Saturninus from 4 to 2 B.C., and then followed *again* by Varus from 2 B.C. to at least A.D. 1.

The Two Governorships of Quintilius Varus

If it can be shown historically that Quintilius Varus was in fact twice governor of Syria, it would give a great deal of validity to the chronological reconstruction I am presenting in this book. And truly, that proof can be given.

In the year 1764, an inscription was found near Tibur (Tivoli), about 20 miles east of Rome. It described in Latin the exploits of a Roman military commander who held several important offices during the emperorship of Augustus. Though the complete inscription has not come down to us (all data on its peripheries have worn away), it does afford some interesting details about the man it describes. What remains of the text is reproduced in this book at the top of page 171. The inscription itself is shown with some supplements by Professor Mommsen given in italics. The inscription tells us several things which narrow its applications to only a few men who were military commanders in the time of Augustus. It is not a difficult matter to find out who the man was. Let us see.

Chapter 11 - The Two Governorships of Quintilius Varus

rEGEM · QVA · REDACTA · IN · POT*estatem*   *imp. caesaris*
AVGVSTI · POPVLIQVE · ROMANI · SENATV*s*   *dis immortalibus*
SVPPLICATIONES · BINAS · OB · RES · PROS*Pere ab eo gestas et*
IPS1 · ORNAMENTA · TRIVMPH*alia*   *decreuit*
PRO · CONSVL · ASIAM · PROVINCIAM · OP*tinuit*   *legatus pr. pr.*
DIVI · AVGVSTI · *i*TERVM · SYRIAM · ET · PH*oenicen optinuit.*

For one, the man referred to had been a proconsul of the province of Asia. This province was located in the western part of modern Turkey. It was one of two senatorial provinces in the Roman Empire during the time of Augustus which was governed by men who were normally former consuls.[289]

This tells us something about the man of the inscription. He had been a consul. Of the four million or so Roman citizens, fewer than 100 men were consuls during the rule of Augustus. Indeed, Augustus mentioned that his principate had witnessed 83 consuls in office.[290] This fact narrows the identification of the man to one of those 83 or so consuls. But even more narrowing can be made. Professor Syme has proved that an award of the *ornamento triumphalia* which the man of the inscription received was only bestowed on victorious generals after 12 B.C.[291] This probably shows that nearly half of the 83 Augustan consuls could be eliminated for consideration because of being politically active only before that year. However, Quintilius Varus was consul in 13 B.C., and was an ex-consular (and able to be proconsul of Asia) for 15 years or so after 12 B.C. This fact indicates that Quintilius Varus could be considered as one of the men described on the stone of Tibur.

Secondly, the inscription gives another clue to the man's identity. It states he had been governor of Syria. Though there are a few periods of time during the emperorship of Augustus when no one knows who was governing Syria, there are names of nine or ten men revealed in history.[292] If one reckons only the governors after 12 B.C. (to agree with the time of the *ornamento triumphalia*, the number would be reduced to six or seven men. Again, Quintilius

Varus was one of them.

Thirdly, the word *regem* is used at the beginning of the inscription. This denotes that a king (living or dead) had been described. The government of the king had been conquered or restored.[293] This specification could precisely tally with the career of Quintilius Varus. Soon after the death of King Herod, a general insurrection took place among the Jews in Galilee and Judaea. Varus stepped in with three legions to quell the rebellion and to restore Herod's kingdom to Rome. Quintilius Varus is a candidate in this point as well.

Fourthly, the inscription specifically says the man was given decorations for securing two victories in that war (*supplicationes binas*). And that's exactly what Quintilius Varus did in Palestine. Josephus clearly distinguished his victory in Galilee and the one in Judaea.[294] Again, the inscription is appropriate to Quintilius Varus to a tee.

Fifthly, and most importantly, the stone of Tibur says the man was *twice* governor of Syria. I have given historical and numismatical data, completely independent of the inscription, to show that Quintilius Varus was *twice* governor of Syria. Interestingly, the inscription implies that the man's governorship was in two non-consecutive terms. It could hardly be said he was twice governor when he simply had two terms in succession. Even in this point, Quintilius Varus fits the man of the inscription perfectly.

Sixthly, the mention of the man having two non-consecutive terms of office narrows the men to be considered dramatically. How many people had been *twice* governor of Syria in the time of Augustus? There are really only two candidates. One is Sulpicius Quirinius (whom we will speak about in the next chapter) and, as we have shown in this book, the other was Quintilius Varus. To be sure, others have been suggested. L.R. Taylor thought that Titius could be considered. Yet there is not the slightest hint that he was twice governor of Syria and Syme has shown that Titius would

Chapter 11 - The Two Governorships of Quintilius Varus

have been much too old to receive the *ornamento triumphalia* given only after 12 B.C.[295] Professor Groag thought Plautius Silvanus might be the man of the inscription. One of his main reasons for suggesting this was because the inscription was found in the vicinity of the tomb of the Plautii family. (The truth is, it was discovered east of the Plautii sepulchre and on the slopes of the hill leading up to Tibur, not near the Plautii monument in the plains area near the Lucano bridge.) Besides this, there is no proof that Plautius Silvanus was ever governor of Syria, let alone twice in office. Other scholars have thought that Calpurnius Piso may be the man. Still, like Plautius Silvanus, nothing shows he was governor of Syria during the reign of Augustus.

With Sulpicius Quirinius, however, it is a different story. Everyone knows he was governor of Syria in A.D. 6/7, and Luke attributes to him a former tenure (as many feel today) at an earlier time when Jesus was born. These two governorships make Quirinius a definite contender. Yet, there are problems. The inscription mentions a war against a king or kingdom. The war in which Quirinius has been singled out for praise by the ancient writers was that against the Homonadenses in Asia Minor north of the Taurus mountains. But the fact is, as Sherwin-White points out, the Homonadenses *had no king*.[296] Some have thought that Quirinius conducted the Homonadensian War when he was first governor of Syria, but to wage war against people living on the northern parts of the Taurus Mountains from the region of Syria makes not the slightest military sense.[297]

Another point concerning Quirinius is this: It could be rationally said that he had three "governorships" of Syria, not simply two. His first rule would have been at the nativity of Jesus, as testified by Luke; his second when he became rector to Gaius Caesar from A.D. 1 to 4; his third when he assumed a governorship of Syria in A.D. 6/7. The inscription, however, records *"twice,"* not thrice.

A final point speaks decidedly against Quirinius being the man of the inscription. The ancestral home of Quirinius was at Lanuvium,[298] while the inscription was found about 30 miles northeastwards at Tibur. There is no historical record to show that Quirinius was ever associated with the city of Tibur. Since Quirinius died without descendants,[299] it is reasonable that a monument to his career could have been raised up in Rome or in Lanuvium (or in any other area where he had been prominent), but there is no reason for a memorial to be in Tibur. Yet, for Quintilius Varus it is different. The ancestral home of Varus, and where he had a magnificent estate, was at the very place where the inscription was found—it was at Tibur!

Seventhly, this fact that the inscription was found in the area of Tibur is powerful evidence in favor of Quintilius Varus. His family had long lived in the vicinity. Horace, who resided just east of Tibur, referred to Varus' father (Ode 18) and mentioned his death with familiar terms by calling him Quintilius (Ode 24). See Smith, *Dict. of Greek and Roman Geography*, vol.III, p.1231. Though Varus' family was well-born and of patrician rank, it was not elevated in prestige until Quintilius Varus was made consul in 13 B.C. From then on, their fortunes began to change. This was especially so when Varus was appointed governor of Syria. Velleius Paterculus said that Varus entered the rich province of Syria as a poor man, but left the province a rich man and the province poor.[300]

And rich he was. On a low ridge just across the River Anio from Tibur, Varus built one of the grandest villas of the time. The foundational remains and the remnants of three walls surrounding the interior of the residential villa are still to be seen, and they witness to its former grandeur. The extent of his living quarters was about 200 by 300 yards (or meters) —a little over 12 acres.

And what a beautiful spot it was! The villa was situated on the ridge so that those looking southeastwards towards Tibur could observe the verdant canyon of the Anio and the several waterfalls plummeting to the valley below. The western area gave a panoram-

Chapter 11 - The Two Governorships of Quintilius Varus

ic view of the plains which reached to the Mediterranean and Rome could be seen 20 miles [32 kilometers] in the distance. There was hardly a more favorable site for a villa.

The fact that this location was the home of Quintilius Varus has been recognized by those in Tibur for generations. A tract on the declivity of *Monte Peschiavatore* bore the name of Quintiliolo as far back as the 10th century, and the little church at this spot is called *La Madonna di Quintiliolo*, an appellation which may possibly have been derived from the family name of Varus.[301]

The agricultural lands supporting such a large residential villa no doubt embraced many surrounding acres. It was normal for the governors of Roman provinces to bring back to their ancestral estates or their other lands great quantities of money. They bought up hundreds, thousands, even tens of thousands of acres and formed gigantic estates. "Agrippa rose out of nothing: he came to own the whole of the peninsula of Gallipoli. Statilius possessed a variety of properties in Istria, whole armies of slaves at Rome.... Lollius left millions to his family—the spoil of the provinces."[302] And when Quintilius Varus came back from the province of Syria, he had its riches in his possession. This would have allowed him to buy thousands of acres around his residential villa, and this would have made his estate one of the most majestic in the area. (As a sidelight, even after Varus' death, his son was described by Tacitus as being very rich.[303])

All of this surely means that Varus secured much land in the western part of Tibur where his villa was located. This brings us to an important point concerning the inscription. Just where was it discovered?

Sanclemente, writing about 30 years after it was found, said the inscription was discovered "outside the Roman gate" of the western wall of Tibur. He also said it was located "in the hill of Tiburtina" (that is, on the slopes of the hill leading up to the town), and "between the Via Tiburtina [the Roman road to the city] and the Villa Hadriana located southwest of the city."[304] It is unfortunate that Sanclemente did not give a more precise location, but he gave enough that a reasonable area for marking the discovery is ascertainable. Since it was found outside the Roman gate, this surely means it was not far from the gate. He also said it was on the slopes of the hill and not in the plains area to the west. This also brings it close to the city.

Since it was located between the Roman road and the Villa Hadriana, it was found in a southwesterly direction from the city gate. The circle on the accompanying map (page 177) gives a reasonable area for the discovery.

Why is this factor important? Simply because it shows that the inscription was found about half a mile south of the doorstep of Quintilius Varus' residential villa. And since Varus must have had extensive land holdings around his villa, it could be said, with a great deal of confidence, that the inscription was found either on or certainly adjacent to the very estate of Varus. The location of the discovery makes this a powerful witness that the man of the inscription was Quintilius Varus.

A Difficulty

While all the above information seems in favor of the inscription of Tibur (called the *lapis tiburtinus*) as referring to Quintilius Varus, there is a problem with it. The phrase "divi Augusti" is part of the text. This title, showing that the Senate reckoned Augustus as divine, was only bestowed on him after Augustus' death in A.D. 14, but Quintilius Varus died in A.D. 9. This was one of the main reasons for Mommsen and Ramsay to conclude that the inscription was Quirinius' because he died in Rome seven years after the death of Augustus. However, the theory will not stand. L.R. Taylor and Meyer Reinhold both maintained that the phrase "divi Augusti" only means the inscription itself was composed after the death of

Chapter 11 - The Two Governorships of Quintilius Varus

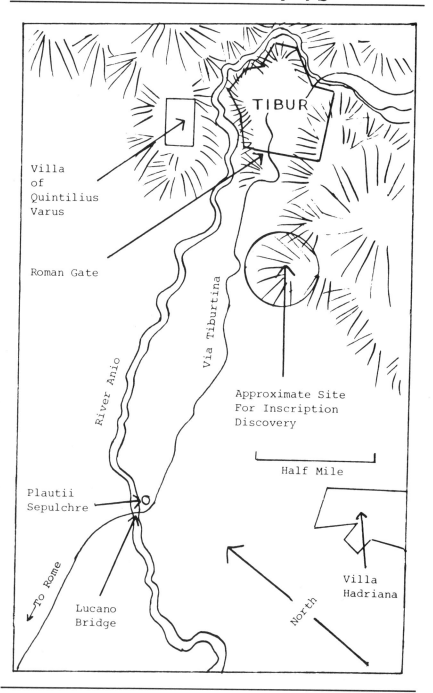

Augustus—not that the man himself lived after A.D. 14.³⁰⁵ And this is true. Indeed, the fact that it was produced after the death of Augustus is a point in favor of it being an inscription to the honor of Quintilius Varus.

Let us now look at some historical information which can indicate that the inscription does refer to Quintilius Varus. To do so, we must recount an important historical event in Varus' later life.

After Varus' two tenures in Syria, he was given a command on the frontier of Germany. In the year A.D. 9, he and three legions met with a disastrous defeat in the Teutoburg forest of Germany. The troops were massacred and Varus himself committed suicide. His body was buried with the last remnant of his army but it was later disinterred, his body humiliated, and his head finally sent to Augustus by the Germans.

This was considered a major disaster by Rome, and so it was. Augustus was so upset with the defeat, and with Varus himself, that for the rest of his life (from A.D. 9 to 14) he commemorated the day of defeat with lamentation. He would often dash his head against the wall and proclaim: "Oh, Quintilius Varus, give me back my legions."³⁰⁶ Until the death of Augustus, who was so distraught with the defeat of Varus, there would have been little desire for anyone to raise up a monument to him, even at his ancestral home. But something different happened with the accession of Tiberius to the emperorship in August of A.D. 14.

One year after the death of Augustus, the new emperor Tiberius ordered Germanicus to muster nine legions to avenge the defeat.³⁰⁷ Germanicus and his legions approached the region of the Teutoburg forest. When he and his troops got to the area, they found the whole of the landscape littered with the whitened bones of the dead Romans. "Touched by this affecting circumstance, Germanicus resolved to pay the last human office to the relics of that unfortunate commander [Quintilius Varus] and his slaughtered soldiers."³⁰⁸

Chapter 11 - The Two Governorships of Quintilius Varus

They found the place where Varus was killed and buried. They also gathered up the bones of their former comrades, buried them with honor, and then raised up "a monument to the memory of the dead."[309] Germanicus and all the troops considered themselves as performing the last obsequies to their kindred, and their brother soldiers. Thus, Quintilius Varus and his fallen legions were all given an honorable Roman burial.

What has this, however, to do with the inscription found at Tibur? In every way, a great deal. Sufficient time had passed for Quintilius Varus and his troops to be honored for their defense of the homeland.

There are good reasons for believing this. Quintilius Varus had been close to Tiberius. He was co-consul with him in 13 B.C. Not only that, a recent discovery of a fragment of papyrus, which gives a funeral oration of Augustus at the death of Agrippa (in 12 B.C.), records that Quintilius Varus and Tiberius were brothers-in-law.[310]

Normally, one would think such relationships would make the two men close friends. And besides that, the son of Varus was the son-in-law of Germanicus, who honored Varus in Germany. Varus' son was also a great-nephew of Tiberius, as Tacitus said he was "nearly related to the emperor."[311] There would have been every reason for a sepulchre inscription of some kind to be raised up at Tibur for Varus after the death of Augustus. And indeed, we have the express statement by Velleius Paterculus that Varus was given a burial with honor at the tomb of his family.[312]

A perfect time for such things would have arrived after Germanicus secured his victories over the Germans (A.D. 16). While Augustus was still alive such an honor for Varus would have been difficult. But after A.D. 16 it would have been a different story. Thus, the phrase "divi Augusti" is no problem in identifying the man of the *lapis tiburtinus* with Quintilius Varus. In fact, it helps to confirm that it belongs to Varus. [See Appendix One for more historical information which supports this.]

What is the outcome of these historical indications? They help to show that Luke was right in placing Jesus' nativity in 3 or 2 B.C.; that Tertullian was right in saying the censuses which brought Joseph and Mary to Bethlehem were during the governorship of Saturninus (3/2 B.C.); that the coins are right in showing a Syrian governorship of Varus from 6 to 4 B.C., and that Josephus was correct in showing another governorship for Varus from 2 B.C. to A.D. 1; and that the *lapis tiburtinus* shows the validity of the matter by confirming the dual governorship of Varus. All the data taken together provide a reasonable picture of what was happening in Palestine and Syria during the period of Jesus' nativity.

With this information, we can logically show who the governors of Syria were for the period from 7 B.C. to A.D. 1.

    Titius.. Prior to 7 B.C.

    Q. Varus......................................7 or 6 to 4 B.C.

    S. Saturninus..............................4 B.C. to 2 B.C.

    Q. Varus (a second time)........2 B.C. to A.D. 1.

    G. Caesar...................................A.D. 1 to A.D. 4.

Chapter 12

THE CENSUS OF QUIRINIUS

Luke said that Jesus was born at a census when Quirinius (KJV: Cyrenius) was a ruler in Syria. This reference has been an enigma to historians for generations because no such census of Quirinius has been found by historians which could have occurred from 7 to 1 B.C. Scholars have stated that Luke simply did not know what he was talking about, and that he probably got his facts mixed-up with the census of Quirinius that took place in A.D. 6/7. There is undisputed evidence that Quirinius was governor beginning in A.D. 6/7 and that he conducted a census at that time (even Luke mentioned it—Acts 5:37). But up to now, no available information has been discovered to show that Quirinius was an administrator (and a census taker) in 3/2 B.C. or in previous years. This new historical research, however, can find that census of Quirinius in the historical records which took place at Jesus' nativity. In the New Testament, Luke actually states that the "census" was an enrollment or a registration of some kind. He does not say what Quirinius' census was for. But we now can discover the reason for his census.

Let us recall from the last chapter that Tertullian said that

The Star that Astonished the World

Roman records supported the fact that censuses (he used the plural) were conducted in Palestine at the time of Jesus' birth. Tertullian said they took place at the time when Saturninus was governor of Syria. Tertullian, though, said nothing about Quirinius as conducting those censuses. This early Christian scholar also identified the year with that which we now reckon as 3/2 B.C. If the biblical narrative given to us by Luke and that of Tertullian can be married together, how could it be that two governors (Saturninus and Quirinius) were then in Syria at the same time? This poses a problem and it has been one of long standing.

Perhaps Josephus provides a clue to help straighten out the mystery. The historian mentioned that actually there were "governors" (plural) in Syria during the rule of Saturninus.[313] While during the earlier governorships of Titius and Quintilius Varus, Josephus spoke of a "governor" (singular),[314] but during the administration of Saturninus why does he mention the plural "governors"?

How many governors were there at this time? Josephus mentions the names of Saturninus and Volumnius. Were these the only men to whom Josephus was referring? Or, could Quirinius be considered as well? This is the very time Luke in his Gospel places the administration of a census by Quirinius. Since it is clear that Saturninus was the regular governor, it must be held that the rule of Quirinius was of a different and special nature. Such special status could well accord with the other types of commands that Quirinius held as attested in the historical records. His war against the Homonadenses, for which Tacitus singled him out for praise, has been called a "special command."[315] This status is also reflected in an inscription which mentions Quirinius "as holding an honorary municipal office at Antioch-by-Pisidia."[316] And it was certainly a special command for Quirinius when he became rector of the young Gaius Caesar when Gaius acquired residential authority at Antioch over the eastern provinces in A.D. 1. Gaius was probably not strictly called the governor of Syria at the time (A.D. 1 to 4),

Chapter 12 - The Census of Quirinius

and it may well be that Quirinius was responsible for running the everyday affairs of government. Tacitus said that Quirinius was one having "considerable talents for business."[318] This could account for his selection as being "guardian" of Gaius who was the heir to the Empire. Too, as our historical reconstruction shows, Quirinius already had experience in Syria by administering the censuses Tertullian talked about in 3/2 B.C. which took place during the time when Saturninus was governor. All these references indicate special commands for Quirinius throughout all his governmental career. There are other historical records about Quirinius which show his special assignments.

Quirinius Was a Special Delegate

This special status of Quirinius is also suggested when he later became governor of Syria in A.D. 6/7. Josephus said he was given the rank of *dikaiodotes* — a governor, but in the sense of one having extraordinary judicial powers (the word *dikaiodotes* means "judge"). And Professor Feldman quoting J.A.O. Larson in the Loeb translation of Josephus states "that the word *dikaiodotes* is found only in *Antiquities*, XVIII. 1 and in inscriptions from Lycia in the sense of 'governor.' Larson plausibly suggests that the word was not so much a title for a governor as *an honorary appellation* [italics mine], much like *soter* or *euergetes*. It would emphasize the high regard with which the governor was held as an honest judge, the duties of the governor (in Lydia, at least) being largely judicial."

Quirinius, then, was even an unusual type of administrator in Syria during the period A.D. 6/7. It could be said that he had special (and probably extensive) powers directly from Augustus. He could have been called, in contemporary terms, a powerful "man-Friday" for Augustus or, officially, a *Legatus Augusti*. This certainly must be the case. When Quirinius conducted the census at the time of Saturninus, Justin Martyr said that Roman historical records showed Quirinius as being the *procurator* in Judaea.[319] Justin dated this political role of Quirinius to the time when Jesus was born.

Since Justin was a second century author referring to Roman records, it is reasonable that he must have been acquainted with the various Roman political titles afforded to eminent officials. It is a shame that Justin's reference that Quirinius was a *procurator* at the time of Jesus' nativity (and not a governor) has seldom been mentioned by historians. But its implication is of profound importance. A *procurator* was normally a personal advocate of the emperor with special authority quite distinct from the residential governor.

This indication of Justin may have significance to our question concerning Quirinius. The *Cambridge Ancient History*, vol, X, p. 216, has an interesting comment on the role of a Roman *procurator*. "Each province had its equestrian procurator who in the eyes of the provincials was almost as important as the governor himself."[320] These *procurators* were appointed by the Emperor quite independently of the *legatus* (governor) and the relations between the two were frequently none too friendly. The fact that Justin said that Quirinius was a *procurator* while conducting the "census" gives much weight to the belief that a resident governor also ruled Syria at the same time. It looks like Luke was well aware of the fact that Quirinius was in Palestine conducting a registration of peoples when Saturninus was the actual governor of Syria. (I will soon discuss why biblical translators erroneously call Quirinius a governor.)

Why A Census or Registration in 3/2 B.C.?

We have no early historical information other than Luke and Tertullian that a census of the Roman world took place in 3/2 B.C. Augustus, with his own hand, composed an account of major events in his life. He wrote of the official censuses in 28 B.C., 8 B.C., and A.D. 14,[321] but nothing in our year of discussion. Yet in his Gospel, Luke said the whole Roman world was involved in some kind of "census." Why was there an Empire registration of peoples in 3/2 B.C. of which Luke speaks? When one recalls the history of that period—particularly what happened in 2 B.C.—we may well have the reason for such a registration.

Chapter 12 - The Census of Quirinius

Let us recall that in chapter one of this book it was pointed out that the year 2 B.C. was one of the most important and glorious in the career of Augustus. It was the Silver Jubilee of his supreme rule over the Empire and the year in which the Senate awarded him the country's highest decoration "the *Pater Patriae*" (Father of the Country). There was no year like it for majestic celebrations in Rome, and since the significance of the festivities involved the entirety of the Empire, there can be little doubt that similar anniversary ceremonies were ordained by Augustus and the Senate for all the provinces.

It should be remembered that back in 27 B.C. Augustus was given complete and absolute allegiance by the Senate and people of Rome. Would there not have been a renewal of their loyalty to Augustus in the Jubilee year? If so, we could well have a reference to an Empire-wide registration of loyalty to the emperor. Josephus mentioned that an oath of allegiance was demanded by Augustus about twelve or fifteen months before the death of Herod. This event would fit nicely with a decree going out from Augustus in 3 B.C. that all were to give an oath of allegiance to him at some designated time during the year. Obviously, the recording of oaths (where people ascribed their names) was a type of registration. That is what Luke said the census was. It was an enrollment of people.

The Oath Was a Census

If the oath of loyalty mentioned by Josephus is what brought Joseph and Mary to Bethlehem (I will quote the text in a moment), then it makes sense why Mary had to accompany Joseph. In a regular census Mary would not have needed to go with Joseph, nor would Joseph have needed to travel so far. Some have suspected that both Joseph and Mary were descendants of David, and were legitimate claimants to the throne of Israel (had such a throne existed). It could easily be seen why Mary, as well as Joseph, was expected to sign the oath of loyalty to Augustus. All "royal claimants" would have especially been singled out to give the oath of allegiance. This would even have involved Mary. It was possible in Jewish circles for female descendants of David to have the rights of primogeniture and kingship for their offspring (cf. Antiquities, XVIII.124 and also Acts 16:1-3 where the principle of legal maternal descent is shown).

Luke tells us that the reason why both Joseph and Mary went to Bethlehem was because he was reckoned as belonging to the house of David. While everyone else went "into his own city" (Luke 2:3) no doubt in their own local neighborhoods, those of royal Judaic lineage because of political implications had to register in Bethlehem. This requirement would allow Herod to know who all claimants were in Judaea to the royal throne of David. He was anxious to know who all these people were (in order to keep them subjected to thorough non-political functions) so that his own dynasty would survive. This was especially important at this time in history because there was then a great deal of messianic expectation among the Jews. Registering David's descendants in Bethlehem, the city of David, would have been a ploy not only to get all the people to attend for prestige purposes but for Herod to find out who they were. Since Augustus had ordered that an oath of allegiance be given to him, Herod simply included himself and the legitimacy of his kingdom within the same oath. And since females among the Jews could give Davidic heirship to descendants, Herod included the women as well. This would have given him a complete record of all such claimants to the throne. This could well be why Mary was expected to accompany Joseph. Let us now look at that oath of loyalty mentioned by Josephus in greater detail.

Josephus and the Census of Quirinius

Josephus referred to the second (and the ordinary) census conducted by Quirinius in A.D. 6, but what about the first one which Tertullian said took place in the time of Saturninus who was governor of Syria in 3/2 B.C.? Lardner, as early as the eighteenth century, was convinced that Josephus mentioned this earlier one as

Chapter 12 - The Census of Quirinius

well.[322] The oath referred to in Josephus and the registration of Luke may be one and the same. The best thing to do is to quote the remarks of Josephus about the oath in their entirety.

> "There was moreover a certain sect of Jews who valued themselves highly for their exact knowledge of the law; and talking much of their contact with God, were greatly in favor with the women of Herod's court. They are called Pharisees. They are men who had it in their power to control kings; extremely subtle, and ready to attempt any thing against those whom they did not like. When therefore the whole Jewish nation took an OATH to be faithful to Caesar, and [to] the interests of the king, these men, to the number of above six thousand, refused to swear. The king having laid a fine upon them, Pheroras' wife [Herod's sister-in-law] paid the money for them. They, in requital for her kindness (for they were supposed, by their great intimacy with God, to have attained to the gift of prophecy), prophesied that God having decreed to put an end to the government of Herod and his race, the kingdom would be transferred to her and Pheroras and their children. Salome [Herod's sister], who was aware of all that was being said, came and told the king of them. She also told him that many of the court [of Herod] were corrupted by them. Then the king put to death the most guilty of the Pharisees, and Bagoas the eunuch, and one Carus, the most beautiful young man about the court, and the great instrument in the king's unlawful pleasures. He [Herod] likewise slew every one in his own family, who adhered to those things which were said by the Pharisee. But Bagoas had been elevated by them and was told that he should some day be called father and benefactor of the [new] king, who was to be appointed according to their prediction, for this king would have all things in his power, and that he [the king] would give him [Bagoas] the capacity of marriage, and of having children of his own."[323]

More than 6000 Pharisees refused to take the *oath* of allegiance to Augustus and Herod. And as Josephus stated, this was because of their belief that the Messiah and his age was just on the horizon. As said before, Lardner went so far as to suggest that this oath of allegiance and the census mentioned by Luke were one and the same. It may well be true. There is a similarity in the wording within the two sources. Note how the two texts are worded when placed beside each other. First notice Josephus.

> "When therefore *the whole Jewish nation* TOOK AN OATH to be faithful to Caesar and to the interests of the king [Herod]... above six thousand Pharisees refused to swear."

Compared with the comments of Luke from original Greek:

> "Now in those days a decree was issued by Caesar Augustus *that all the world* SHOULD BE REGISTERED [enrolled]. This was the first registration when Quirinius *was ruling* from Syria."[324]

Certainly, the reference in Josephus to the oath must be looked on as some kind of a registration—a swearing of loyalty to Augustus and to Herod. How does one show loyalty? It is done by doing the will of the ruler, giving him devotion, paying one's share of taxes for the upkeep of the government, and recognizing the legality of the regime. And, no time in the Roman world would have been better for such an oath than the year preceding the Silver Jubilee celebrations. It could even have been called a census, as well as a registration, because the recording of an oath of allegiance from all people required the ascribing of their names to obey Augustus and Herod. How else did Josephus know that over 6000 Pharisees refused to take the oath unless some kind of record of their number had been made?

The Census is Now Identified

Once the chronology of the period is properly understood it can be seen that the oath would have been required about twelve to fifteen months before the death of Herod. Anyone reading the narrative of Josephus without pre-conceived opinions, would have to put it somewhere in that range of time. This oath would have been given during the governorship of Saturninus, and that is the exact period when Tertullian said the registration of Judaea was conducted. Coupled with this is the fact that Luke called this "census" the *first registration*. It could mean that he was distinguishing this "census" from the *second* (and ordinary) census of Quirinius which took place in A.D. 6/7, or that this was the *first registration* of its kind that ever took place. The latter reason has the best credentials.

The truth is, the "oath" mentioned by Josephus and the "census" of Luke are no doubt one and the same. All fits perfectly if the registration was ordered by Augustus in the Summer of 3 B.C. to be completed by Autumn of 2 B.C. during the year in which he was acclaimed the *Pater Patriae*. We will see that this was the *first time* that Augustus ever ordered *all in the Empire* to show such loyalty.

When the universal registration mentioned by Luke is dated to 3 B.C., a flood of light comes on the scene showing several Roman references to it. Since Luke said it was Augustus who gave the decree for an Empire-wide registration, perhaps we should let Augustus tell us with his personal statement about a political accounting of peoples that involved the whole Empire. It took place in 3 B.C. just when Luke said a registration occurred and when Josephus shows the Jews gave their oath to Augustus. This was the *first time* the emperor had the whole Roman Empire award him the title *Pater Patriae* (Father of the Country). We have a record from Augustus that an Empire-wide registration took place in 3 B.C.

The Empire-wide Registration

Augustus received his most prestigious title, the *Pater Pat*riae, on February 5, 2 B.C. which was the Day of Concord on the Roman religious calendar. But in what legal way did Augustus obtain this title? In the *Res Gestae*, composed by Augustus himself, he wrote: "While I was administering my thirteenth consulship the senate and the equestrian order *and the entire Roman people* [italics mine] gave me the title Father of my Country."[325] Within the Empire there were over 4 million Roman citizens. For the totality of the citizenry to approve the bestowal of the *Pater Patriae* must have involved an Empire-wide accounting. Since Augustus was officially given the award in early 2 B.C., the registering of the citizens must have been decreed and began to be carried out sometime in 3 B.C.

189

The Star that Astonished the World

In this universal registration of citizen approval regarding the "Fatherhood" of Augustus and the recognition of Supreme authority that the title signified, it is reasonable that all non-citizens in the Empire also gave some kind of recognizable approbation within the same period of time. Since most people in Judaea and the Empire were not Roman citizens, Augustus could well have decreed in 3 B.C. that everyone should swear an oath of absolute obedience to him to accompany his majestic award as being "Father of the Country." This would have been an appropriate gesture from all peoples in acknowledging their obedience to him by the time of his Jubilee Year of supreme power in 2 B.C.

Remarkably, an inscription found in Paphlagonia (north central Asia Minor) that is clearly dated to 3 B.C. records an oath of obedience "taken by the inhabitants of Paphlagonia and the Roman businessmen dwelling among them."[326] The inscription states that Romans as well as non-citizens took the oath. And importantly, the whole of the population were required to swear it. "The same oath was sworn also *by all the people in the land* [italics mine] at the altars of Augustus in the temples of Augustus in the various districts."[327] This was in 3 B.C. Also, in Judaea an oath was required of all the people at the same time (as shown by my chronological reconstruction).[328] This is a reasonable hint that the oath mentioned by Josephus was the same that the people of Paphlagonia were required to render. If so, then it could have been a part of the Empire-wide recognition of Augustus' *Pater Patriae*.

Others Records About the Census

There is yet another point. The Armenian historian Moses of Khorene said that the native sources he had available showed that in the second year of Abgar, king of Armenia in 3 B.C., the census mentioned by Luke brought Roman agents "to Armenia, bringing the image of Augustus Caesar, which they set up in every temple."[329] It is implied that people had to go to the temples to register for the census. This information is very similar to that engraved on the Paphlagonian inscription (also referring to 3 B.C.), that recorded the "oath" given to Augustus. The same oath was sworn by all the people in the land at the altars of Augustus in the temples of Augustus in the various districts. The similarity of language is so striking (and since the year is exactly the same), it may mean that we have Armenian history showing that the registration mentioned by Luke did indeed occur in the year 3 B.C.

The fact that the census of Luke was actually an Empire-wide oath to Augustus was recognized by Orosius, who lived in the fifth century. He must have had early sources for his evidence. He wrote:

> "[Augustus] ordered that a census be taken of each province everywhere and that all men be enrolled.... This is the earliest and most famous public acknowledgment which marked Caesar <u>as the first of all men</u> and the Romans as lords of the world, a published list of all men entered individually.... This first and greatest census was taken, since in this one name of Caesar all the peoples of the great nations <u>took oath</u>, and at the same time, through the participation in the census, were made apart of one society"[330] (underlining mine).

Orosius also identified the year for this enrollment and oath as being 3 B.C. He said the oath was taken to enroll Augustus "as the first of all men"—an apt description of the bestowal of the *Pater Patriae* in his Silver Jubilee year and when the priestly celebrations for the 750th anniversary of Rome took place. The fact that Orosius equaled the census with an oath of allegiance to Augustus may well mean that he had historical records that substantiated it.

Oaths Were Given at Censuses

The fact that oaths and censuses should go together should be no strange thing. Most Roman census declarations required an oath of allegiance to the emperor. One such declaration for property tax ended with: "We swear by the fortune of the Emperor Caesar Trajanus Hadrian Augustus.... *under oath*."[331] "And I swear by the Emperor Nero Claudius Caesar Augustus that I have kept nothing back."[332] It is thus very reasonable that the "census" mentioned by Luke could well have been the "oath" referred to by Josephus, as well as Orosius, and the Paphlagonian inscription.

It thus seems highly probable that all people in the Empire registered an oath of obedience and an approval of the *Pater Patriae* to Augustus at this time,[333] and that Quirinius had been sent to the East to conduct it for that section of the Empire. This would mean that Quirinius possessed special powers that were different than those of the resident governor. And though the registration was decreed in 3 B.C. (and many took the oath at that time), there was no doubt a few months allowed for peoples to register their oaths because it was universal in application with all people involved in the matter. It is reasonable that a period of about a year was allowed for the complete enrollment. Thus, Augustus' information in his *Res Gestae*, the Paphlagonian inscription, the history of Armenia, Orosius, Josephus and the statement of Luke historically blend together well.

The Registration Was Not For Taxation

Luke said that "all the [Roman] world should be registered" (Luke 2:1). Some have assumed that this "registering" was for taxation purposes. But Luke nowhere states that the payment of moneys was the reason for the enrollment, though an oath of obedience certainly involved financial accountability.

There is clear evidence that the registration conducted by Quirinius was not for taxation. While King Herod was alive none of the Jews in Judaea paid taxes to Rome. They paid them to Herod himself. This is made clear in the events immediately following Herod's death. The Jews asked Archelaus (Herod's successor) to relieve them of excessive taxes.[334] Had the Jews been paying taxes directly to Rome (brought about by the census of Quirinius) this request would have been irrelevant. From 63 B.C. to 47 B.C. Judaea was a part of the province of Syria and paid tribute directly

Chapter 12 - The Census of Quirinius

to Rome. From 47 B.C. to 40 B.C. Hyrcanus was the "ruler of a free republic,"[335] but the Jews still paid direct taxes to Rome. When Herod became king, however, the tribute to Rome ceased and Herod collected all taxes. This continued until A.D. 6/7 when direct taxation was again imposed upon those in Judaea.[336] This means that the registration by Quirinius in 3/2 B.C. was not strictly for tax purposes. This helps to show that it was primarily a census of loyalty to Augustus that all in the Empire had to undertake in honor of Augustus' "Fatherhood." The Paphlagonian inscription called it an "oath," Josephus called it an "oath," and Luke simply called it a "registration."

There may be more evidence to support this. It was common for Roman citizens to have their citizenship records checked every five years. There were both municipal records in Italy and in the provinces that registered citizenship status for Romans. When new citizens were enrolled, they were registered in the official tribal lists at Rome, and in many cases in the archives of their own native cities or other important "Roman centers" throughout the Empire.[337] Roman citizenship at that time was a prized possession and people wanted credentials of some kind to vouch for the title (*cf.* Acts 22:25-28). The registrations were checked and adjusted as to present circumstances every five years. Interestingly, we have clear evidence that Augustus had official censuses in 28 and 8 B.C.[338] This was a twenty year interval, and, of course, divisible by periods of five years. The next five year time for checking would have been 3 B.C. This was the precise year that the imperial oath recorded on the Paphlagonian inscription took place (sworn by both Roman citizens and natives).

Professor Sherwin-White of Oxford University said it was customary for provincial Romans to have their citizenships "checked" or to renew imperial privileges at certain cities to which citizens politically belonged. The normal thing for Roman provincials was to "be registered at his native city."[339] In Asia Minor there were

193

"archive cities" throughout the area where Roman imperial records were deposited. Many Roman provincials could prove their citizenship status by reference to those records. If the "oath" in Paphlagonia was the same as the "oath" that Josephus said took place in Judaea, and if both "oaths" were a part of the "census" mentioned by Luke, then perhaps Luke's remark that "everyone went into his own city" (Luke 2:3) might make sense for Roman provincials as well as non-Romans. This fits in well chronologically because all people periodically (and normally it was every five years) had to have their legal privileges or limitations checked at the "archive cities." And 3 B.C. was an exact five year period from the last Roman census. This would help to show that this particular year was indeed a year in which a "census" or a "registration" would have occurred even under ordinary circumstances.

The Twenty Years Census Period

Recall that the official censuses involving taxation were in 28 B.C. and 8 B.C. This was an exact 20 year period between the two censuses. The next official census according to Augustus was in A.D. 14. That is 21 years after 8 B.C.—not 20 years as one might expect. Could it be that a whole year was dropped out of taxation accounting in that period? Was the majestic Silver Jubilee year of 2 B.C. a non-taxable year? If so, note what would then have happened. The next five year period for checking the personal affairs and effects of Romans would have been in A.D. 4 and the next in A.D. 9, followed, of course, by the regular census five years later in A.D. 14. Interestingly, A.D. 4 and A.D. 9 were the exact years in which Augustus passed the social legislation pertaining to Roman citizens.[340] If what I am saying is true then we have, in the time of Augustus, official censuses occurring every 20 years. This must be the case because professors Vermes and Millar report that the earliest actually attested census for taxation was in A.D. 33/34, and that is 20 years after the last official census of Augustus in A.D. 14.[341] All of the five year periods between the main 20 year census-

Chapter 12 - The Census of Quirinius

es could be called minor censuses.

The year 2 B.C., however, was reckoned so glorious—a new beginning for Augustus and Rome—that it looks like imperial taxation and evaluation ceased during that year if people would give their oath of allegiance to Augustus as their *Pater Patriae* and that they reckoned him as their universal lord. This could well be the case. It was not uncommon to remit some or all taxes at times.

Remitting part or all taxes was no new thing, especially if special circumstances were involved. Herod in order to honor his good fortune and because he was in a cheerful mood canceled a fourth part of taxes to the delight of his subjects. They went away with the greatest joy, wishing the king all sorts of good things.[342] The Romans remitted taxes from the Jews in their sabbatical years.[343] Even within the Empire it was not uncommon to cancel taxes at times of national joy at the accession of an emperor. Note that Alexander Severus cited a precedent of earlier emperors of remitting certain taxations at times of accession.[344] And, if there was ever a time when Rome was in joy, a feeling that a "new beginning" and a new "Golden Age" was happening, it was the year 2 B.C. Thus, it seems possible that the people taking the census/oath for the *Pater Patriae* of Augustus were granted many fiscal immunities to accompany the joyful Silver Jubilee of the princeps and the 750th anniversary of Rome as shown by the priestly records.

This helps to show that the census of Luke was not for taxation purposes. It was for Augustus' exaltation to the *Pater Patriae*. All of this indicates that the *first* census conducted by Quirinius in Herod's kingdom was for this reason. After all, while Herod was alive, it was he who collected his own taxes, not Roman officials. But in 3 B.C., Quirinius was a *procurator* with unique powers from Augustus and responsible for conducting the special registration concerning the *Pater Patriae* for Augustus. It is just that simple.

Was Quirinius Governor in 2 B.C.?

There is one question that needs answering. Many translators of the New Testament render Luke 2:1 as though Quirinius were governor of Syria. In no way does Luke state this in his original Greek text, though I used to believe he did. Luke simply said that Quirinius was *ruling* or *administrating* this *first registration* from Syria, not that he was the governor of the province. The Greek word Luke used to show the rulership of Quirinius was *hegemoneuontos*. It is a present participle which simply means that Quirinius was *ruling* or *administrating* his duties from the region of Syria. There is not the slightest indication in Luke's narrative that identifies the specific office being held by Quirinius while he was *administrating* his official duties. In normal Greek usage at the time, the word *hegemoneuontos* could refer to any type of rulership from that of an exalted President or a military commander on down through various lesser offices to that of the local dog catcher for the city. The word could very well refer to the fact that Quirinius was a *procurator* as Justin Martyr attests. Certainly, Quirinius was NOT the resident govenor as so many assume. In no way do the words of Luke mean such a thing. Indeed, shortly afterward, Luke in chapter 3 verse 1 referred to Pontius Pilate by the exact same word (and in the exact grammatical structure) and we know from a recent monumental discovery that Pontius Pilate was a *Praefectus Judaeae,* not a senatorial *Legatus* (Governor) who controlled one of the major provinces of the Empire. The fact is, Luke's administrative description of Quirinius' powers could dovetail nicely with those of a special *Procurator* of Augustus precisely as Justin Martyr said that Quirinius was. It is wrong to assume that Luke meant that Quirinius was the governor of the province of Syria.

There is, however, one possibility that could have made Quirinius to be a temporary governor of sorts. Note that Josephus tells us that Saturninus was still governor of Syria in the latter part of Spring in 2 B.C.[345] But by the following November, Quintilius Varus was then governor and hearing the charges in Jerusalem

Chapter 12 - The Census of Quirinius

against Antipater the son of Herod. Josephus tells us specifically that Varus had lately taken over the governorship from Saturninus.[346] This allows for a six month period in which no one knows who was governor of Syria. This was the Summer change-over period from one governor to the next. Could it be that Saturninus left Syria in late Spring, handed affairs over to Quirinius for the change-over interval, and then Varus took charge in late September or October of 2 B.C.? This is possible.

There was yet no established custom near the time of Augustus for governors to be in their provincial seats of authority at set times of the year. Cicero left his province before May 1st in 58 B.C.[347] His brother, however, did not leave Rome to take up his proconsulship until the early part of May.[348] This example shows that sometimes parts of the Summer period saw a province without its resident governor. Obviously, a lieutenant would have been in charge in some capacity. In fact, Atkinson shows that it was common practice for some of the Summer months not to have provincial governors in residence.[349] Perhaps this is what occurred in the change-over period from Saturninus to Varus. In truth, there was a good reason why both Saturninus and Varus would have wanted to be in Rome for the Summer of 2 B.C. That year was one of great significance to the citizens of Rome and to those who lived within the Empire. It was the Silver Jubilee of Augustus' accession to total power and the year he was proclaimed the *Pater Patriae*. This year was looked on as the apex of the Augustan Peace.

The Celebrations at Rome

Both Saturninus and Varus would have wanted to be in Rome for the Summer months. And both had an ace in hand to do it. Quirinius was then in Syria having conducted his procuratorial role of conducting a registration of peoples. Since Quirinius was a man of high rank, and with the province having peace and security on all sides, there would not have been the slightest reason for not having Quirinius assume the supreme command while concluding his procuratorial responsibilities. With Saturninus gone to Rome in late Spring of 2 B.C., this would have left Quirinius as the full administrator until October or so. Something approaching this explanation might make some people think that Quirinius could have been considered the temporary governor of the province of Syria. Luke, however, in no way said that he was. The office that best suits Quirinius while he was performing his duties in conducting the registration of the people would be that of *Procurator*.

It is true that later, in A.D. 6/7, Quirinius himself became what could more appropriately be called an official governor of Syria (which then included Palestine). Though even here, he seemed to have special powers that normal governors did not have. A "census" was also taken at that time (and Luke referred to it—Acts 5:37) because the province officially became a part of the Roman Empire in that year. But Justin's remark that Quirinius was a *Procurator* when the "census" was taken at the nativity of Jesus, yet he was full (and undisputed) governor at the census for taxation in A.D. 6/7, helps to distinguish the two different "censuses."

The explanation given in this chapter is reasonable and solves the difficulty at once. The statement of Luke can make good historical sense. Indeed, it could be said that Luke provides the key that shows who governed Syria from 3 B.C. on through the Summer months of 2 B.C. And indeed, why shouldn't Luke be accepted? He was probably a native of Antioch (or certainly familiar with the area). He was writing to a Roman nobleman who would surely have been knowledgeable of Roman affairs. Luke was also a writer who lived much closer to the events than either Josephus or Dio Cassius the early Roman historian.

The simplicity and reasonableness of the explanation in this chapter is a strong point in its favor. And interestingly, this historical information harmonizes the Paphlagonian inscription with Tertullian (quoting Roman records), and this agrees with Justin Martyr (quoting Roman records) and with Luke (writing to a

Chapter 12 - The Census of Quirinius

Roman nobleman), and it is confirmed by Orosius and Moses of Khorene the Armenian historian.

This means that the "census" of Quirinius which has eluded any positive identification by modern historians is now found in several historical sources and some of them right at the time the "census" occurred according to the chronology of the New Testament and that of secular history. In a word, the "census" of Quirinius associated with the nativity of Jesus has been found.

Chapter 13
THE CHRONOLOGY OF JOSEPHUS

The new historical information which has now come to light focuses on the fact of Herod's death in 1 B.C. and the birth of Jesus in 3 B.C. But the main reason historians have accepted the 13 March, 4 B.C. eclipse as the one associated with Herod's death is primarily because of two factors: the first is a chronological indication made by Josephus concerning Herod's length of reign, and the second involves the lengths of reign of the sons of Herod who were his successors.

Let us note what Josephus said about the year lengths of Herod's reign. We have to say "lengths" (in the plural) because Josephus gave two such indications. He said that Herod had a reign of 37 years from the time he was proclaimed king by the Romans and 34 years from the death of Antigonus which occurred after Herod captured Jerusalem.[350] Scholars have been prone to say that these indications would date the death of Herod to the year 3 B.C., but there was no eclipse of the Moon in that year. The nearest eclipse was that of 13 March, 4 B.C. Since astronomical data are such powerful evidences, many scholars within the last hundred years have felt it necessary to *stretch* the chronological statements of Josephus to make them fit the time of this eclipse. They do not mind *stretching* the facts in this regard because they have to in order to rescue the 13 March eclipse as the one associated with Herod's death. This is why professors Vermes and Millar acknowledged that Josephus reckoned one year too many.[351]

All scholars recognize this discrepancy in trying to resolve Josephus' chronological statements. To mend the disparity, it is assumed that Josephus has adopted a scheme of reckoning parts of one year (only the first few days of a year) as answering in a legal sense to a whole year. If two or three days can be accepted as representing a whole year in Josephus' account of the number of years for Herod's reign, then these few days could allow Herod's last year to be extended back to the first of Nisan on the Jewish calendar (March 29) in 4 B.C. and then a whole year can be awarded to him in a *de jure* sense.

With this type of reasoning, modern scholars suggest that Herod would have died two or three days after 1 Nisan (the start of the Jewish ecclesiastical year), but for legal reasons in reckoning Herod's reign, the whole year from 1 Nisan, 4 B.C. to 1 Nisan, 3 B.C. is considered by them as the last regnal year of Herod. Not everyone, however, buys this explanation. Professor Barnes will not accept the eclipse of 13 March, 4 B.C. as proper. Barnes made it clear that the time between Herod's death and the next Passover (which Josephus said occurred after Herod's death) is too short an interval to witness all the recorded events associated with Herod's funeral procession, the period for his mourning, and the other events that occurred before that Passover.[352]

This does not end the matter however. The second reason many scholars have placed Herod's death in 4 B.C. is because it has been supposed that Herod's three successors seem to have their reigns commencing in that year. But this is not so. I have shown previously in this book that David W. Beyer in his work titled: "Josephus Reexamined: Unraveling the Twenty-Second Year of Tiberius" has demonstrated with a great deal of competent research into the manuscripts of Josephus that shows Herod's son Philip began his reign in 1 B.C. and had a 37 year reign, dying in the twenty-second year of Tiberius (as the older manuscripts of Josephus show) and not the twentieth year of Tiberius that scholars have accepted today. (I will discuss the seeming chronological disparities regarding Herod's other two sons shortly.)

These disparities have allowed scholars in the past to accept the eclipse of 13 March, 4 B.C. (as untenable as it is!). They felt justified in *stretching* the historical records almost beyond recognition to make them fit their chronological interpretations. While they were well aware that their assumptions had considerable difficulties associated with them, they did not think it necessary to tell the public in most of their general works or encyclopaedias that there were major "problems" in accepting these appraisals. But the public has a right to know the facts involving the historical circumstances concerning this important period of time. If scholars would simply state that their appraisals are *mere possibilities* among other explanations, then their guessing might be acceptable as offering their conjectures to explain the difficulties. But more often than not, this is the time when scholars express their blatant dogmatisms. They do this in spite of the fact that classical historians state that the period from 6 B.C. to A.D. 4 is one of the most *obscure decades* in the history of the Roman Empire as far as reliable records are concerned. This is where the difficulty arises in evaluating the historical events of this obscure period. Still, utter dogmatism prevails. The theologians who make their dogmatic assumptions that they expect the general public to accept have thrown caution to the wind.

It is now time to bring these problems out into the open for all to evaluate. Thankfully, it is gratifying to see that some scholars are

Chapter 13 - The Chronology of Josephus

now beginning to recognize that their past assumptions are not compatible with the facts of history. This is a welcome trend. When finally all professionals seriously join the quest to attempt to sort out the truth, I do not have the slightest doubt that it will be seen that Herod died not long after an eclipse of the Moon on 10 January, 1 B.C., and *not* a few days after the eclipse of 13 March, 4 B.C.

The Anomalies of Josephus

Josephus is not an easy author to understand relative to his chronological statements regarding earlier historical events of which he was not an eyewitness. As mentioned in an earlier chapter, besides the clear editing that has happened in the manuscripts that make many of his chronological indications suspect, even the text of Josephus that can be reasonably trusted as being unedited is at times inconsistent in his chronological information. For certain periods he avoids giving any chronological details at all, often at the very times when the modern historian needs them the most. For example, the main years of Archelaus, Herod's successor, are glossed over with one or two general statements, and the period from A.D. 6 to the time of Pilate in A.D. 26 is practically blank. No one knows why these discrepancies exist in Josephus, but they are there.

There are, without doubt, several anomalies in Josephus' treatment of Herod's reign. During the first years of Herod, he buttressed his history with known and reliable chronological eras of time. He equated Herod's seventh year with the year following the Battle of Actium and he also gave reference to the Olympiads.[353] Josephus continued giving exact dates supported by internationally known benchmarks until Herod's twenty-eighth year (a few years before the birth of Jesus).[354] But from then on, for some strange reason, Josephus stopped giving chronological indications which would link the latter years of Herod's reign with known historical eras. He did not resume his normal international cross-references until the tenth year of Archelaus (son of Herod) in A.D. 6. From

203

then until the Jewish War of A.D. 66 to A.D. 73, when Josephus gives chronological references, they are sensible.

Why did Josephus abandon prime chronological indications in the latter years of Herod and the beginning of Archelaus' reign? This is a mystery. The fact is, some of the most important events in Palestinian history were occurring during that period: When the sons of Mariamme (one of Herod's wives) were slain, when the oath of loyalty took place and over 6000 Pharisees refused to sign the oath, when Antipater (Herod's rebellious son) went to Rome, when Herod's brother Pheroras died, when the trial of Antipater happened, when the golden eagle was destroyed, when the two rabbis were executed and when Antipater was slain. For these events, there is not one cross-reference to the Olympiads, the Battle of Actium, or other international benchmarks. This lack gives the historian a great deal of difficulty in precisely dating the events.

Harmonizing the Chronological Difficulties

Let us now look at some possible reasons why Josephus in the period of Herod treated chronological matters in the way he did. Josephus tells us that Herod died after a reign of 37 years from the time he was made king by the Romans and 34 years from the death of Antigonus. On the surface scholars think this leads us to the year 3 B.C. for Herod's death (or by reckoning two or three days of a year as a whole year, it could be stretched back to 4 B.C.). But other historical data I will show in this book will not allow either 4 or 3 B.C. for Herod's death. I give historical information in Appendix Four that shows the sequence of Sabbatical Years for our period under discussion. Without doubt, the evidence indicates that Herod captured Jerusalem in the Sabbatical Year ending in late Summer of 36 B.C. (indeed, it was on the Day of Atonement at the conclusion of that Sabbatical Year). Since Antigonus was killed at a later period, Herod's rule of 34 years from the death of Antigonus works out nicely with what I am showing in this book—his year 34 would be from 2 to 1 B.C. Galloway in the last century saw the problem and

Chapter 13 - The Chronology of Josephus

suggested that Herod's 34 years mentioned by Josephus were to be counted from the death of Antigonus some three years later. He did not believe Antony killed Antigonus immediately after Herod's conquest of Jerusalem, but had him executed three years later when Antony went to war against the Armenians.[355] This explanation was also maintained by Cunninghame.[356] The fact is, however, the interval of three years for Antigonus' death that these historians have suggested is not required and there is no substantiation of it in the records. As a matter of fact, Antigonus could have been killed a few months after Herod captured Jerusalem in 36 B.C. and still Herod's death would work out to 1 B.C.

Yet there are problems with these appraisals. Josephus called Herod a "king" at least a dozen times between the day he was proclaimed king by the Romans and when he actually began to rule after capturing Jerusalem. His 37 years must be reckoned from the proclamation of his kingship by the Romans, and this would seemingly bring Herod's last regnal year to 3 B.C. And there are the indications that two of Herod's sons who succeeded him in his government seemingly have their reigns dated from 4 B.C.

The Suggestions of W.E. Filmer

An ingenious solution has been offered. In October, 1966, the *Journal of Theological Studies* carried an article by W.E. Filmer which suggested a solution to the problem concerning the years of Herod's reign—especially the year of his death. His suggestions can be summarized as follows: most scholars feel that Herod's 37 years' reign began in 40 B.C. and his 34 years from the capture of Jerusalem which they think was in 37 B.C. This brings us to 3 B.C. for Herod's death. But this is one year beyond the 13 March, 4 B.C. eclipse. Most scholars today have failed to take this disparity into account. This is not the case with Professors Vermes and Millar. They have noticed this major fault and it prompts them to write: "We know that Josephus reckons one year too many."[357] The reason that they are willing to admit that Josephus is off one year is in order (one would surmise) to protect the eclipse of 13 March, 4 B.C. as being the one referred to by Josephus. The acceptance of that eclipse as the proper one has forced scholars to bend the rules in several ways. That is why that early eclipse deserves no protection. Look at what the retention of this wrong eclipse has done.

To accommodate the eclipse of 4 B.C., scholars have been forced to count Josephus' years inclusively. This means they are willing to allow a mere two or three days of Nisan in 4 B.C. (when the Jewish ecclesiastical year began) to be counted as a whole year in the reckoning of Josephus. Filmer, however, has given good evidence to show that Josephus did not count his years in this inclusive manner. This is also shown by Ormund Edwards in his "A New Chronology of the Gospels" (pp., 27-33). Furthermore, Filmer also showed reasons that the capture of Jerusalem by Herod was not in 37 B.C., but in 36 B.C. and I have demonstrated in Appendix Four of this book that the Sabbatical Year at that time in which Jerusalem was captured was truly in 36 B.C.

Filmer's suggestion is absolutely correct. Herod's 34 years of reign from the time of Antigonus' death after he captured Jerusalem must be reckoned from 36 B.C. — not from 37 B.C. Filmer showed several reasons for this. Two of them involved sacred seasons of the Jews. When such seasons are mentioned in the historical sources, a greater amount of credibility can be given to the chronological statements in the records because the Jewish authorities would have long remembered important events that occurred on their holy days or sacred seasons. It was not uncommon for the general populace to place theological or prophetical significance to such occasions. So, what were the two sacred seasons that happened when Herod finally captured Jerusalem?

Josephus said that Herod's siege was during a Sabbatical Year and that a great scarcity of food was evident because of it.[358] Sabbatical Years occur every seventh year on the Jewish calendar. Modern studies of Wacholder and others clearly demonstrate that

Chapter 13 - The Chronology of Josephus

36 B.C. was indeed the end of a Sabbatical Year,[359] and I show the results of that new research in Appendix Four. And, Professor Marcus in his notes to the Loeb edition of Josephus shows that there are very good reasons for believing that the Sabbatical Year under discussion was to be reckoned from October, 37 B.C. to October, 36 B.C. Herod would have captured Jerusalem at the end of that sacred period.

And there is one other historical reference involving a Jewish sacred day that substantiates this conclusion even more. All Sabbatical Years according to the Law of Moses ended on the Day of Atonement (*Yom Kippur*), and Josephus said that Herod's capture of Jerusalem coincided exactly with a Day of Atonement.[360] He further stated that it was precisely to the very day, 27 years after the Roman general Pompey conquered Jerusalem in 63 B.C.[361] Clearly, this chronological fact leads one to 25 October, 36 B.C. for Herod's capture of Jerusalem.

This indication is powerful evidence in which any scholar can place the highest confidence that Herod's 34 years of reign from Antigonus' death has to have 36 B.C. as a beginning benchmark. This is because Sabbatical Years stood out very remarkably to Jews who lived in Palestine at the time. This was a time when food was in short supply and when the whole of agricultural activity ceased. When a major event like Herod capturing Jerusalem took place in a Sabbatical Year, that would have been long remembered. This was especially so because his capture was also on the Day of Atonement.

Actually, though, Josephus got even more precise than simply the time Herod captured Jerusalem. He said that Herod's 34 years are to be reckoned from the death of Antigonus (which happened at a later period) and *not* simply from the day of Herod's conquest of Jerusalem. There were at least a few months after Jerusalem's fall before Antigonus was executed. By using the ordinary accession method of counting regnal years of Judaean rulers, the actual date for the commencing of Herod's 34 years was with the first of Nisan in 35 B.C. This makes Herod's 34th year to start with Nisan in 2 B.C. and it ends with Nisan in 1 B.C.

It must be remembered that all priestly years were reckoned from Nisan and not from the autumn month of Tishri. The Hasmoneans who ruled Judaea before Herod (and whom Herod succeeded) were of priestly origin. It became common under their priestly rule for the kings in Jerusalem to reckon their years from Nisan and not from Tishri. In the Talmud, the later Jews understood this fact and stated that the later kings of Judah were accustomed to the Nisan to Nisan reckoning.[362] In the earlier biblical period, the custom for Judah was a Tishri to Tishri reckoning.[363]

The Reasonableness of These Historical References

These historical indications are powerful witnesses that Herod's conquest of Jerusalem was in late 36 B.C. and Antigonus' death was some time later. And remember, Josephus said Herod's 34 years commenced with the death of Antigonus, *not* at Herod's capture of Jerusalem.

Professors Vermes and Millar state that these historical indications represent "a considerable difficulty" to those scholars who wish to maintain either the year 38 B.C. or 37 B.C. as the year Herod took Jerusalem.[364] In truth, these factors make it *impossible* to consider the earlier years of 38 and 37 B.C. that have been guessed by some theologians.

The Jewish people would have long remembered that Sabbatical Year and the holy day season regarding the taking of Jerusalem by Herod. Pressing the siege especially at the very end of a Sabbatical Year and on the Day of Atonement would have made Herod an abominable character as far as the Jews were concerned, and they would never have forgotten the outrage. Even Josephus remembered it well and he stated that it was precisely 27 years *to the day* that Pompey previously committed his abominations.

Chapter 13 - The Chronology of Josephus

The Major Problem with Filmer's Suggestions

While Filmer's treatment of Josephus' reckoning for Herod's years of reign appears reasonable, there is one major stumbling-block to it. Barnes, in his review of Filmer's position,[365] made it pretty clear that the historical records show that some of Herod's successors began their reigns in 4 B.C., and not as one might expect in 1 B.C. The Roman historian Dio said that Herod's son Archelaus was deposed in his tenth year of reign in the consulship of Aemalius Lepidus and L. Arruntuis.[366] This answers to A.D. 6 and it means that Archelaus took over from Herod sometime in 4 B.C.—or at least it looks that way. There is even more evidence of this. Antipas was deposed by Caligula in A.D. 39, and there are coins which record his forty-third year. This evidence also leads one back to 4 B.C. for the beginning of Antipas' reign.

The fact that these two sons of Herod (Archelaus and Antipas) seem to be reigning in 4 B.C. is the main problem to the thesis of Filmer. If Herod died in early 1 B.C. (as Filmer and the evidence of this book suggest), why were two of Herod's successors reckoned as reigning as early as 4 B.C.? This, on the other hand, is not the case with Herod's son Philip. I have shown how David W. Beyer has made it clear that the early manuscripts of Josephus show Philip to have started his 37 years of rule in 1 B.C. But why do the other two sons of Herod seemingly show 4 B.C.? There are historical reasons why this happened. And once they are understood, it shows that Filmer is right after all in his solutions to the problem.

Toward An Answer

Josephus said that in the Summer before Herod's death, Varus became governor of Syria. He had taken over the position from Saturninus. We have shown that this tenure would have been Varus' *second* governorship (2 B.C. to A.D. 1). Saturninus had been governor the previous two years (from early 4 B.C. to the Summer of 2 B.C.). Varus had also been governor the *first* time before the rule of Saturninus (from 7 or 6 B.C. to 4 B.C.). Josephus said the gov-

209

ernor before Varus' first governorship was a man named Titius.[367]

Let us now notice what Josephus said occurred just after Saturninus assumed the governorship of Syria (which would have been in early 4 B.C. according to my dating in this book). Herod sent a part of his army to Arabia to put an end to the activities of robbers who were hiding in the area and to collect a major debt that was owed him by the Arabian ruler. And though the governors of Syria had given Herod permission for the action, Augustus was misinformed by Syllaeus the Arabian about the whole affair. Augustus responded by sending a stinging rebuke to Herod. The message from Caesar was devastating: "Whereas of old he [Augustus] had used him *as his friend*, he should now use him *as his subject*."[368]

This declaration of Augustus was not a simple displeasure at Herod's actions. It had very serious political implications attached to it. To be a friend of Caesar was a title (*amici Caesaris*) which was awarded to special individuals by the Roman government to show a close political relationship to the emperor. So pleased was Herod of Chalcis to have the designation that he had the title stamped on the coins of his realm.[369] At the time of Jesus' crucifixion, Pilate must have had the same honor because "the Jews cried out, saying, If thou let this man go, thou art not Caesar's friend."[370] In regard to Pilate, this was tantamount to saying he did not respect his title as "Caesar's Friend." Pilate took the charge seriously. But Herod took it even more so. Herod had now not only been stripped of his honorable title by the emperor himself, but he was further relegated to an even lower position by being reckoned as a "subject." True enough, Herod was later reconciled to Augustus, but not before some tactical and strategic damage had been done to Herod's governmental standing with Augustus.

This official reduction of Herod's authority may well have prompted some major revisions in the way Rome looked on his government. Remarkably, a short time after Herod's power was diminished, we find that Antipater, Herod's eldest son, was now being acknowledged as *reigning jointly* with his father.[371] Antipater was allowed to wear the purple robe, the symbol of rulership.[372] Even Herod later admitted that his son had been given one-half the kingdom.[373] It could well be that Roman authorities began (from the Summer of 4 B.C.) to acknowledge a permanent joint rulership over the region of Judaea. Obviously, Antipater could not have assumed such authority by himself and Herod was also unable to bestow these honors on any of his sons unless Augustus gave permission. Josephus could well have figured this event into his reckoning of the reigns of Herod's successors. If Antipater could have a joint-rule with his father, why not the other two sons?

But Josephus' assessments may have been swayed by another important occasion that occurred about two years before Herod's death (in 4 B.C.). This was an event that angered Josephus so much and most of the Jewish nation that he never forgave Herod for it.

Herod's Murder of His Sons

From the time of Judas Maccabeus to that of Herod, the Jewish nation had been governed by the priestly family of the Hasmoneans. When Herod came to power, he wished to solidify his political position in the nation by marrying Mariamme, one of the surviving descendants of this dynasty. She was considered a "queen." Herod had two sons by her—Alexander and Aristobulus. As these sons grew up they became very popular with the people, and many in the nation were hoping that they would gain the crown upon the death of Herod. This would have meant a legitimate continuation of the Hasmonean dynasty. The designated heir of Herod, however, was Antipater. This older son saw the two sons of Mariamme as a danger to his own aspirations to rule. According to Josephus, Antipater concocted many false accusations against them and finally got the Hasmoneans alienated from the affection of Herod. In his reflections about Antipater's schemes, Josephus waxed hot in anger. He also castigated Herod for going along with the false invectives of Antipater and for having the monstrous gall of finally having the two "royal" sons killed about two years before Herod died.

Josephus spent considerable space in his histories utterly abhorring the whole affair. Indeed, it could well be said that he went overboard in his condemnation of Herod and Antipater. Why he did so is not difficult to answer. He had a double reason to be indignant with them both. First, he felt that the mistreatment of the Hasmonean sons and their consequent executions were completely unjust. Secondly, Josephus was himself a descendant on his mother's side from this same Hasmonean family. So, when Herod came under "subjection" to Caesar, and with the legitimate heirs to Herod's kingdom now dead, Josephus, as well as the Jewish people, could have considered legal government at an end in Jerusalem. Even Augustus may have been deeply concerned over Herod's execution of the "royal" sons (though Augustus gave permission for Herod to do it). Professor Hoehner has shown that Augustus must have had a personal acquaintance with the Hasmonean sons and they had been held in high esteem at Rome.[374]

Augustus Assumed Personal Control

Augustus could well have decided that some governmental change was now necessary for the Judaean area of the Empire. After all, Herod was now quite old and with affairs in his own family in chaos, Augustus felt it was time to take more direct control in Judaea. He revoked Herod's award as being "Caesar's Friend" and demoted him further to being one of subject class. And recall, it was just after this time that Augustus also decreed that a registration of the Empire should take place.[375] Such a registration was a direct interference by Augustus into the governmental affairs of Judaea. The oath that accompanied it, as I have said before, was no doubt a part of the registration mentioned by Luke. Such an oath was also administered to the people of Judaea at the accession of Caligula to the emperorship,[376] and it too was prompted by a change

Chapter 13 - The Chronology of Josephus

of government. Professor Burkhill, writing in the revised Schurer, p. 376, states that "the oath of allegiance to the emperor which the people were obliged to take, *presumably on every change of government* [italics mine], was mandatory already in the days of Herod."

The fact that Augustus demanded the direct registration and oath for the people of Judaea is a clear sign that he was becoming concerned over the political state of the area. It was a personal intrusion of the emperor into the government of Herod. The insistence upon the oath was also an indication to the people of Judaea that they now owed their allegiance directly to the emperor and not to Herod alone. By signing the oath, the Judaeans were showing acceptance to the new political status of Rome in their affairs. "The oath was used as the conclusion of all kinds of legal dealings, particularly in political administration, taxation, and public documents."[377]

Rome Took Direct Control

This change of governmental status in Judaea is reflected in another way — a way which is very evident to anyone who studies the judicial powers of Herod during his time of reign. When Herod was first coming to power in Judaea, he was to be tried by the Sanhedrin at Jerusalem (the Supreme Court of the Jews) for high crimes.[378] But notice this important point. This trial was convened without any appeal to Rome for permission to execute Herod if the sentence went in that direction. Later, when Herod himself came to power in Judaea, he and the Sanhedrin executed Hyrcanus without getting authority from Rome to do it.[379] Herod put to death the royal Queen Mariamme[380] and Aristobulus,[381] and the royal sons of Baba[382] without consulting Caesar. And even later, Herod's son Alexander (one well liked by Augustus) admitted that Herod still had power to execute him and his brother if he desired.[383] But, and it is important to note this point, once Herod was demoted from being Caesar's Friend, Herod's power for executive action in regard to capital crimes was invalidated for persons of high rank. When Herod finally decided that Alexander and Aristobulus should be executed for their supposed crimes against him, he had to have Caesar's representatives in the province of Syria hear the case. In fact, Augustus even ordered that the trial be held in Beirut (a major city within the province of Syria) rather than at Jerusalem as one might expect in deference to Herod.

Indeed, at Beirut Augustus ordered a whole battery of important people to judge the case: Saturninus governor of Syria with his sons, Volumnius, the Syrian military administrator, a special envoy named Pedanius (with his own adjudicators).[384] It was these Roman officials who made the final decision in the case, not Herod himself. And even later, when Herod's son Antipater was tried for high crimes, Varus the governor of Syria was in Jerusalem to hear the case.[385] Even then Herod had no power to execute Antipater unless Augustus himself gave the permission. All of this shows a profound reduction of governmental authority for Herod (especially in the judicial sense). His decline in power began with his demotion from being Caesar's Friend, and we have shown this to have happened about two or three years before his death. This demotion would have occurred in 4 B.C. Even the later demand of Augustus for an oath of allegiance from the people of Judaea with a registration of their names is also a clear sign that a governmental change had happened in Herod's realm.

These things show that Herod lost much personal power in 4 B.C. There is another way of demonstrating governmental changes in his administration at this time. Recall that during the rule of Saturninus (4-2 B.C.), Josephus spoke about "governors" in Syria. Why this change to "governors"? Even Quirinius had been sent to the region as a special *procurator* of the emperor to oversee its political affairs. Technically, Herod's kingdom was under the influence of the Syrian governors. If governmental changes were then taking place in Syria, such adjustments could well be reflected in

Herod's domains. This is especially true when one realizes that Herod was near the end of his life and Augustus knew that an unstable political situation was already developing in Judaea. This could have been a factor why Quirinius was sent to conduct the census and the registration of loyalty to Augustus among Herod's subjects. Let us recall that Justin Martyr said that Quirinius was in actual fact a *procurator* when he was in Syria and Palestine. This meant he was a special envoy of Augustus to conduct important governmental duties in these eastern areas. This also shows the concern that Augustus had about this important region of the Empire.

There is also another important reason why the time of 4 to 2 B.C. could have been a period of governmental reorganization in Judaea. From 4 B.C. onward, there was the joint reign of Antipater with Herod. This joint rule is clearly stated by Josephus.

The Two-Year Co-Rulership of Antipater With Herod

From what Josephus records about the evil actions of Antipater (the designated heir of Herod), he must be acknowledged as one of the most iniquitous sons any father ever had. Though Josephus said Antipater was "co-ruler with his father and in no way different from a king,"[386] for the two-year period after the deaths of Alexander and Aristobulus, it was Antipater's constant activity to think up ways to kill his father. He involved many people in his plots and even prompted Herod's brother Pheroras into a plan to poison him. While Antipater was on a trip to Rome, Herod found out about his schemes. Indeed, as time went on, the magnitude of the whole affair and the great number of people involved caused Herod to recall Antipater from Rome. He did not tell him the reason for his return, but Herod's object was to judge Antipater before a court of law and have him executed for his crimes.

When Antipater got back to Jerusalem he was brought to trial at once and in one day was convicted of high treason, murder, and attempted parricide. Herod immediately sent messages to Caesar asking permission to execute Antipater. Herod had to ask the emperor at this time, and this shows his decline in authority.

Herod then altered his will by excluding Antipater from any inheritance. The message finally came back from Caesar that Herod could either banish him to a remote part of the Empire or kill him. Banishment for severe offenses meant a complete loss of all rights—including citizenship, family privileges, and even sonship. When Augustus' daughter Julia was banished about the same time (2 B.C.) he considered her no longer his daughter. When Julia's name would come up in chance conversation, Augustus would sometimes quote a line from Homer: "Better to have never married, and childless to have died."[387] Was there an expunging of such a person's name from official or family documents? This certainly was allowed in a Jewish environment. In the Bible it is mentioned that if a person, family, or tribe left the true religion, he was to be excommunicated from the nation and his name blotted out "from under heaven" (Deuteronomy 29:17-21). Because of the idolatry of the tribe of Dan, it was little heard of in the latter part of the Old Testament, and in the New Testament the tribe is not even reckoned among the twelve tribes of Israel (Revelation 7:4-8).

Erasing Names in Genealogical Lists Was Common

Herod would have found enough biblical precedents for expunging Antipater's name from the public records (including his two years of joint rule with Herod when he was also reckoned as a king). There are historical examples of such things *e.g.*, chiseling away names from the monuments of Egypt (even attempting to destroy the written records of Pharaoh Akenaton) and Nabonassar obliterating the accounts of previous Babylonian kings. And now, Herod had received permission to either banish his son (this could have meant the loss of sonship for Antipater) or to kill him. Herod decided to execute him, but he no doubt stripped him of all family associations in an effort to degrade him completely.

Chapter 13 - The Chronology of Josephus

Note that Herod again changed his will immediately after killing Antipater. Directions for such a "blotting out" could well have been in his final testament. It could have been that Antipater's joint rule with Herod was now awarded retroactively to Herod's true successors to secure the "blotting out" of Antipater's memory. This is even suggested by what Josephus said about Archelaus, the chief successor of Herod. There is the obscure reference that Archelaus was recognized as one that "*had long exercised royal authority.*"[388] This was not actually true to fact. The mind of Herod had been poisoned against Archelaus. Only at the last moment of his life, when in desperation, did Herod appoint Archelaus to be the heir to the kingdom.[389] Why then was Archelaus reckoned as having authority with Herod in the latter years of Herod's reign when everyone knows he wasn't in such power? He was no doubt awarded the years of Antipater's joint rule in a *de jure* sense — replacing Antipater's joint rulership associated with his father in the Judaean kingdom when the two royal Hasmonean sons were killed (4 B.C.).

The Evidence of Coins

The immediate successors to Herod were reckoned in some way as reigning in 4 B.C. But this was the year when Herod was demoted in Augustus' eyes and when Alexander and Aristobulus were slain. This year was not when Herod died. It appears that Herod's successors were awarded regnal years in which they did not rule alone over their lands. When we analyze the historical data after the death of Herod, we find interesting evidence which justifies this appraisal. The first information comes from coins that were minted by Herod's later successors.

The grandson of Herod the Great through his Hasmonean wife Mariamme was Herod Agrippa I. He reigned over Judaea from A.D. 38 to A.D. 44 (a seven-year period). But strange as it may seem, he had coins minted in his eighth and ninth years.[390] There can be little doubt that Herod Agrippa I died in the year of the Caesarean games established by King Herod in 9 B.C. They were held every four years. This makes the seven years' reign of Agrippa I terminate in A.D. 44, just as Josephus attests. But for some reason he had coins dated to his eighth and ninth years. Did he reckon his regnal years as beginning at least two years *before* Josephus allowed him an official reign? It looks like it.

It should also be mentioned that Agrippa I was awarded the government over Palestine by Caligula in A.D. 37. Agrippa, however, did not go immediately to Jerusalem to commence his rule but remained in Rome almost a year and a half after his appointment. He actually governed the area of Judaea in absentia. Then in late Autumn of A.D. 38, he took up personal rulership at Jerusalem. He then began to mint coins. On them he showed his regnal years, yet he reckoned those years as beginning before he actually ruled in Palestine. Others could have done the same thing. At any rate, scholars recognize that the coins often show *de jure* dates. Meyshan says: "This is additional proof that coins always record conditions *de jure* not *de facto*."[391]

When it comes to Herod Agrippa II (the son of Agrippa I) the evidence from his coins shows conclusively that he dated his reign from at least two different eras, and Madden suggested four. On some of his coins he indicated two years of significance, *e.g.,* the sixth and eleventh. His official reign over the small territory of Chalcis near Damascus began in A.D. 50 — and this is the time that Josephus said he assumed the throne.[392] But the coins do not square with this. There are some scholars who feel his regnal years should start as far back as the death of his father in A.D. 44, though Meyshan, one of the main Israeli numismatists who has studied the problems at length, does not think this is possible.[393]

The numismatist Meshorer feels that one of Agrippa's eras should start with A.D. 56, and another in A.D. 61.[394] But there is much confusion in the evidence. Meshorer points out that some of his coins bear the names of three Roman emperors—Vespasian, Titus, and Domitian—and they have identical dates on them.[395]

Chapter 13 - The Chronology of Josephus

How could these be dated from one era while all three emperors reigned at different times? No one really knows why these coins have the doubtful dates they do. But, whatever the case, some of the coins do not agree with the years of Agrippa II as indicated by Josephus. Meshorer has seen the problem and informs us that: "the date mentioned by Josephus as the first regnal year of Agrippa II is incompatible with at least some of his coins."[396]

Even more important, however, are coins that were apparently minted by Antipas—one of the immediate successors of Herod the Great. Antipas was removed from his throne in A.D. 39 and banished to Europe.[397] If one dates his reign from 4 B.C., it means he would have had a reign of 43 years. Indeed, there are three coins of Antipas marked with the regnal year 43.[398] However, there is a coin mentioned by Vaillant (and it is also referred to by Garland in his travel narratives who found it at Jericho in 1674) that has the year 44 inscribed on it.[399] But this would have Antipas commencing his reign in 5 B.C. This seems impossible. Much debate has surrounded the interpretation of the year mentioned on this coin. The general opinion is that the date on the coin was probably misread. Since the coin can no longer be traced, it is conjectured that this explanation is probably the best, but no one can be sure.

Coins Often Give Political Data, Not Real History

Worse yet, during the last century a coin came to light which showed year 45 for Antipas' reign. This would have extended Antipas' rule back to 6 B.C. What can be done with this coin? Some scholars have thought Antipas' reign might be extended beyond A.D. 39, but this explanation is very unsatisfactory and cannot account for these two unknown regnal years. Still, having Antipas reigning in 6 B.C. seems like an absurd assessment. As a result, many scholars simply call the coin a forgery. This is the easy way to cut the Gordian Knot.

But why a forgery? There is not the slightest external evidence for the problem except the date on the coin. But even the coins of Agrippa I and Agrippa II (who lived within the later years of Antipas) also have regnal years recorded on them before Josephus reported them reigning, and few dispute these coins.

No one knows why any of these coins record earlier years than Josephus sometimes allows, but they do. Since inscriptions on coins show legal or governmental recognition about matters of state (often for symbolic reasons), they could be accepted as real evidence that different types of regnal years were in vogue among the sons and grandsons of Herod. Certainly, the years of rule could not have been placed on the coins without the approval of Rome. This is clear evidence that Rome allowed *de jure* regnal years, which Josephus sometimes, or sometimes did not, reckon in his year-lengths of the Herodian successors.

Indeed, even Herod himself had three of his regnal years awarded in the *de jure* manner (from the time he was appointed king by the Romans until his capture of Jerusalem three years later). Should it seem odd that Herod's successors should in similar fashion have years of reign assigned to them by the Romans? Even Archelaus, the immediate successor to Herod, had a reign which was acknowledged by Josephus as nine years in one place and ten years in another.[400]

These discrepancies could legitimately be explained in the *de jure* manner. The fact is, it was common practice to award special years to Herod and his successors. And while the Roman emperors observed no such regnal years in this manner, the practice was widespread in Judaea and in other eastern areas of the Empire.

The Pivotal Problems Resolved

It looks like two or three years were awarded to Archelaus and Antipas in which they did not rule alone over Herod's domains. The coins certainly reveal the existence of *de jure* years, but most historians find such things confusing. In our western world there is a

Chapter 13 - The Chronology of Josephus

natural resistance toward the acceptance of such a reckoning because it is disruptive to a uniform and consistent chronological plan. Anyone with common sense would share a distaste for using "awarded" years. The fact is, however, anyone working with the regnal years of the kings and rulers within the Hellenistic period will have to get used to them. It was common practice in the Hellenistic east (of which the region of Judaea was a part) for rulers to ascribe even in an official way extra years to their lengths of reign that fictitiously gave them more years than they actually ruled.

Antedating Was Commonly Practiced in the Ancient World

Professor E.J. Bickerman has collected a great deal of historical material to show how usual it was for Hellenistic rulers to inflate their lengths of reign, normally by antedating their years of rule. "Like Ptolemaeus I, Seleucus I, etc., Attalus [of Pergamus] antedated his kingship, and computed his regnal years from his succession to Eumenes, in 240 B.C."[401] Bickerman continues: "An official date is not necessarily the authentic one. When a Hellenistic ruler succeeded in gaining the sovereignty, the symbol of which was the royal title, he often antedated the initial year of his kingship. For instance, in the second century B.C. the kings of Pontus computed their regnal years from 336 B.C. when the reputed ancestor Mithridates was established as governor of Cius, although the dynasty had not assumed the royal title before Mithridates III, brother in law of Seleucus II. The Arsacids followed the same patterns."[402] With the rulers of Bithynia there is the evidence of using a *de jure* or a fictitious era.[403]

The Herodian kingdom was a direct outgrowth of this historical and political environment. Antedating reigns (overlapping of years) was certainly nothing new to the Jews. They were well accustomed to it even within the biblical period.[404] And lest one think that antedating of reigns was limited simply to the nations of the east in the Hellenistic period, Bickerman points out that Charles II of England was crowned king on 29 May, 1660 but for political reasons he counted his years of reign from the death of Charles I on 30 January, 1649.[405] It should not seem odd that the Herodian successors would do the same thing—especially since the east had a long history of accepting such a practice. And since the coins certainly do show *de jure* years of reign for the Herodians which cannot be accounted for historically, it would be very unwise to dismiss this deduction as being of little consequence. This is especially so since virtually all the other historical evidence that I have been showing in this book points to Herod's death as being in 1 B.C.

The Reason for Antedating

It appears clear that Archelaus and Antipas reckoned their reigns as commencing in 4 B.C. at the very time their half-brother Antipater became co-ruler with Herod and acted every bit as a "king." Why would these two sons want to adopt the practice of antedating? Though the procedure was often used, there still must be some reason why Herod's successors utilized it for dating the beginning of their reigns. When one understands the political and religious positions which the family of the Hasmoneans had with the general Jewish population (both in Palestine and in the Roman world) a reason for antedating becomes evident. Recall that Alexander and Aristobulus (the two Hasmonean sons of Herod) met their deaths almost three years before Herod himself died. This was a tragic circumstance to all the Jewish people because the two brothers were considered of royal stock and the legitimate heirs to the throne of Judaea. They were considered legal heirs to kingship.

Look at the matter carefully. Herod the Great was a commoner. Actually, he was not even a Jew by race, but a mixture of Idumaean and Arabian stock.[406] He, however, had been made king by the Romans to replace Hyrcanus who was a Hasmonean. The Hasmoneans were descendants of the Maccabees who were of priestly ancestry. These people were reckoned to be of royal, priestly blood.[407] The Jewish population considered the Hasmoneans as the only royal line with legal vouchers until one of the Davidic dynasty could show he had messianic credentials.[408]

This fact was well recognized by the Jews. Even Herod saw the importance of the Hasmoneans in his own time of rulership. Herod, in order to legalize his own rule, married Mariamme of the royal Hasmonean house. She was reckoned by the Jewish people as "Queen."[409] But Herod was regarded as "base of birth."[410] Herod felt he had to marry the royal Mariamme.[411] She gave Herod two sons. They were acknowledged by the Jewish people as the "royal sons" and the only ones who could legally be claimants to the throne.[412] One of the main reasons for this was because the two sons (Alexander and Aristobulus) were born after Herod had assumed the kingship of Judaea.[413] These two sons outshone all the other children of Herod in prestige because they were the only regal children. They were reckoned as being of "noble birth,"[414] of the "royal family,"[415] of "royal lineage,[416] they expressed "royal conceit,"[417] and they exulted in their "pride of birth."[418]

The exclusive feeling of royalty attached to these two sons of Mariamme (at the expense of all the other "common" children of Herod), was accepted by the Jewish people.[419] Both young men had "the goodwill of the masses" behind them because of their regal connections.[420] When these two sons were killed, "*royalty*" ceased in Judaea.

Rome Accepted the Royal Sons

Such lineal attachment to ancient dynastic houses was important to the people who lived in the first century. Both the Jews and Romans looked upon noble lineage as significant. An example of this is seen in the remarks of Glaphyra, the wife of Alexander (the first son of Mariamme and Herod). She expressed pride in the fact that she was the daughter of the King of Cappadocia and was descended on her father's side from Temenus (one of the important kings of ancient Macedonia) and on her mother's side from Darius, the son of Hystapses of Persia.[421] Glaphyra chided Herod, his other wives, and their children, because of "their low birth."[422] Sir Ronald Syme has shown that even the Romans were no less interested in family connections with ancient and modern houses.[423] It might be said that dynastic connections were the main themes that granted reasons to rule. Royal descent was looked on as important.

But what happened to the two Hasmonean sons? It was a real blow to Judaic society when Herod had the two royal sons killed and as a consequence promoted Antipater (born of a common woman from Idumaea) to be his heir. This was almost too much. Antipater knew that he had no right to the throne by any reason of birth.[424] But when the two royal sons were killed, Antipater assumed undisputed claim to the succession.[425] This is when Antipater became joint-ruler with Herod and he began to be considered as a "king" in his own right.

In time, however, Herod came to see the extreme wickedness of Antipater and, just before his own death, Herod executed Antipater and gave his kingdom (his joint-rule with Antipater) to his other three sons — all commoners! They were Archelaus, Antipas and Philip. The first two had a Samaritan woman for a mother and Philip's mother was a common woman of Judah.

Not one of these three successors of Herod had any "royal" connections whatever. To them, this must have represented a great disadvantage in securing the legal right to rule in the eyes of the Jews. It was only the command of Herod and Augustus that gave them their jurisdiction. The Jews themselves would have looked on these commoners as usurpers. In fact, at the death of Herod, many of the Jews went to Rome to plead with Augustus to make Judaea a part of the province of Syria, and no longer ruled by kings.[426] There was then no one of age of prime Hasmonean stock to assume any kingship and many Jews did not want these commoners ruling over them. If someone would have been old enough of Hasmonean stock, it may have been a different story. Witness the false

Chapter 13 - The Chronology of Josephus

Alexander who duped many Jews just after the death of Herod.[427] The Jews didn't mind legal claimants to the throne ruling over them, but not commoners like Archelaus, Antipas and Philip.

What does this show to our question? Very much. It indicates that the Jewish people made a distinct separation between commoners and those of royal lineage. They were willing to accept legitimate Hasmoneans, but others had no legal right to rule. A problem arose, however. Herod and Augustus had accepted the "commoners" Archelaus, Antipas and Philip. They had no biblical, traditional, or dynastic right to rule over the Jews. These three successors of Herod would no doubt have understood the difficulty in the matter. How could they, in some possible way, secure at least a limited amount of legal approbation from the Jews? Since neither they nor their father Herod were of royal Hasmonean stock, some device was needed to gain a measure of legitimate succession.

Antedating Secured Dynastic Continuance

Since the Jews (and most kingdoms of the Hellenistic east) were used to antedating reigns to give political or dynastic significance to present rulership, why not antedate the reigns of the three Herodian successors back to the deaths of the two "royal sons"? Such a thing would have gained some respect in the minds of the Jewish populace. It not only would have "blotted out" Antipater's two year joint rule with Herod when he was reckoned as a "king," but it would have linked up the reigns of the three successors with the two royal children.

Later history of Palestine and the Middle East certainly supports this proposition. Look at what happened with those three successors. Archelaus was deposed in A.D. 6 and banished to Gaul. His region of rule was then annexed to the Empire. No successor to Archelaus was appointed. Judaea became a part of the Syrian province of Rome. Philip died in A.D. 36 and his territory was eventually given to Agrippa I (a Hasmonean). Antipas also died in

225

exile and Agrippa I came to rule his region as well. The fact is, after the reign of these three "commoners" was over, the sovereigns connected with the Herodian family that later ruled in regions of the east were descendants of royal Hasmonean stock. This must be significant. Indeed, when the emperor Claudius bestowed royal power on Agrippa I, he not only gave him all the lands that had formerly been under the rule of his grandfather Herod, but Claudius specifically said he was awarded the grant because it "was due to his family."[428] That family, or dynasty, was that of the Hasmoneans. It was the only family with a legal right to rule in Judaea. Even Josephus (who wrote in the last part of the first century) stated that—in Jewish opinion—a connection with the priesthood is the hallmark of an illustrious line."[429] The Hasmoneans were such priests. Josephus himself said: "On my mother's side I am of royal blood, from the posterity of the Hasmoneans."[430]

There can be no doubt of the importance of the Hasmoneans among the Jews as the only legal heirs to the Judaean throne, and after the deaths of the three successors of Herod (who were all commoners), nothing but Hasmoneans were allowed to rule in Judaea (and even in some other eastern areas) by the Romans. Note the following table of kings and queens.

Agrippa (Hasmonean)
Agrippa II (Hasmonean)
Herod of Calcia (Hasmonean)
Aristobulus of Lesser Armenia (Hasmonean)
Tigranes IV of Armenia (Hasmonean)
Tigranes V of Armenia (Hasmonean)
Alexander of Cilicia (Hasmonean)
Drusilla, Queen of Emesa and then wife of Felix (Hasmonean)
Bernice, Queen of Calcia and then of Cilicia (Hasmonean)

This proclivity to accept only Hasmonean stock for later rulers in certain eastern areas surely shows that the Jews desired the

Chapter 13 - The Chronology of Josephus

Romans to allow only legitimate lineage to reign. Rome consistently accepted the concept as the proper one to follow.

Antedating Was Used to Achieve Dynastic Association

Even as early as the time of Herod the inclination for such legal rule was evident among the Jews. This gives good reason why two of the successors of Herod would have had their regnal years reckoned back to the deaths of the legal recipients to the throne. Since antedating was so prevalent in the Hellenistic east, such a procedure would not have appeared odd at all. Even Herod may have desired it. Just before Herod's death, when he finally came to realize that Antipater had lied about the two royal sons to get them killed, Herod expressed remorse for the deaths of his Hasmonean children.[431] It could well have been recorded in his final will that all recognition of Antipater be expunged from the records (to go along with biblical usage—Deuteronomy 29:17-21). Herod also desired the children of the two "royal sons" to be accepted by the Jews and other members of his family.[432] Antedating the reigns of Archelaus and Antipas (to comprise the two years of the joint-rule of Antipater) could have been one way to secure this recognition as well as giving some legitimacy to the three "commoners" in their own rulerships. With Philip, however, we now know from the research of Beyer,[433] that the early manuscripts of Josephus show that Philip commenced his reign at the exact time of Herod's death in 1 B.C. and ruled for 37 years, dying in A.D.36 (the twenty-second year of Tiberius). All this makes perfectly good sense.

The Reasonableness of These Explanations

Something approaching this explanation must be the reason why the successors of Herod commenced the reckoning of their regnal years in 4 B.C. In no way could Herod have died in 4 B.C. The historical evidence I have provided in this book is decidedly against such a proposition. Perhaps the obscure statement of Josephus that Archelaus, only a few weeks after receiving his right to rule, was accused by his opponents as having "long exercised royal authority"[434] can make better sense. This certainly was not true in actual fact, but through the practice of antedating, such a statement could be accepted in a *de jure* manner. Thus, the obscure chronology of Josephus in regard to Herod's death and the regnal years of his successors can be solved in a satisfactory way and in accord with accepted practices in the Hellenistic east that were in existence at that time.

In closing, it would be profitable to mention that Josephus was well aware of the tendency within the Judaean kingdoms (whether of Herod's or earlier ones) to have joint-rules of some of their sovereigns. Josephus mentioned the early first century B.C. co-rulership of Hyrcanus II when he came to power in 70/69 B.C.[435] with that of his mother Queen Alexandra. For Hyrcanus' first two years, he was jointly ruling with his mother.[436] Such joint-rules were common in this period. Thus, Antipater jointly ruled with Herod, and it appears that the other two "common" sons of Herod also were awarded such rules.

Whatever the case, the evidence of history, archaeology and astronomy is now showing that Herod died in early 1 B.C. and that Jesus was born in 3 B.C. This is the period of time (3 to 2 B.C.) when the majority of early Christian historians place the nativity of Jesus. And they were correct. What we are beginning to discover is that the "obscure decade" from 6 B.C. to A.D. 4 in Roman history is now taking on a great deal of light. And the key to the illumination happens to be the historical and chronological indications contained in the New Testament.

Chronological Rundown

The nativity occurred on September 11, 3 B.C. Note the following sequence of historical events.

1) Joseph and Mary's journey to Bethlehem for the "census" occurred at the very close of the Jewish civil year— an apt time for

Chapter 13 - The Chronology of Josephus

a registration of peoples to happen. It was in the Summer season and before the rains set in that would have made it difficult.

2) Jesus was born in a stable in the twilight period of September 11th, the Day of Trumpets, 3 B.C.

3) He was circumcised on September 18, 3 B.C. (the eighth day for the circumcision rite is reckoned inclusively).

4) He was dedicated in the temple on October 20/21, 3 B.C.

5) Luke says: They returned into Galilee, to their own city Nazareth (2:39). This means they did not go to Egypt after the birth of Jesus. After all, they had only gone to Bethlehem for the "census," not to move there. So, the family returned to Nazareth in the latter part of October, 3 B.C.

6) Then for some reason, they decided to move to Bethlehem. This could have been in the Spring or Summer of 2 B.C. They set up house, having no need for the temporary type of shelter they had when Jesus was born (Matthew 2:11).

7) On December 5th (Kislev 7) of 2 B.C. the youth tore down the eagle from the east entrance to the temple.

8) Then on December 25, 2 B.C., when the King planet Jupiter came to its stationary point in mid-Virgo the Virgin, it would have been seen "stopped over Bethlehem" as viewed from Jerusalem. The Magi then went to Bethlehem and gave the child the gifts they brought from the east. Jesus was now a *paidion* (Greek: toddler) not a *brephos* (Greek: infant, as in Luke). He was old enough to stand and to walk. In the papyrus codex Bodmer V of the *Proto-Evangelium of James* written in Egypt in the fourth century, it even states that the Magi were able to see Jesus "*standing* by the side of his mother Mary" (21:3). This shows early opinion that the visit of the Magi to give gifts to Jesus was long after his birth. This giving of gifts by the Magi would have occurred during the days of Hanukkah when Jewish fathers were accustomed to give gifts to

their children. This would have appeared quite proper to Jewish people.

9) With the warnings of the Magi, Joseph and Mary immediately took Jesus to Egypt in late December of 2 B.C.

10) Immediately after this, Herod killed all the male children "from two years old and under" (Matthew 2:16). This matter of killing children two years old can now make better sense. If Jesus was born on 11 September, 3 B.C., the slaying of the innocents was about 15 months after his birth. If the conception period were also considered, it comes to 24 months exactly. This may be a helpful clue that Jesus was indeed born in September, 3 B.C. and why the Magi saw Jesus "*standing* by the side of his mother Mary."

11) Soon afterward, the two illustrious rabbis were tried and sentenced by the Sanhedrin. This could have been in early January of 1 B.C., and then a few days later (on January 10th) the eclipse of the Moon occurred that Josephus mentioned.

12) Herod then died about January 28th (Schebat 2) in 1 B.C.

13) Later, in the Spring of 1 B.C., the Passover occurred during which 3000 Jewish worshippers lost their lives in the temple.

14) In the Summer and Autumn of that year (1 B.C.) *The War of Varus* took place.

15) Then, about twenty-eight years later, Jesus was baptized by John the Baptist sometime in either October or November of A.D. 27 at the beginning of a Sabbatical Year. Jesus then began his official ministry with the Passover and Pentecost season of A.D. 28 and was finally crucified in A.D. 30.

If what I am suggesting in this book is true, a new understanding in the life of Jesus emerges. Not only do many obscure passages in Josephus make sense, but the chronological and theological indications of the New Testament about the birth of Jesus also become clearer. Roman history as well becomes more understandable for

Chapter 13 - The Chronology of Josephus

the middle years of Augustus. And while none of us was living some 2000 years ago to prove these points as an eyewitness, there is enough evidence available to give us some reasonable assurance that this new information brings us pretty close to the truth.

This means that the Star of Bethlehem can be identified and that it fits into the over-all historical theme to make this period in human history more understandable. This is just another reason why all historians who want to comprehend the proper history of Rome in the early Empire period need to focus their attention on "The Star that Astonished the World."

Appendix One

QUINTILIUS VARUS AND THE LAPIS TIBURTINUS

The man of the inscription now in the Vatican Museum was once governor of the province of Asia and two coins have been found which show at one time that Quintilius Varus was proconsul of Africa (Grant, *FITA*, pp.228,230). It is held by some that the same consular could not be proconsul of Africa as well as Asia because, for one thing, the two offices were selected by lot from among the ex-consulars (Schurer, *The Jewish People in the Time of Jesus Christ*, Div.I. vol.I, p.347, note 16). True enough, if one believes that a fixed system of lot drawings for yearly consularships was in operation for Africa and Asia in the time of Augustus, then this would present a problem. Yet no exact uniform and rigid *modus operandi* for such things was then in evidence (Atkinson, *Historia* [1958], p.301; Syme, *The Titulus Tiburtinus*, p.590), For example, Agrippa governed Asia while in charge of other provinces (Atkinson, p.302). Also, Asian consulars were sometimes chosen without the lot (pp.304,307,308) or with the lot manipulated (Syme, *The Roman Revolution*, p.395). The governorship was even given to a person not of consular rank (Atkinson, p.305), and governors for two or even three years in succession are acknowledged

Appendix One - Quintilius Varus and the Lapis Tiburtinus

(while the "rule" demanded a one-year tenure) (pp.308,309). These points refer to the province of Asia, but they are equally pertinent to proconsular Africa.

This shows there was no consistent system yet worked out for the governorships of these provinces. "The reign of Augustus was marked by the absence of rigidity and fixed rules" (Atkinson, p.302). It would have been possible for Quintilius Varus, if the emperor wished it, to have been governor of Africa in, say 8/7 B.C., of Syria in 6 to 4 B.C., of Asia in 3/2 B.C., and Syria again from 2 B.C. to A D. 1. If some insist that regulations would not allow it, then perhaps the remarks of Sir Ronald Syme would be appropriate: "Who ordained the rules for Caesar Augustus in the management of the *provincia?*" (*The Titulus Tiburtinus*, p. 590). The point is, Augustus was emperor and he did as he jolly well pleased.

If the *lapis tiburtinus*, however, refers to Varus, why doesn't it record his African governorship? This can hardly be a problem. The inscription is in such a fragmentary state (only parts of six lines have come down to us), that his African residence could have been mentioned near the top or bottom no longer extant. Even those who accept Quirinius as the man of the inscription are aware that there is no mention of the emperor Tiberius—an unforgivable omission if Quirinius were the man of the inscription. Yet again, the top and bottom parts of the *lapis* are gone, so these "omissions" allow no argument one way or the other. Another point. The parts of the six lines seem, at first glance, to be giving an order of events in chronological sequence. This is maintained by Syme because he reads the word *iterum* as "second," not "twice." On the other hand, Professor Groag did not feel the *lapis* is chronologically arranged, and he was followed by Magie and A.E. Gordon (*The Titulus Tiburtinus*, p. 594). If *iterum* truly means "twice" (as I have shown in this book), then it would call for two non-consecutive terms of office over Syria, and this would favor the belief that the events of the inscription are not chronologically disposed. This would allow the conquered kingdom to have been that of Herod by Varus, and the two victories (the *supplicationes binas*) to have been his subjection of Galilee and Judaea. This would account well with the central period of Varus' career, though it is not strictly in accord with an ordered chronology from top to bottom. The same is reflected in the "Queen of Inscriptions" (the *Monumentum Ancyranum*—otherwise called the *Res Gestae Divi Augusti*). Augustus did not compose this work in chronological order from top to bottom. He introduced a subject, treated it in general chronological fashion, returned to another subject, and then to another, etc. Even within the contexts of his subjects he was not always consistent in a chronological way. In the section dealing with payment of moneys to the Roman plebs, he mentioned his penultimate donation, and then, abruptly, recorded an event which happened 24 years earlier—completely out of chronological order (II. 15). On buildings, he interjected, out of sequence, an event 16 years before the context allows (IV. 20). In his record of embassies from foreign kings and rulers, he mentioned events in 26 B.C., 20 B.C., then back to 31 B.C., and finally 10 B.C. (VI. 32). Again, Augustus was not paying attention to sequential chronology.

It is precarious business to demand that the *lapis tiburtinus* has within it a strict descending chronology from top to bottom. This is especially true since the word *iterum* signifies "twice." All this helps to show that the inscription could well refer to Quintilius Varus and his exploits in Palestine at the death of Herod. This is the very part of Varus' career that his family would have wanted to relate to all around Tibur and at Rome. And, with the *lapis tiburtinus* found about half a mile from the doorstep of Varus' villa, surely he must be the one it describes.

Appendix Two

THE QUESTION OF GAIUS CAESAR

The history surrounding the question of Gaius being by the side of Augustus when he heard the case for and against the kingship of Archelaus has caused some scholars to believe that the death of Herod must have been in 5 B.C. It concerns the use of the Greek words *protos/proton* in Josephus (*War*, II.25; *Antiquities*, XVII. 229). Does it mean that Gaius was for the first time in an official role, or does it mean in first place beside Augustus? The argument has long been discussed and there are proponents for each interpretation (Barnes, *Journal of Theological Studies*, vol. XIX, pp. 207, 208).

No matter how one looks on the issue, it is a very flimsy piece of evidence on which to base chronological exactitudes. I, of course, take the position that Josephus meant that Gaius took "the first place" next to Augustus. If the other interpretation is accepted it might add weight to a 5 or 4 B.C. death for Herod, because "the first time" Gaius sat with Augustus in judgment was probably in one of those earlier years. Whiston in his translation of Josephus rendered the words as we accept them—and he has been followed

235

by many others. The point is, it is very unwise to make profound chronological decisions based on the meanings of disputed words. I feel, however, that the overwhelming evidence for a 1 B.C. date for Herod's death, qualifies the translation "the first place" as being the proper one.

Appendix Three

THE BANISHMENT OF JULIA

Philip the Tetrarch built a city in his territory east of the Sea of Galilee and called it Julias after the emperor's daughter Julia. But late in 2 B.C., Julia was disgraced and banished by her father Augustus for openly practicing wantonness. It has been suggested by modern historians that the naming of this city after Julia had to have taken place before she was banished in late 2 B.C. But there are major difficulties with this hypothesis. Is it possible that a complete city could be built for thousands of people in a year and a half from the Summer of 4 B.C. to the Winter of 2 B.C.? This is highly doubtful because we have the plain testimony of Josephus that it took Herod twelve years to build Caesarea, and it was only given its name after it was finished (*War*, I.414).

We are not told how long it took Philip to build Julias, but if it were only a quarter of the size of Caesarea it would have taken at a bare minimum three years. With Philip beginning his tetrarchy in 1 B.C., the completion of the city would have occurred long after Julia was disinherited late in 2 B.C. Most probably, the city of Julias was not finished and dedicated until at least A.D. 4 or 5.

This date would fit quite favorably with the overall history of this period. In A.D. 4 it is recorded that Julia's father Augustus relaxed the strict requirements he had imposed on his daughter. Dio said that Julia "was restored from banishment" at that time (LV, 13.1a). And though Augustus never forgave his daughter in the absolute sense for her wayward behavior, he did allow her to enjoy more freedom and to do good works from A.D. 4 until his death in A.D. 14.

It is said that in this period of mercy from her father, Julia and her own daughter concentrated their activities to engaging in many benevolent enterprises. They helped the poor and the unfortunate as best they could. This won a love and respect from the people of Rome. And though her father Augustus remained adamant in his refusal to allow her a full reprieve, there was no doubt in Rome that Julia was now reckoned an honorable and repentant woman and admired by the people of Rome and the Empire.

It could have been in this period of time that Philip built a new city on the east coast of the sea of Galilee and named it Julias—after the daughter of the emperor. This would have been quite feasible from A.D. 4 to 14. Since Philip had spent his youth in Rome, he could well have known Julia and her daughter (and others near the imperial family), and the ten-year period of her "relaxed" confinement could have been an appropriate time to name a new city after her. Surely, Augustus would not have minded, though his firm stand on his early judgment did not allow him to relinquish his sentence of banishment.

Thus, Philip named his new city Julias. It was only when Tiberius (the former husband of Julia, and one who hated her very much) came to the emperorship in A.D. 14 that Julia again fell out of favor with the ruling powers. Within a year after Tiberius took over the imperial authority, Julia died—apparently of starvation ordered by Tiberius. One thing is certain, the building and naming of the city of Julias nowhere interferes with the suggestions in this book that Herod died in 1 B.C.

Appendix Four

THE SABBATICAL YEARS AND CHRONOLOGY

The correct dating of Jesus' birth is primarily a chronological matter. What one must do is to use all avenues of investigation that contain chronological evidences (or even hints) that can reasonably establish a proper chronological background to that historical event. The prime evidence comes from those individuals who were eyewitnesses (or record information from eyewitnesses). This is why the information in the Bible itself is so important in understanding the chronology associated with the nativity of Jesus. And the information in the Bible does not disappoint us. Indeed, there is a further method found in the Bible and history for determining the time of the birth of Jesus. This is the Old Testament legislation which demanded that the Jews let their lands in the region of Palestine lie fallow each seventh year.[437] Every seventh year, all commercial farming or agricultural activity came to a halt. These years (every seventh year) were known as Sabbatical Years. These Sabbatical Years are important, especially in determining the length of Herod's reign. Josephus tells us that the battle in which Herod captured Jerusalem took place during a Sabbatical Year, and that he captured the city on the Day of Atonement. We now have abundant evidence that the occurrence of this Sabbatical Year when this well-known conquest of Jerusalem occurred was in 36 B.C. The Jewish king Antigonus was killed a few months later. Josephus tells us that Herod reigned 34 years after the death of Antigonus. This means that Herod reigned unto 2 to 1 B.C. This is precisely what I am showing in this book. What I will do in this appendix is to reveal that the New Testament itself supports the fact that the Sabbatical Cycle of years makes the summer of 36 B.C. to have been a Sabbatical Year. This will show Herod's death to be in 1 B.C.

The Jews and Sabbatical Years

The Jews before and during the time of Jesus were following the Mosaic Law for agricultural inactivity every seventh year in the land of Palestine. Because of this practice, it affords us some excellent chronological clues regarding the time certain historical events occurred in Palestine because the records show them to have happened in association with Sabbatical Years. Thankfully, it is possible from the Bible and history to accurately determine those years in which the Jews refrained from agricultural activity. Once the cycle of those seven years is understood, then those Sabbatical Years can be used as chronological benchmarks in determining important events in Jewish history during the time of Jesus.

The Cycle of Sabbatical Years Can Be Known

New evidence has become available which gives powerful proof for properly dating the years of Jesus' ministry and even the year of his crucifixion is able to be determined. This new information from the New Testament itself provides a major key which makes other chronological indications of the New Testament more understandable. It also shows that the Sabbatical Year in which Herod captured Jerusalem was indeed 36 B.C.

The Gospel of John records some prime chronological references for reckoning the years of Jesus' ministry that the other three Gospels do not report. For example, John mentions three Passovers

Appendix Four - The Sabbatical Years and Chronology

which occurred during the ministry of Jesus (2:13; 6:4; 13:1). Other Jewish festivals were acknowledged as well. There was the "unknown feast" between the first two Passovers (5:1), and after the second Passover he mentions the feasts of Tabernacles (7:1) and Dedication (10:22). These feasts provide some chronological indications for establishing the proper sequence of years associated with Jesus' ministry.

The new evidence that I am presenting in this book centers on a statement given by Jesus that John positions between his first two Passovers (2:13 and 6:4) and before his "unknown" feast (5:1). This reference is an important piece of historical information that up to now has been completely overlooked and misunderstood. But when the new research is recognized, we will have one of the most significant chronological keys for ironing out the historical difficulties associated with the chronology of Jesus' life.

A New Testament Chronological Indication

It is first essential to understand the historical environment in which this new chronological evidence occurs. Once this is understood, the year in which Jesus began his ministry can then be determined, which in turn will also reveal the exact year in which Jesus was born according to New Testament historical indications. This new biblical evidence is important. Let us look at it.

At the end of the third chapter of John's Gospel we are told that Jesus left Jerusalem after the first Passover mentioned by John and he started on his journey toward Galilee (John 4:3). His route necessitated traveling through Samaria. Upon his arrival at Jacob's Well, being weary from his journey, Jesus talked to a Samaritan woman while his disciples went into the village to fetch food. No other people were around when the discussion mentioned by John took place (John 4:6-26). However, upon the conclusion of the dialogue, the disciples returned with food. Jesus then gave them some spiritual teaching about what true food actually represented. It is this particular teaching (when the woman had left and no other Samaritans were around) that solves a major chronological problem regarding the time and length of Jesus' ministry. Jesus said:

> "Say ye not, 'There are yet four months and then cometh the harvest?' behold, I say unto you, lift up your eyes and look on the fields; for they are white [ripe] already for harvest."[438]

The real meaning of Jesus' words has not been understood, yet his intention is so easy to comprehend if the legal requirements governing Palestinian agriculture in the first century are taken into account. In a moment I will show what Jesus had in mind when he made this statement, but let us first review the normal interpretations given by scholars to explain what Jesus meant.

Some Opinions of Theologians

There are two explanations normally proffered by theologians.

1) Since Jesus was speaking within a context of sowing and reaping, it is recognized (correctly) that Jesus was calling attention to the barley and wheat harvest which farmers reaped between Passover and Pentecost (from late March to early June). Scholars have seen significance in the phrase "four months unto the harvest." If Jesus meant that there were yet four months until the time of the Palestinian grain harvest, then it is supposed he must have uttered his statement about late December or early January. This would allow the phrase four months to harvest to make reasonable sense. If this is the case, scholars have surmised, it would mean that Jesus gave this illustration to the disciples some 8 or 9 months after John's first Passover, and about 4 months before the beginning of the regular grain harvest which started about late March. So, most conservative theologians have felt that this is a chronological statement which can be placed within the months of December or January near the end of Jesus' first year of ministry.

2) The other theory, however, suggests that Jesus was simply stating a well-known proverb about some four month interval of

Appendix Four - The Sabbatical Years and Chronology

time from sowing to harvest, and that no chronological significance is to be interpreted from this so-called "proverbial" reference.

There are flaws in both suppositions. For one, Jesus' statement could hardly have been made some 8 or 9 months after John's first Passover because in verse 45 (given shortly after he had returned to Galilee) his Galilean acquaintances recalled the signs he had recently accomplished at John's first Passover. These were Galileans who had gone to the FEAST "for they also went unto the FEAST." Anyone should recognize that this refers to the first Passover mentioned by John which happened about six or seven weeks before. If this is not the case, then the words of John's Gospel are incomprehensible. To say that the Galileans were referring to an unmentioned feast of Pentecost, or an unnamed feast of Tabernacles (or even the feasts of Dedication or Purim) is stretching the matter beyond reasonable belief. Truly, the Galileans must have been talking about the previous feast of Passover during which they had seen Jesus perform certain miracles and that Passover had occurred no more than 40 or 50 days before. This means that Jesus' statement (made at Jacob's Well, about a week before he met the Galileans in Nazareth) was not uttered in the months of December or January, and not 8 or 9 months after John's first Passover. Clearly, Jesus stated his remark in late May or early June. (The reason he did so at that time will be shown shortly.)

The second explanation offered by many scholars is also suspect because no proverb has been found in Jewish literature which refers to a four month season from sowing to harvest. The period for wheat was more like six months according to the Jewish Mishnah.[439]

The Real Meaning of Jesus' Statement

Jesus said that his disciples would reckon four more months to the harvest, yet his statement was proclaimed in late May or early June, right in the midst of the wheat harvest. There is really no doubt that this is the case. Origen who lived in Palestine in the third century recognized that Jesus' teachings in John 4:35 were stated in the middle of the actual harvest season.[440] Even Jesus himself acknowledged that this time was during the regular grain harvest.

"Lift up your eyes, and look on the fields for they are white [ripe] already for harvest."[441]

This reference by Jesus shows that the grain was already available for harvest (after all, it was late May or early June), but for some reason he put it in the mouths of the disciples that they would not expect anyone to harvest the grain for another four months. Why on earth did Jesus say there were yet four more months before harvest, when the harvest season was at its height?

The answer is simple if one remembers the agricultural legislation that Moses imposed on Jews and Samaritans living in the Holyland. There were agricultural rules that both groups observed in the first century. The truth is, Jesus made his statement in the midst of what the Jews and Samaritans called a Sabbatical Year. Such a year was one in which no sowing or reaping were permitted, from the New Year of one Autumn to the New Year of the next. When this is realized and understood, all chronological difficulties associated with John 4:35 thoroughly disappear (though they appear to be outright contradictions on the surface).

The Simple Answer

Notice how plain the whole matter can become. Jesus gave his teaching near the end of the second Hebrew month or the start of the third (late May or early June). When a person counts forward four more months, the month of Tishri is reached. This is the month in which all Sabbatical Years ended and people could legally begin to harvest once again. Jesus was saying what the apostles and the general population were aware of. That year was a Sabbatical Year. No one could commence any harvesting (even though one were in the midst of the harvest season for grain) until the Sabbatical Year

Appendix Four - The Sabbatical Years and Chronology

was over. This is the reason Jesus said it was still "four months" to the period of harvest.

There is more evidence to support this interpretation. Jesus elaborated on his teaching about the harvest by saying in John 4:

"And herein is this saying true, 'One soweth and another reapeth.' I send you to reap that which ye bestowed no labor" (verses 37,38).

Even Jesus adopted the theme of a Sabbatical Year by telling his disciples that the harvest he asked them to engage in was one in which they HAD DONE NO LABOR. How true this illustration would have been even for the physical harvest of a Sabbatical Year. During Sabbatical Years no one could labor on the land. No sowing, plowing, pruning or harvesting were permitted. So even Jesus' statement that the disciples had bestowed no labor on the harvest that he was talking about, is indicative of the fact that that year was sabbatical. Jesus used terms only applicable to Sabbatical Years.

Another point needs to be made. Since Jesus gave his illustrations in John 4:35-38 at the time the fields were already white for harvest, he strongly implies that no one was in the fields doing any reaping. If all the fields were then ripe for harvest (and that is what Jesus said), this is a powerful suggestion that none of the fields (no matter how many there were) was then being harvested by the people. And, of course, this would have been the case in a Sabbatical Year. All the fields were not then being harvested.

In case some might doubt that fields in Sabbatical Years would produce much grain, since they had not been sowed in the previous Autumn and Winter, all one has to do is to recall that Leviticus 25:5 indicates there would always be a crop during the fallow Sabbatical Year from the grains that fell on the ground in the sixth year of harvest. Grain was in the stalks, but unharvested.

The Day of Pentecost?

There is yet another piece of evidence that the event which

occurred at Jacob's Well happened in a Sabbatical Year. This is Luke's parallel account of what transpired in Galilee soon after Jesus had returned to his hometown of Nazareth from the Passover at Jerusalem. Luke tells us in the Greek that on "The Day of the Sabbaths" (or, "The Day of the Weeks") [another possible way of saying Pentecost to agree with the terminology of Exodus 34:22; Deuteronomy 16:10; II Chronicles 8:13], Jesus was handed the scroll of Isaiah and he read chapter 61, verses 1 and 2. Luke recorded the occasion. [I am translating from the Greek.]

> "And he came to Nazareth, where he had been brought up, and he entered, as his custom was, into the synagogue on *the Day of the Sabbaths* [or, The Day of the Weeks] and stood up to read. And he was handed the scroll of the prophet Isaiah. And he opened the scroll, and found the place where it was written: 'The Lord's Spirit is upon me, because he anointed me to preach good tidings to the poor; hath sent me to proclaim release to the captives, and sight to the blind, to set free the bruised, to proclaim the Lord's acceptable year.' And he rolled up the scroll, and gave it back to the attendant and sat down, and the eyes of all in the synagogue were fixed upon him. And he began to say unto them, 'Today hath this scripture been fulfilled in your ears'."[442]

It should be noted that the synagogue attendant handed Jesus the scroll of Isaiah. This hints that the synagogue liturgy required Isaiah to be read that day. If so, this could indicate that Jesus read the regular triennial cycle selection from the prophets that accompanied the sequential readings from the five books of Moses. It is interesting that the section that Jesus quoted was that which paralleled the readings from the Law of Moses for Pentecost on the second year of the triennial cycle. (See the chart accompanying the article on the Triennial Cycle in the Jewish Encyclopedia, Funk and Wagnalls, 1906.) This is just another indication that this event in the synagogue in Nazareth occurred on Pentecost.

Though I am in no way insisting that the phrase "The Day of the Weeks" on which Jesus read Isaiah 61:1,2 was Pentecost (yet it may have been), it is still clear that the event happened in the late Springtime just after Jesus had returned from Jerusalem from

Appendix Four - The Sabbatical Years and Chronology

John's first Passover. It was certainly the same year that Jesus gave his teaching about the Sabbatical Year in John 4:35. With this in mind, we have a further reference that that year was sabbatical. Note that Jesus called that year *"the acceptable year of the Lord."* This is a phrase indicating the time of release. Even the use of this phrase shows that this year was a Sabbatical Year.

The First Year of Jesus' Ministry was Sabbatical

These terms Jesus was using in his discourse at the synagogue at Nazareth were those associated with Sabbatical Years (and with the Jubilee which was a type of Sabbatical Year). [Jubilee Years were not being celebrated by the Jews in the first century, yet the ordinary seven year sabbatical cycle was very much in evidence among the Jews and Samaritans.]

Look at the factors within Jesus' quote from Isaiah which suggest this. He said that he was anointed (1) to preach good tidings to the poor. This is a reflection on the sabbatical regulations that the poor and the stranger could eat from the fields without hinder. (2) He was to proclaim a release and to free the bruised. This recalls the sabbatical release regulations and being free of debt as mentioned in Deuteronomy 15:1-6. And (3), Jesus was ordained to proclaim the acceptable year of the Lord. This is a reference to a sabbatical period (which years officially commenced on the Day of Atonement, Leviticus 25:9 and Isaiah 58:1-14). Such years are always associated with "unloosing the bands of wickedness, undoing heavy burdens, letting the oppressed go free, and the breaking of every yoke" (Isaiah 58:6). This is the type of "acceptable year" that Jesus was proclaiming at the synagogue in Nazareth, and the theme is clearly that of a Sabbatical Year.

There is even more proof to show that this year was a Sabbatical Year. This is because Luke states that a few weeks later the disciples found themselves on a day that Luke called the "second-first Sabbath" and they began to eat from the grain that was in the ears

The Star that Astonished the World

of the wheat. What is the "second-first" Sabbath? The "second-first Sabbath" was the first weekly Sabbath of the month of Tishri (in the Autumn of the year) in which the twenty-four priestly courses commenced their second annual cycle (from weekly Sabbath to weekly Sabbath) for administrating in the Temple. See my proof of this in chapter five of this book.

The fact is, in normal harvest years, ALL the grain found in barley and wheat stalks would have long been harvested. But here were the disciples on the first weekly Sabbath of the month of Tishri and they were still finding plenty of stalks of wheat with grain in them. This again shows that the year in which this happened was a Sabbatical Year. That Sabbatical Year lasted until the Day of Atonement.[443] This indication in Luke 6:1 shows that there was still plenty of wheat in the fields by the first week of Tishri (as late as Autumn). This would have been an extraordinary thing in normal agricultural years because the wheat harvest would have been completed by around Pentecost time, three months earlier. But again, that Summer in Palestine in which all of this happened was a Sabbatical Year.

This means that we have several biblical proofs that the beginning of John the Baptist's ministry and that of Jesus' teaching started in a Sabbatical Year. This is why it makes excellent sense why so many people were able to follow both of them during the times of their preaching. Many of the people would have been off from their farm labor and able to travel at leisure over the land of Palestine.

The Sequence of Sabbatical Years

Though over the past few centuries historians studying the records about Sabbatical Years have been able to arrive at their former sequence within a year or two, only within the last 50 years (and especially the last 30), has it become possible, through archaeological discoveries, etc., to determine with an almost certainty

Appendix Four - The Sabbatical Years and Chronology

what the exact Sabbatical Years' sequence was and is. This can be known from 163 B.C. to the present. Two brilliant historical studies by Prof. Wacholder of Hebrew Union College, Cincinnati, have solved the riddle of when the Sabbatical Years occurred in ancient times, and when they ought to be observed today. His first study is in the Hebrew Union College Annual, 1973, titled "The Calendar of Sabbatical Cycles During the Second Temple and the Early Rabbinic Period" (pp.183-196), and the same Annual for 1975 has his "The Timing of Messianic Movements and the Calendar of Sabbatical Cycles" (pp. 201-218). In this book I will summarize the results of Prof. Wacholder's excellent studies. I also will give some research material of my own from three further references in Josephus which substantiates the conclusions of Wacholder. It will demonstrate the number of precise years over the centuries which were reckoned as Sabbaticals, and how we can know the exact sequence of the seventh years for the period we are discussing.

1) We are told by I Maccabees 6:49 that Judas Maccabee's defeat at Beth-Zur was in a Sabbatical Year. And this can be dated to the Sabbatical Year from the Autumn of 163 to Autumn 162 B.C.

2) Josephus, the Jewish historian, shows the murder of Simon the Hasmonean as happening in the Sabbatical Year of Autumn 135 to Autumn 134 B.C.

3) Josephus shows Herod's conquest of Jerusalem as occurring in the last part of the Sabbatical Year of 37 to 36 B.C.

4) King Agrippa the First recited the section of Deuteronomy which a king was required to do as associated with the Sabbatical Year (Deuteronomy 31:10-13). He performed it at a time which historically shows that Agrippa's Sabbatical Year was A.D.41 to 42.

5) A papyrus document written in Aramaic has recently been found in Palestine which is dated to the second year of Nero, and it says that that year was a Sabbatical Year. Thus, A.D.55 to 56 was Sabbatical.

6) A reference in the second century Jewish work called the *Seder Olam* can be interpreted as showing the Temple at Jerusalem being destroyed in a Sabbatical Year. That would have been A.D.69 to 70.

7) Dated documents have been found concerning the Bar Kokhba revolt of the Jews against the Romans which show that the year A.D.132 to 133 was also a Sabbatical Year.

8) The ruins of an ancient synagogue have recently been uncovered which have a date, in a mosaic, for the Jewish year 4000, and that it was the second year of a Sabbatical cycle. This answers to A.D.237 to 238.

9) There is a reference in the Jewish Talmud (*Sanhedrin* 97b) that the Messiah will release the world from its bondage of corruption in the year after 4291 of the Jewish calendar. Since it was believed this would occur in a Sabbatical Year, this reference becomes important (though the prophecy did not occur) because the year after 4291 was A.D.531 to 532, and it was Sabbatical.

The Sequence of Sabbatical Years is now Known

The interesting thing about these Sabbatical Years is the fact that they are all in proper sequence. This gives the historian a great deal of confidence that they are correct. This would mean that all the Sabbatical Years in between can be known. (Schurer, following Zuckermann, felt that the Sabbatical Years' cycle was a year earlier than the one presented above, but Wacholder has shown this to be untenable. For example, in Schurer's sequence, the year A.D.40 to 41 was Sabbatical, but Josephus says that crops were able to be harvested that year (*Antiquities* XVIII.271-284).[444] Even Schurer admits to the difficulty.[445] Indeed, to use Zuckermann's and Schurer's cycle of years, A.D. 61 to 62 would have been Sabbatical, but Josephus makes it clear that in the Spring of A.D.62 people were working at the threshing floors.[446] But, in the very next year (A.D.62 to 63), Agrippa II started to rebuild Caesarea Philippi

Appendix Four - The Sabbatical Years and Chronology

which is what would ordinarily have happened when many farmers were seeking work in the building trade during a Sabbatical Year.[447] Prof. Wacholder has given us the proper sequence of Sabbatical Years, and my references to Josephus given above corroborate his findings. (See also "The Interpreter's Dictionary of the Bible," Suppl. Vol., pp.762,763.)

Historical Events in Judaea Can Now Make Better Sense

Once the proper annual occurrences of Sabbaticals are understood, all other intervening years in sequence can be tallied. We then discover how important events occurred on them. Those years were times when the majority of the population (being mostly in agriculture) were off from their ordinary jobs, and something had to be done in order to keep them busy at earning a proper living. There was a simple answer to this that many people have not thought of. During the six years of farm labor the government took some grain and foodstuffs (like Joseph did in Egypt) and when the Sabbatical Year came around, they paid the people this produce to work at construction or other types of work. Since there was a vast reservoir of workers then available, new buildings, cities, walls, roads, irrigation projects were undertaken. And for the most part the people did the work willingly because they believed God to be behind their efforts of keeping the Sabbatical Years. Note examples of these building activities.

Herod commenced his work on the outer parts of the great Temple of God on the Sabbatical Year of 23/22 B.C.[448] This was also the exact year he commenced work on building the new city of Caesarea on the Mediterranean coast.[449] And later, Herod's son Philip started to build Caesarea Philippi[450] in the Sabbatical Year 2/1 B.C. The city of Tiberias probably had its founding in A.D.20, which was also the beginning of a Sabbatical Year.[451] Also the expansive third wall around the northern parts of Jerusalem (which, if finished, Josephus said would have made Jerusalem impregnable) was no doubt started by King Agrippa the First in the

Sabbatical Year of A.D. 41/42.[452] And, as I stated earlier, his son Agrippa II also began huge construction projects in similar circumstances in the Sabbatical Year of A.D. 62/63. Josephus said that "King Agrippa enlarged Caesarea Philippi and renamed it in honor of Nero. He furthermore built at great expense a theatre for the people of Beirut and presented them with animal spectacles, spending many tens of thousands of drachmas upon this project."[453]

It is because so many Jews had to take different types of jobs in Sabbatical Years that it was common for most of them in the first century to have two trades. Recall that the apostle Paul was a trained tentmaker.[454] Most learned these secondary trades during the Sabbatical Years when so many new construction projects were then underway. This is one of the main reasons that the Jewish people went along with many of the building endeavors of Herod during Sabbatical Years.

The Sabbatical Year of Jesus' Ministry

The sequence of Sabbatical Years is now established with almost certainty by Professor Wacholder. His information, with the new interpretation of John 4:35 that I am giving in this book, provide a logical chronology for the years of Jesus' ministry. We can now know that Jesus gave his information about the "four months to harvest" in a Sabbatical Year and that year is the one from the Autumn of A.D.27 to the Autumn of A.D.28.

There is another chronological indication in Luke's Gospel that helps substantiate this. Luke said that John the Baptist began his ministry in the fifteenth year of Tiberius Caesar.[455] Scholars have recognized several ways of reckoning this fifteenth year, but with our new information identifying Jesus' first year of teaching as the Sabbatical Year of A.D.27 to A.D.28, we are now helped in understanding the regnal years of Tiberius as reckoned by Luke. (For a full discussion on the various ways that Tiberius' fifteenth year have been reckoned, see the works of Prof. Jack Finegan,

Appendix Four - The Sabbatical Years and Chronology

Handbook of Biblical Chronology, pp.259-273, and Prof. Harold W. Hoehner, *Chronological Aspects of the Life of Christ*, pp.29-37.) We can now consider two of the explanations which blend in perfectly well with this new chronological information.

If one acknowledges the fifteenth year of Tiberius as being in conformity with the non-accession method based on the official Roman Year (called the Julian), that fifteenth year would be from January 1, A.D.28 to December 31, A.D.28. This would dovetail nicely with our new proposal, yet it would mean that John the Baptist began baptizing in January A.D.28 in the Jordan Valley. This would be acceptable since it was not excessively cold in the Jordan depression even during mid-winter. However, it does press events between January and the next Passover (which occurred in late March or early April) into a "hurry up" situation. (Recall that Jesus spent 40 days in the wilderness after his baptism.) Though this reckoning for the fifteenth year is not improbable, it is not to be preferred over the following determination which fits in much better with all factors. Let's notice it.

Since Luke was a Gentile and writing to a nobleman named Theophilus (traditionally both were from Antioch, Syria), it is possible that Luke was using the non-accession method of reckoning regnal years in Syria from the time of Augustus to Nerva. The fifteenth year of Tiberius was then from Tishri 1, A.D.27 to Tishri 1, A.D.28. This would mean that Luke was calculating the beginning of John the Baptist's ministry (and consequently that of Jesus') according to the calendar with which he and Theophilus would have been familiar (Hoehner, pp.34,35). It also has the advantage of paralleling the Jewish Year which also commenced with Tishri 1 (near our September). And more than that, this reckoning would also correspond precisely with the Sabbatical Year from the Autumn of A.D.27 to the Autumn of A.D.28. The Jewish authorities in the Talmud state clearly that this is the very method used by Gentile rulers in relationship to the calendar of the Jews. The

253

Gentile Romans commonly reckoned Jewish years from Tishri One.[456]

Chronological Importance of Sabbatical Years

What a significant symbolic time for John and Jesus to start their ministries. The Jewish people were keenly aware of the prophetic significance of Sabbatical Years as they related to prominent people of the Old Testament periods, and also to the advent of the Messiah into the world. In literature written not long before Jesus began to preach, we have these symbolic features about Sabbatical Years emphasized. The Book of Enoch presents an apocalyptic account based on the seven sabbatical ages, and in 91:12-17 it adds three more, a total of ten sabbatical periods. The Book of Jubilees records that at the creation God partitioned off time periods into Sabbatical and Jubilee cycles.[457] The births of significant people such as Adam, Noah, Abraham, and other patriarchs were timed to dovetail precisely with Sabbatical eras.[458] The Dead Sea sectarians recognized future reigns of the Kings of Wickedness and Righteousness relative to a Sabbatical calendar, and believing that the last year of the cycle would be the start of the Messianic age.[459]

These early opinions on the symbolic teaching concerning Sabbatical Years were no doubt prompted by the Sabbatical periods recorded by the Prophet Daniel. His Seventy Weeks' prophecy was an extension of a Sabbatical Years' theme, and this prophecy was the prime reference point for the advent of the Messianic age that the Jews were expecting in the first century. "Passover of the Sabbatical Year became the period when the redeemer's coming was expected most."[460]

Many People Were Off Work During Sabbatical Years

It is thus no surprise that vast crowds of people came out in the Sabbatical Year of A.D.27 to A.D.28 to be baptized of John the Baptist and Jesus. This was not only a time when a great percentage of the people would have been free of agricultural duties and

Appendix Four - The Sabbatical Years and Chronology

able to travel at leisure following the great teachers around Palestine, but it was also the Sabbatical Year when many of them were expecting Messianic signs to occur.

It makes perfectly good sense that John the Baptist would have started his ministry in the Autumn, at the beginning of the Sabbatical Year, and that Jesus would have commenced his own teaching a little later.

This would indicate that John the Baptist inaugurated his teaching ministry at the beginning of a Sabbatical Year. Soon after that, Jesus went into the wilderness for 40 days and then returned to Galilee. It appears that he was waiting for Passover in A.D.28 to begin officially his ministry. As Prof. Wacholder states, "Passover of the Sabbatical Year became the period when the redeemer's coming was expected most."

It was also in the Sabbatical Year of A.D.27 to A.D.28 that Jesus was 30 years of age. At the Passover of A.D.28, when he officially began his ministry, he was within his year 30. There was rather a strange way to us westerns of reckoning the years of a person's life. During the whole of a person's 30th year the word meaning "about" or "as if" was used to denote the year. Luke records: "Jesus began [his ministry] *about* thirty years of age."[461] Irenaeus, however, shows what Luke meant. "For when he [Jesus] was baptized, he had not yet completed his thirtieth year [he was indeed 30 already, but he had not completed year 30], but was beginning to be about thirty years of age."[462] Irenaeus had just said he was already 30 in paragraph 4. So, "beginning to be about 30" was used of a person all the way from the beginning to the ending of a person's year 30. During the whole of a person's year 30, the word meaning "about" or "as if" was applied. When his year 30 ended, he had then concluded his year 30. This means that Jesus was indeed 30 when he began his ministry, but he had not yet completed his 30th year. Irenaeus said this was the time that the Jews called a man a "Master."[463] It may appear strange to us that the word "about" is used to indicate something like our word "being," but this is the way it was interpreted by Irenaeus and he spoke Greek in the idiom that was near that of the New Testament. Gregory Nazianzen also understood the idiom to signify the fact that Jesus was a full 30 years of age. He said: "Christ was thirty years old when he was baptized" (*Oration on Baptism,* XXIX). A man had to be fully 30 to be a "Master."

More Evidence from the Apostle Paul

In the Book of Galatians the apostle Paul said the Gentile Galatians were suddenly going over to keeping the Mosaic law because people from Jerusalem taught them the need to do so. Indeed, the Galatians were "observing days, months, times, and *years.*"[464] Note the italicized word "years." Within the context of Paul's rebuke to the Galatian Gentiles, this can only refer to their observing (the verb is in the present tense) the Sabbatical Years of the Mosaic law. This, again, is an important chronological clue.

The sequence of Sabbatical Years in the period when the Book of Galatians could have been written was A.D.41/42, A.D.48/49; and A.D.55/56. Since A.D.55/56 is well after the Jerusalem Council of A.D.49, this could not be the Sabbatical Year the Galatians were observing. It is manifestly too early for A.D.41/42 to be considered. The only possibility is the Sabbatical Year of A.D.48/49. If this were the Sabbatical Year they were actively observing (and note that Paul used the present tense "observing"), one can understand the apostle Paul's urgent concern for their behavior. The truth is, it was not even necessary for Jews to observe Sabbatical Years outside the designated lands associated with Palestine, but here were the Galatians (and Gentiles at that) now observing the official Sabbatical Year of A.D.48/49 in Asia Minor. And only that year fits.

Important New Testament Deductions

Once the proper sequence of Sabbatical Years is understood, we can now appraise some significant New Testament historical state-

Appendix Four - The Sabbatical Years and Chronology

ments in a much better way. For one, we now know that the Autumn of A.D.48 to Autumn A.D.49 was a Sabbatical Year. This is a time when all agricultural activity in Palestine would have ceased. Such ritualistic requirements were often very traumatic for the Jewish people who lived in the Holyland and this was especially true in the six months' period that succeeded any Sabbatical Year. The fact is, they had effectively been cut off from earning any money from land products during the Sabbatical period. This point is a major one in interpreting several statements in various sections of the New Testament. Since Palestinian Jews were usually in dire economic straits during Sabbatical Years, and the six months that followed, it was customary for Jews in the Diaspora (those living outside Palestine) to send money and foodstuffs to their brethren in the Holyland. However, when Palestine was not undergoing drought or keeping Sabbatical Years, there is ample evidence to show that the region was very productive in which to live. Even Titus, the later Roman emperor, said that Judaea was proportionately more prosperous than Rome itself.[465] But when the Jews ceased agricultural pursuits in Sabbatical Years, many of them became poor as the Scriptures attest. It may seem like a moot point, but when Paul and Barnabas were given the right hand of fellowship that they should go to the Gentiles and the "pillar" apostles were assigned to the circumcision, the only extra requirement imposed on Paul was that he "remember the poor."[466] The poor in question, as the context certainly shows, were the poor among the Jews in Palestine because Paul and Barnabas would surely have considered it incumbent on them to show benevolence upon the Gentiles to whom they were commissioned to preach. But why were the Jews poor? The answer should be evident once the sequence of Sabbatical Years is recognized. The truth is, A.D.48 to A.D.49 was a Sabbatical Year, and the apostle Paul had the conference with the "pillar" apostles sometime in A.D.48 right at the start of a Sabbatical Year. There would have indeed been many poor in Palestine during the next year or so. It was always the year after a

Sabbatical that was most severe in food shortages. Yet there is more.

The apostle Paul went to Corinth while on his second journey, arriving there near the Autumn of A.D.50 or early A.D.51. He spent 18 months in Corinth.[467] There is archaeological information which shows that Gallio, the Roman proconsul, was in office between January 25, A.D.52 and before August 1, A.D.52.[468] Paul went before Gallio at that time.[469] Afterward, in the middle part of A.D.52, Paul went to Jerusalem, and finally back to his homebase in Antioch of Syria.[470] Then in the Spring of A.D.53, Paul started out on his third journey,[471] reaching Ephesus in late Spring of A.D.53. He stayed there for two years[472] and near that end of that period, and just before the Passover season in A.D.55, he wrote his first epistle to the Corinthians.[473] He ordered them, as he had those in Galatia, to save up money and goods to give to the poor saints at Jerusalem.[474] Afterwards, he went to Macedonia (from whence he wrote II Corinthians in late A.D.55). He again wrote the Corinthians (two long chapters) about the collection for the poor saints in Jerusalem, praising them that even "from before" the Sabbatical Year began with Tishri in A.D.55, the Corinthians had started to save their money and produce.[475] Then, in late A.D.55, Paul went on to Corinth, where he wintered with them for three months (Acts 20:3). This is when he wrote his epistle to the Romans, telling them he was soon journeying to Jerusalem to deliver the collections he had secured from Galatia, Macedonia, and Greece.[476] The Book of Romans was written in the early Spring of A.D.56. He then left Corinth and went to Ephesus, now telling them it had been three years since he started preaching to them.[477] He got to Jerusalem about Pentecost in A.D.56[478] approaching the end of the Sabbatical Year.

Why are these chronological data important to know? Because they show that Paul was taking produce and money to Jerusalem to help them through the Sabbatical Year from Autumn A.D.55 to Autumn A.D.56. Not only does this information help us date the

Appendix Four - The Sabbatical Years and Chronology

times when the epistles I and II Corinthians (as well as Romans) were written, but the evidence helps to confirm the sequence of Sabbatical Years which Professor Wacholder has provided. When the complete ramifications of this chronological subject are recognized, it will be seen how important the proper interpretation of John 4:35-38 really is. Jesus in that verse is talking about a Sabbatical Year. That indication represents a powerful chronological benchmark which can help us identify the years when the festivals took place that John mentioned in his Gospel. When it is realized that the Sabbatical Year of A.D.27 to A.D.28 is the first year of Jesus' ministry, most of the other chronological indications in the Gospels and epistles can make much better sense. It especially denotes that 30 years before this Sabbatical Year, one arrives at 3 B.C. for the birth of the Jesus. All makes sense when these things are understood.

SELECT BIBLIOGRAPHY

Bahat, Dan, The Illustrated Atlas of Jerusalem (New York:Simon & Schuster, 1990).

Beyer, David, W., Josephus Re-examined: Unraveling the Twenty-Second Year of Tiberius, (soon to be published research:1996).

Boa, K., & Proctor, W., The Return of the Star of Bethlehem (Garden City: Doubleday, 1980).

Brown, R.E., The Birth of the Messiah (New York:Doubleday, 1977).

Bullinger, E. W., The Witness of the Stars (Grand Rapids:Kregel, 1972).

Cumont, F., Astrology and Religion Among the Greeks and Romans (New York: Dover, 1960).

Devore, N., Encyclopedia of Astrology (New York:Philosophical Library, 1947).

Select Bibliography

Edwards, O., A New Chronology of the Gospels (London:Floris, 1972).

Eliade, M., Cosmos and History (New York:Harper & Row, 1959).

Finegan, J., Handbook of Biblical Chronology (Princeton:University Press, 1964).

Hendriksen, W., New Testament Commentary, (Grand Rapids:Baker Book House, 1973).

Hoehner, H.W., Chronological Aspects of the Life of Christ (Grand Rapids: Zondervan, 1977).

Hoehner, H.W., Herod Antipas (Cambridge:University Press, 1972).

Hughes, D., The Star of Bethlehem Mystery (London:J.M. Dent, 1979).

Jeremias, J., Jerusalem in the Time of Jesus (London:SCM, 1969).

Keresztes, Paul, Imperial Rome and the Christians (New York:University Press, 1989).

Kittel, G., Theological Dictionary of the New Testament (Grand Rapids: Eerdmans, 1964).

Kudlek, M. & Mickler, E.H., Solar and Lunar Eclipses (Neukirchen-Vluyn:Verlag Butzon & Bercker Kevelaer, 1971).

Lewin, T., Fasti Sacri (London:1865).

Lindsay, J., Origins of Astrology (New York:Barnes and Noble, 1972).

Madden, F., History of Jewish Coinage (San Diego:Pegasus, 1970).

Maier, P., The First Christmas (New York:Harper & Row, 1971).

Martin, Ernest L., The Birth of Christ Recalculated (Pasadena:FBR Publications, 1978, 1980 second edition).

Meshorer, Y., Jewish Coins of the Second Temple Period (Tel-Aviv:1972).

Meyshan, J., Essays in Jewish Numismatics (Jerusalem:1960).

Mosley, John, The Christmas Star (Los Angeles:Griffith Observatory, 1987).

Nicoll, W.R., The Expositor's Greek Testament (Grand Rapids:Eerdmans, n.d.).

Parker and Dubberstein, Babylonian Chronology (Providence:University, Brown, 1969).

Reifenberg, A., Ancient Jewish Coins (1947).

Schurer, E., History of the Jewish People in the Time of Jesus Christ (Edinburgh:Clark, 1896). Rev. Ed. (The New Schurer), G. Vermes & F. Millar (Edinburgh:Clark, 1973).

Seiss, J.A., The Gospel in the Stars (Grand Rapids:Kregel, 1972).

Sherwin-White, A.N., Roman Society and Roman Law in the New Testament (Oxford:Clarendon, 1963).

Smith, W., Dictionary of Greek and Roman Biography (London:Walton, 1870).

Smith, W., Dictionary of Greek and Roman Geography (London:Walton, 1876).

Select Bibliography

Syme, Sir Ronald, The Roman Revolution (Oxford:1939).

Syme, Sir Ronald, "The Titulus Tiburtinus," in Vestigia Akten des VI Internationalen Kongresses fur Griedchische und Lateinische Epigraphik (Munich:Beck, 1972).

Syme, Sir Ronald, "The Crisis of 2 B.C.," in Verlag Der Bayerischen Akademie Der Wissenschaften (Munich:Beck, 1974).

Tuckerman, B., Planetary, Lunar, and Solar Positions 601 B.C. to A.D. 1 (Philadelphia:American Philosophical Society, 1962).

Van Goudoever, J., Biblical Calendars (Leiden:Brill, 1959).

Vardaman and Yamauchi, Chronos, Kairos, Christos (Winona Lake:Eisenbrauns, 1989).

Yamauchi, Edwin M., Persia and the Bible (Grand Rapids:Baker, 1990).

ZPEB, Zondervan Pictorial Encyclopedia of the Bible (Grand Rapids:Zondervan, 1975).

FOOTNOTES

Chapter One

1 Sky and Telescope, Dec., 1968, 384-386.
2 Zondervan's Pictorial Encyclopedia of the Bible, I.398.
3 Lindsay, Jack, Origins of Astrology, 246.
4 Matthew 2:2.
5 Suetonius, Tiberias, 69.
6 The Oxford Classical Dictionary, 149.
7 Bickerman, E.J., Chronology of the Ancient World, 77.
8 Allan, B., Augustus Caesar, 216-218.
9 Syme, Sir Ronald, The Crisis of 2 B.C., 3.
10 Ibid.
11 Res Gestae of Augustus, 16.
12 Lewin, T., Fasti Sacri, 135.
13 Res Gestae of Augustus, 35.1.
14 Lewin, T., Fasti Sacri, 135
15 Ovid, Fasti, II.637,638.
16 The Encyclopaedia of Religion and Ethics, XII.51.
17 The Encyclopaedia of Religion and Ethics, XII.49f.
18 The Oxford Classical Dictionary, 569.
19 Syme, Sir Ronald, The Crisis of 2 B.C., 3.
20 The Oxford Classical Dictionary, 569.
21 Martin, E.L., The Birth of Christ Recalculated, 17-19.
22 The Encyclopaedia of Religion and Ethics, XII.51.
23 Mosley, John, The Christmas Star, Griffith Observatory, 45.
24 The Encyclopaedia of Religion and Ethics, XII.51.
25 The Los Angeles Times, December 10, 1980.
26 Asimov, Isaac, The Planet that Wasn't, 222.

27 Suetonius, Vespasian IV and Tacitus, Histories, V.13.
28 Luke 1:78.
29 Thorley, Dr. John, "Greece and Rome" (April, 1981), Oxford University.
30 Hallett, P.H., The National Catholic Register, January 13, 1980.
31 Mosley, John, The Christmas Star, Griffith Observatory, 20.
32 Guideposts, December, 1988.
33 Imprimis, December, 1993, 3.
34 Sky and Telescope, December, 1968, editorial.
35 Mosley, John, The Griffith Observer, December, 1980.

Chapter Two

36 e.g. The New English Bible.
37 Isaiah 47:13; Daniel 1:20; 2:27.
38 Matthew 2:3.
39 Pliny, Natural History, XXX.6.
40 Matthew 2:3.
41 As it was with Tiridates when he and the Magi visited Nero at Rome.
42 Herodotus, I.101; Pliny, Natural History, V.29.
43 Diog. Laert., IX.7.2.
44 Herodotus, III.61sq.
45 Daniel 5:11.
46 Jeremiah 39:3,13 see Hebrew.
47 Daniel 9:24-27.
48 Josephus, War, VI.313.
49 Many scholars hold that the theological beliefs of the Persians and Jews were similar.
50 Suetonius, Vespasian, 4.
51 Tacitus, History, V.13.
52 Suetonius, Nero, 40.
53 Josephus, Antiquities, XI.133; War, II.398; VII.43.
54 The Encyclopaedia of Religion and Ethics, art. Zoroastrianism, XII.862-868.
55 Ibid.
56 Philo, Quo. Probus Liber, 74.
57 Diodorus Siculus, II.31; Ephraem, Syrus, II.488.
58 Diog. Laert. IX.7.2.
59 Zondervan Pictorial Encyclopedia of the Bible, IV.34.
60 Strabo, XVI.762; Cicero, De.Divin., I.41.
61 Strabo, XI.9.3.
62 Tertullian, C. Marc. 5.
63 Some have thought this number was invented to equate them with the 12 tribes of Israel.
64 Genesis 43:11; Psalm 72:15; I Kings 10:2,10; II Chronicles 9:24; Song of Songs 3:6; 4:16
65 Kittel, Theological Dictionary, I.352
66 Vincent, Word Studies, I.21.

Chapter Three

67 Finegan, Jack, Handbook of Biblical Chronology, 229.
68 The Oxford Classical Dictionary, art. Libraries, 606,608.
69 By the end of the fourth century all such records were in the hands of Christians.
70 Finegan, ibid.
71 Luke 1:26.
72 Revelation 12:4 is an example.
73 Numbers 9:15-18.
74 Mark 14:62; Acts 22:6-11.

75 Josephus, War, VI.290.
76 Genesis 1:14.
77 Genesis 37:9,10.
78 Psalm 19:3,4.
79 Romans 10:18.
80 Job 38:31.
81 II John 13.
82 Matthew 25:1-10.
83 Matthew 24:27.
84 Malachi 4:2.
85 See also Revelation 6:1-8 where the four beasts are similarly described.
86 Numbers chapter two.
87 Revelation 12:1-5.
88 Chapter Five of this book explains this in detail.
89 Charlesworth, James, The Old Testament Pseudepigrapha, I.476.
90 Ibid.
91 Isaiah 47:13.
92 Jubilee 8:1-4.
93 Luke 21:11,25.
94 Romans 10:18.
95 Daniel 5:11.
96 Revelation 22:16.

Chapter Four

97 II Peter 1:19.
98 Isaiah 60:3.
99 Luke 1:78,79.
100 Hendriksen, Matthew 153.
101 Revelation 5:5.
102 Olcott, Star Lore of All Ages, 233.
103 Mark 1:2.
104 Numbers 24:17.
105 Numbers 24:19.
106 Genesis 49:9,10.
107 Genesis 49:10.
108 Jeremias, The Old Testament in the Light of the Ancient East, 148.
109 Sinnott, Sky and Telescope, December, 1968, 384-386.
110 Asimov, Isaac, The Planet That Wasn't, 222.
111 The Encyclopaedia of Religion and Ethics, XII.51.
112 Jeremiah 30:6,7.
113 Matthew 2:2.
114 Luke 2:21-24.
115 Matthew 2:11.
116 Matthew 2:16.
117 Matthew 2:9.
118 Kittel, Theological Dictionary, VII.648.
119 Matthew 2:9.
120 Irish Theological Quarterly, VII.61.
121 Matthew, Homily, VI.3.
122 Expositor's Greek Testament, I.73.
123 Cumont, F., Astrology and Religion Among the Greeks and Romans, 89.
124 Luke 1:78,79.
125 Malachi 4:2.
126 Eliade, Cosmos and History, 51-62.
127 Jeremiah 10:1-4.
128 John 10:22.
129 Rockland, J.S., The Hanukkah Book, passim.
130 Ibid.
131 Ibid.

Chapter Five

132 Josephus, Life 1-3.

133 For an excellent description of this type of regnal reckoning, see Harold W. Hoehner's "Chronological Aspects of the Life of Christ," 34,35.
134 Res Gestae, VI.35.
135 Lewin, T., Fasti Sacri, 135.
136 Ovid, Fast., 2.119; Suetonius, Augustus, 58.
137 Josephus, Antiquities, XVII.41-45.
138 Ramsay, Born at Bethlehem, 193.
139 The barley was always early near Jericho, but usually the crops were judged in the region of Jerusalem.
140 Parker and Dubberstein, Babylonian Chronology, 25.
141 Van Goudoever, J., Biblical Calendars, 274.
142 Ibid.
143 The Qumran sects were not in charge of the Temple and their opinions should not lead the way in our inquiries on the course of Abijah.
144 Ramsay, ibid.
145 Hendriksen, Matthew, 182.
146 Philo, Op. Mund., 55; Rashi, Commentary, I.5.
147 Lange's Commentary, X.34.
148 Liddell and Scott., Lexicon, 1448.
149 Devore, Encyclopedia of Astrology, 366.
150 M'Clintock and Strong, Cyclopedia, X.568.

Chapter Six

151 Gaster, Festivals of the Jewish Year, 109.
152 Thiele, The Mysterious Numbers of the Hebrew Kings, 28,31,161,163.
153 Gaster, ibid., 108.
154 Ibid., 113.
155 Ibid., 115.
156 Ibid.
157 Ibid., 114,115.
158 Zondervan Pictorial Encyclopedia of the Bible, II.524.
159 Barnes, T., Journal of Roman Studies, LXIV (1974), 22.

Chapter Seven

160 Syme, Sir Ronald, The Crisis of 2 B.C., 30.
161 Ibid., 5,6.
162 Ibid.
163 See notes to the Loeb edition of Dio Cassius.
164 Res Gestae, III.14.
165 Finegan, J., Handbook of Biblical Chronology, 229.
166 Josephus, Antiquities, XVI.136.
167 Stauffer, Jesus and History, 22.
168 The Dictionary of Christian Biography, III.449.
169 War, 70.
170 Antiquities, X.233.
171 Ibid., XIII.301.
172 Corbishley, The Journal of Roman Studies, XXXVI.22.
173 Antiquities, XIV.158,159.
174 Dio Cassius, XLIV.22.
175 Antiquities, XIV.487.

176 The notes to the Loeb edition of Josephus explain many of these problems.
177 Antiquities, XVII.342; Life, 5.
178 Antiquities, XVII.342.
179 War, II.111.
180 War, II.115.
181 Life, 424.
182 War, IV.622.
183 Life, 38.
184 Antiquities, XVIII.106.
185 Beyer, Josephus Re-Examined: Unraveling the Twenty-Second Year of Tiberius, 8,9.

Chapter Eight

186 Antiquities, XVII.167.
187 Ibid.
188 War, I.657.
189 Antiquities, XVII.174.
190 Ibid., 177.
191 Ibid. and also War, I.670.
192 Antiquities, XVII.196.
193 War, I.670.
194 Antiquities, XVII.198.
195 War, I.184.
196 Antiquities, I.196.
197 Ibid., 198.
198 Ibid., 199.
199 The Encyclopaedia of Religion and Ethics, XI.475.
200 This was suggested by Douglas Johnson in "Chronos, Kairos, Christos."
201 Suetonius, Augustus, 100.
202 Toybee, Death and Burial in the Roman World, 45.
203 Ibid., 50,51.
204 Antiquities, XVII.177.
205 Ibid.
206 Ibid.
207 Ibid.
208 Ibid.
209 Antiquities, IV.78.
210 War, III.437.
211 Antiquities, XVII.311.
212 Ibid.
213 Antiquities, XVII.200.
214 Ibid., 232,233; War, II.27,28.
215 Antiquities, XVII.233.
216 Barnes, T., Journal of Theological Studies, XIX (1968) 209.
217 Antiquities, XVII.218,219.
218 Ibid.
219 At the defeat of Antiochus Epiphanes.

Chapter Nine

220 Antiquities, XVII.164-167.
221 Ibid.
222 Leviticus 20:14; 21:9; Joshua 7:25,26.
223 Sanhedrin XI.4.
224 Kraus, Die Mischna, Sanhedrin, 302.
225 Sanhedrin, 64.
226 The Theodosian Code, XVI.viii.18.
227 Gaster, Theodore H., Festivals of the Jewish Year, 227.
228 Josephus, War I.35 with 562,563 and Esther 9:10.
229 Ibid., I.400.
230 Philo, Quod. Deus, 144,148,166,180.
231 Rashi, Commentary on Genesis 27:39 and Numbers 24:19.
232 Josephus, War I.123,181.
233 e.g. Livy, XLIV.37.

234 Josephus, War II.18.
235 Ibid., Antiquities, XVII.221.
236 Ibid., War II.40.
237 Ibid., Antiquities, XVII.222.
238 Ibid.
239 Josephus, War II.52.
240 Ibid., 46; Antiquities, XVII.257.
241 Josephus, War II.23.
242 Ibid.
243 Josephus, Antiquities, XVII.264.
244 Barnes, T., Journal of Theological Studies, XIX (1968), 209.
245 Vermes and Millar, The New Schurer, 326.
246 Jeremias, Jerusalem in the Time of Jesus, 162.
247 Josephus, Antiquities, XVII.82; War I.606.
248 Horayoth, 12b; Yoma 12b; Megilla 9b.
249 These factors may be technical, but they are real proofs to the experts.
250 Burnaby, S., The Jewish Calendar, 261.
251 Josephus, Antiquities, XVII.149.
252 Ibid., 155.
253 Josephus, War I.649.
254 Ibid., 660.
255 Kudlek, M. and Mickler, E., Solar and Lunar Eclipses of the Ancient Near East, 156.
256 Josephus, Antiquities, XVII.218.
257 Josephus, Contra Apion I.34.
258 Josephus, Contra Apion I.34.

Chapter Ten

259 Josephus, Antiquities, XVII.41-45.
260 Josephus, War I.284,285.
261 Res Gestae, 16.
262 Syme, Sir Ronald, The Crisis of 2 B.C., 3.
263 Barnes, T., The Journal of Roman Studies, (1974). 23.
264 Josephus, Antiquities, XVII.229; War II.25.
265 Dio, LV.10.6.
266 Tacitus, Annals, IV.1.
267 Ibid., IV.5.
268 Dio Cassius, LV.10.6.
269 Vellius Paterculus, II.101.1.
270 Dio Cassius, LV.10.6.
271 Tacitus, ibid.
272 Syme, Sir Ronald, History in Ovid, 68.
273 Pliny, Natural History, XII.55ff.
274 Strabo, XVI,4.23.
275 Josephus, Antiquities, XVII.295-298; War II.76-79.
276 Ibid.
277 Pliny, Natural History, VI.31.
278 Suetonius, Augustus, 93.
279 Assumption of Moses, 6:8.
280 Zetzel, Greek, Roman, Byzantine Studies, XI (1970), 250ff.
281 Bowersock, The Journal of Roman Studies, LXI (1971), 227.
282 Zetzel., ibid.
283 I Thessalonians 2:15.
284 Josephus, Contra Apion, passim.
285 Lewis and Reinhold, Roman Civilization, 369.
286 See note in my second edition of "Birth of Christ Recalculated," 85.
287 Josephus, Antiquities, XVII.89.

Chapter Eleven

288 Tertullian, An Answer to the Jews, ch.8.
289 Vermes and Millar, The New Schurer, I.255.
290 Res Gestae, V.25.
291 Syme, Sir Ronald, The Titulus Tiburtinus, 586.
292 Vermes and Millar. The New Schurer, I.254-260.
293 Sherwin-White, Roman Society and Roman Law in the New Testament, 165.
294 Josephus, War, II.68,72-79.
295 Syme, Sir Ronald, The Titulus Tiburtinus, 594.
296 Sherwin-White, ibid., 165.
297 Syme, Sir Ronald, Klio, XXVII (1934), 133f.
298 Tacitus, Annals, III.48.
299 Ibid., 22.
300 Vellius Paterculus, II.117.2.
301 Smith, Dictionary of Greek and Roman Geography, II.1204.
302 Syme, Sir Ronald, The Roman Revolution, 381.
303 Tacitus, Annals, IV.66.
304 De vulgaris aerae emendatione, Rome (1793), 414.
305 Taylor and Reinhold, the Journal of Roman Studies, (1936), 161ff.
306 Suetonius, Augustus, 23.
307 Tacitus, Annals, I.62.
308 Ibid., 61.
309 Ibid., 62.
310 Syme, Sir Ronald, The Crisis of 2 B.C., 8.
311 Tacitus, Annals, IV.66.
312 Vellius Paterculus, II.119.5.
313 Josephus, Antiquities, XVI.280,285,357,361.

Chapter Twelve

314 Ibid., XVII.89.
315 Last, Hugh, Quoted by Rice Holmes in "Architect of the Roman Empire," II.89, note 1.
316 Sherwin-White, ibid., 165.
317 Tacitus, Annals, III.48.
318 Ibid.
319 Justin Martyr, Apology, I.34.
320 See Tacitus, Agric., 15.
321 Res Gestae, II.8.
322 Lardner, Credibility, I.292-313.
323 Josephus, Antiquities, XVII.41-45.
324 Luke 2:1.
325 Res Gestae, VI.35.
326 Lewis and Reinhold, Roman Civilization, II.34,35.
327 Ibid.
328 Josephus, Antiquities, XVII.41-45.
329 Thomson, R.W., Moses of Khorene's History of the Armenians, II.26.
330 Orosius, VI.22 and VII.2.
331 Lewis and Reinhold, Roman Civilization, II.387.
332 Ibid., 388.
333 Res Gestae, VI.35.
334 Josephus, Antiquities, XVII.205.
335 Ibid., XIV.117.
336 Sands, P.C., The Client Princes of the Roman Empire, 222-228.
337 Sherwin-White, ibid., 148.
338 Res Gestae, II.8.
339 Sherwin-White, ibid., 148.
340 Ibid.

341 Vermes and Millar, The New Schurer, I.404.
342 Josephus, Antiquities, XVI.65.
343 Ibid., XIV.202-206.
344 Lewis and Reinhold, ibid., II.444.
345 Josephus, Antiquities, XVII.57.
346 Ibid., 89.
347 Att., III.9.1
348 Att., IV.2.1 cf. V.3.
349 Atkinson, Historia, VII (1958), 310-312.
350 Josephus, Antiquities, XVII.190; War I.665.

Chapter Thirteen

351 Vermes and Millar, ibid., 326.
352 Barnes, T., The Journal of Theological Studies, XIX (1968), 209.
353 Josephus, Antiquities, XV.121.
354 Ibid., XVI.136.
355 Galloway, The Chain of Ages (c.1860), 460-465.
356 Cunninghame, The Fullness of Times (1836), 94-97.
357 Vermes and Millar, ibid., 326.
358 Josephus, Antiquities, XIV.475.
359 See Appendix Four of this book.
360 Josephus, Antiquities, XIV.487.
361 Ibid.
362 Abodah Zarah, 10a.
363 See my chapter six of this book for details.
364 Vermes and Millar, op.cit., 285.
365 Barnes, T., The Journal of Theological Studies, XIX (1968), 204-209.
366 Dio, LV.27.6.
367 Josephus, Antiquities, XVI.270.
368 Ibid., 291.
369 Reifenberg, A., Ancient Jewish Coins (1947), 15.
370 John 19:12.
371 Josephus, Antiquities, XVII.2.
372 Ibid., 90.
373 Ibid., 96.
374 Hoehner, Herod Antipas, 271.
375 Luke 2:1-5.
376 Josephus, Antiquities, XVIII.124.
377 Kittel, Theological Dictionary of the New Testament, V.459.
378 Josephus, Antiquities, XIV.168-176; War I.210,211.
379 Ibid., XV.164-178.
380 Ibid., 232-236.
381 Ibid., 247-252.
382 Ibid., 259-266.
383 Ibid., XVI.106,109.
384 Josephus, War I.538,539.
385 Ibid., 620-640.
386 Josephus, Antiquities, XVII.2.
387 Suetonius, Augustus, 65.
388 Josephus, War II.26.
389 Ibid., 168; Antiquities, XVII.188.
390 Thompson, W.R., Zondervan Pictorial Encyclopedia of the Bible, I.822.
391 Meyshan, Essays in Jewish Numismatics, 72.
392 Josephus, Antiquities, XX.104; War II.223.
393 Ibid., 73.
394 Meshorer, Y., Jewish Coins of the Second Temple Period, 82-84.
395 Ibid., 81.
396 Ibid.

397 Josephus, Antiquities, XVIII.252.
398 Madden, Coins of the Jews, (1881), 121f.
399 Vermes and Millar, op. cit., 327.
400 Josephus, Antiquities, XVII.345; War II.112.
401 Bickerman, E.J., Beryutus (1944), 77.
402 Ibid., 81.
403 Robert, Etudes Anatoliennes (1937), 231.
404 Thiele, The Mysterious Numbers of the Hebrew Kings, 207.
405 Bickerman, E. J., Chronology of the Ancient World, 90.
406 Josephus, Antiquities, XIV.121.
407 Josephus, Life I.1.
408 Klausner, The Messianic Idea in Israel, 256f,313,455f, 469,514.
409 Josephus, Antiquities, XVI.381.
410 Josephus, War I.522.
411 Ibid., 241.
412 Ibid., 521,546.
413 Ibid., 435,436.
414 Ibid., 458.
415 Ibid., 483.
416 Ibid., 522.
417 Josephus, Antiquities, XVI.399.
418 Josephus, War I.449,468.
419 Ibid., 560.
420 Josephus, Antiquities, XV.167,168.
421 Josephus, War I.476.
422 Ibid., 467.
423 Syme, Sir Ronald, The Roman Revolution, 378.
424 Josephus, Antiquities, XVI.78-81.
425 Josephus, War I.552.
426 Josephus, Antiquities, XVII.299-314.
427 Josephus, War II.101-110.
428 Josephus, Antiquities, XIX.275.
429 Josephus, Life I.1.
430 Ibid., 2.
431 Josephus, Antiquities, XVII.120.
432 Ibid., 12-15.
433 Beyer, Josephus Re-examined: Unraveling the Twenty-Second Year of Tiberius.
434 Josephus, War II.26.
435 Josephus, Antiquities, XIV.4.
436 Josephus, War I.120.
437 Leviticus 25:1-7.

Appendix Four

438 John 4:35.
439 Mishnah, Ta'anith, I.7.
440 Commentary on John, tom.xiii.39,41.
441 John 4:35.
442 Luke 4:17-21.
443 Leviticus 25:1-22, see especially verse 9 which shows that Sabbatical Years began and ended on the Day of Atonement.
444 War II.200; Antiquities, XVIII.271-284.
445 JPJC, I.I., 42,43.
446 Antiquities, XX.206.
447 Ibid., 211-214.
448 War, I.101 and Loeb, vol.VIII, p.184 note c.
449 cf. Antiquities, XV.341 and Loeb note d.
450 cf. Schurer, revised., II.169-171.
451 Ibid., 179.
452 War II.218.
453 Antiquities, XX.211.

454 Acts 18:3.
455 Luke 3:1.
456 Abodah Zarah, 10a.
457 Jubilees 1:27-29.
458 4Q181, fragments 1,2.
459 1 Qmelch.3:2.
460 Wacholder, Inter.Dictionary, One Vol., supplement, 763.
461 Luke 3:23.
462 Against Heresies, II,xxii,5.
463 Ibid.
464 Galatians 4:10.
465 War III.516-521; VI.317,333-336; Antiquities, V.76-79.
466 Galatians 2:10.
467 Acts 18:11.
468 Finegan, ibid., 316-318.
469 Acts 18:12-17.
470 Acts 18:21,22.
471 Acts 18:23.
472 Acts 19:10.
473 I Corinthians 16.
474 I Corinthians 16:15.
475 II Corinthians 8:10; 9:2.
476 Romans 15:25-33.
477 Acts 20:31.
478 Acts 20:16.

INDEX

Aaron	68-69, 133	Alexandrian	34-35
Abarbanel	33, 37	Amalekite	141-142
Abgar	190	Amalgamation	104
Abia	69	Ancyranum	234
Abijah	68-69, 71, 76-78, 84, 267	Antedating	221-222, 225-227
		Antiochus	63, 268
Abodah	272, 274	Antony	204-205
Abraham	26, 29, 63-64, 100, 253	Apostles	41, 90, 244, 256-257
Actaion	128	Aqaba	163
Actian	169	Arabia	49, 163, 210
Actium	106-107, 115, 203-204	Aristobulus	211, 213, 215, 217, 222-223, 226
Adam	94, 99-100, 253		
Adar	139-140	Arruntuis	209
Adonis	128	Arsacids	221
Aegean	163-164	Asia	26, 171, 173, 190, 194, 232, 256
Aemalius	209		
Agagite	141	Asimov	17-18, 53
Ahasuerus	139	Astrologer	10, 44
Akenaton	216	Astrology	6-7, 22, 33, 42-43,
Alexander	195, 211, 213, 215, 217, 222-224, 226	Astronomer	4-5, 19-20
		Atkinson	196, 232
Alexandra	228	Babylon	3-5, 25, 28, 44, 52-53, 77, 142
Alexandria	27, 168		

274

Babylonian	44, 77, 216	Claudius	168, 192, 225
Babylonians	24-25, 69, 77	Comets	37
Bagoas	187	Commagene	159
Bahat	259	Conder	117
Balaam	49-50	Conjunctions	10, 14, 33, 36, 49, 51-52, 55, 66, 93
Barnabas	256-257		
Barnes	103, 136, 161, 201, 209, 235	Consul	171, 174
		Consularships	232
Beirut	145, 214, 251	Consuls	107, 109, 115, 171
Belus	28	Corbishley	108
Beta	98	Corinth	257-258
Bethzur	248	Corinthians	81, 96, 101, 257-258,
Beyer	112-113, 202, 209, 227, 259	Crossan	113
		Cumont	61, 259
Bickerman	221	Cunninghame	205
Bier	126-130	Cyrenius	181
Bithynia	221	Cyrus	108
Boaz	83	Dalmatia	162
Brephos	54, 67, 229	Damascus	117, 122, 126, 134, 137, 149, 218
Brown	259, 261		
Bullinger	84, 99, 259	Dan	216, 259
Cairo	142	Darius	223
Caligula	209, 212, 218	Davidic	186, 222
Callirrhoe	123	Delta	98
Calvinus	109	Deuteronomy	79, 132, 141, 216, 227, 245, 247, 249
Calvisius	117		
Cappadocia	159, 223	Diadem	126
Caspari	117	Diaspora	256
Cassius	104-105, 109, 162, 198,	Dikaiodotes	183
Census	182-183, 185, 187, 189, 191, 193, 195, 197, 199	Diodorus	264
		Dionysius	35
Chaldeans	7, 25, 31, 44, 47	Domitian	218
Chanukkah	62	Drusilla	226
Charlesworth	42	Dubberstein	77
Chester, C.	19	Edersheim	107
Christmas	17, 19, 154	Edom	141, 143
Chronicles	69-72, 245	Edomites	142
Chronos	116	Egyptian	44, 101, 132
Chrysostom	60	Elam	142
Cicero	28, 196	Eliade	61, 259
Cilicia	226	Elizabeth	68, 71, 78, 197

275

Emesa	226	Hanukkah	62-65, 229
Enoch	253	Hasmoneans	208, 211, 222, 225-226
Enrollment	75, 181, 185, 191-192	Hebrew	42, 48, 83, 244, 248
Ephesus	257-258	Hebrews	128
Ephraem	264	Heifer	99
Epiphanes	63, 268	Hendriksen	259
Esther	139-141, 143	Herodians	222
Euergetes	183	Herodotus	24
Eumenes	221	Hezekiah	83
Eunuch	158, 187	Hillel	110-111
Exiguus	35	Hoehner	212, 253
Ezekiel	41, 128	Homer	216
Ezra	69-70, 95, 111	Homonadenses	173, 182
Federer	20	Hyrcanus	109, 193, 213, 222, 228
Feldman	183	Hystapses	223
Felix	226	Ideler	33-34
Festivals	62, 90, 95, 101, 141, 165, 240, 258	Idolatry	63-64, 152, 216
		Idumaea	157, 164, 166-168, 224
Festschrift	116	Idumaean	222
Filmer	117, 205-206, 208-209	Imprimis	19
Finegan	5, 116, 252, 259	Iota	98
Gabriel	38	Irenaeus	255
Galatians	126, 255-256	Isaac	17-18, 53, 100
Galilee	108, 133, 157, 166, 172, 229, 234, 236-237, 241-242, 245, 254	Ishtar	47
		Israelites	24, 132
		Italy	130, 193
Gallio	257	Iterum	233-234
Gaster	95-97	James	30, 73, 229
Genetrix	11	Janus	8, 160
Genizah	142	Jehoash	95
Germanicus	178-179	Jehoiarib	69, 77
Gingerich	19	Jehu	95
Glaphyra	223	Jeremiah	25, 62, 81, 95, 128
Greece	17-18, 165, 258	Jeremias	50, 149
Greeks	49, 128, 259	Joazar	140
Griffith	5, 16-17, 19-20	Job	26, 40, 113, 116
Guideposts	19	Jordan	139, 148, 166, 252
Hadrian	192	Joshua	128, 141
Hadriana	176	Josephus	112-113
Haman	141-144	Jubilees	43, 253
Hannah	100	Judaean	207, 212, 217, 226, 228

Judaism	95, 98, 111	Mauritania	164
Judas	211, 248	Medes	24
Julian	252	Megillath	151-153
Julias	236-237	Mercury	11-12, 48, 53-55, 93
Julius	6	Meshorer	218
Jupiter	*passim*	Mesopotamia	3, 17, 25, 52
Justin	183-184, 196, 198-199, 215	Mesopotamian	2, 21
		Meyer	176
Kepler	20, 33	Meyshan	218
Keresztes	117	Mickler	121
Khorene	75, 190, 199, 271	Millar	109, 194, 200, 205, 208
Kislev	63, 151, 153, 229	Mishnah	243
Kokhba	249	Mitzvah	25
Kudlek	121	Mommsen	170, 176
Lardner	187	Mosley	5, 20
Latin	49, 170	Mowinckel	98
Lawgiver	50	Nabataean	163
Legatus	183-184	Nabonassar	216
Legion	145-146, 164	Nazareth	42, 111, 229, 243, 245-247
Lepidus	209		
Levites	24	Nebuchadnezzar	24, 44
Lewin	75	Nero	24, 26, 28, 192, 249, 251
Liddell	267		
Lucius	105	Nerva	253
Lycia	183	Nicanor	139
Lydia	183	Nicolas	117, 122, 126, 134, 137, 149
Maccabean	109, 139		
Maccabee	248	Noah	94, 100, 253
Maccabees	63, 152, 222, 248	Norton	98
Maccabeus	211	Nova	37
Macedonia	223, 257-258	Olcott	48
Madden	218	Olympiad	109
Magian	23-26, 28, 31, 44, 55	Olympiads	106-107, 115, 203-204
Magicians	24	Origin	26, 208, 243
Magie	233	Orosius	76, 191-192, 199
Malachi	48, 61	Paidion	54, 67, 229
Marathus	6	Palestinian	2, 21, 34, 90, 107, 143, 160, 162, 204, 241-242, 256
Marcus	108, 206		
Mariamme	110, 204, 211, 217, 223		
Mars	8, 11-12, 29, 33, 53-55	Paphlagonian	75-76, 191-193, 198
Martius	130		

277

Papyrus	179, 229, 249	Reinhold	176
Parthia	28, 158-159, 162, 167	Reiss	117
Parthian	23, 26, 28	Sabbaths	73, 245
Parthians	159, 161	Sabbaticals	248, 250
Passovers	240	Salome	187
Paterculus	104, 162-163, 174, 179,	Samaria	241
Patmos	86	Samaritan	224, 241
Pedanius	214	Samaritans	241, 243, 246
Peraea	166	Sanhedrin	23-24, 111, 139, 150,
Pergamus	34, 221		152, 213, 230, 249
Persia	139, 223	Sarah	100
Persian	141, 143	Saturn	12, 29, 33, 36-37, 54
Persians	24	Scaliger	117
Peschiavatore	175	Schebat	151, 153, 230
Peter	46	Schurer	109, 194, 212, 232, 250
Pharaoh	44, 97, 216	Schuster	259
Pharisee	187	Schwab	151
Pharisees	158, 187-188, 204	Scorpio	41
Pheroras	131, 158, 187, 204, 215	Scroll	151, 245-246
Philadelphia	113	Scrolls	35, 42
Philippi	250-251	Seleucus	221
Philo	27	Senate	6, 9, 15, 31, 75, 176,
Pilate	106, 203, 210		185, 189
Pisces	33, 37	Sentius	169-170
Piso	173	Shekinah	39
Plautii	173	Sheloshim	127, 130-135
Pleiades	41	Sherwin-White	173, 193
Pliny	125, 163	Shiloh	50
Plutarch	28	Sibylline	42
Pompey	109, 154, 158, 207-208	Sigma	98
Proconsul	171, 232, 257	Silvanus	173
Proconsulship	196	Sinnott	4, 20, 50
Procurator	184, 195-196, 198, 214-215	Solar	4, 25, 62-63, 70, 87, 121
Procuratorial	197	Solomon	95
Protoevangelium	229	Spica	84
Ptolemaeus	221	Stades	127-128
Ptolemy	145-146	Steinmetzer	57
Qumran	77	Suetonius	26, 128
Rab Mag	25	Sulpicius	172-173
Ramsay	76, 79, 176	Syllaeus	210

Syrian	136, 163, 180, 214, 225	Whiston	235
Talmud	100, 142, 150, 208, 249, 253	Wikgren	127
		Yahweh	40-41, 97-98
Tax	191, 193	Yamauchi	116
Taylor	172, 176, 270	Zeiss	5
Tertullian	170, 180-181, 183-184, 188, 198	Zodiacal	12-13, 40-42, 51-52, 81-82, 84, 99
Tetrarch	236	Zoroaster	26, 35
Theodosian	142	Zoroastrian	26
Theophilus	18, 253	Zuckermann	250
Thessalonians	96, 101		
Theta	98		
Thorley	18, 98		
Thracians	126		
Tiberias	251		
Tibertine	8		
Tiburtina	175-176		
Tiburtinus	176, 179-180, 232-235		
Tigranes	226		
Timothy	103, 136		
Tion	128		
Tiridates	24, 28		
Titius	172, 180, 182, 209		
Titulature	160		
Titulus	232-233		
Titus	218, 256		
Tivoli	170		
Trajanus	192		
Triennial	246		
Triumphalia	171, 173		
Tuckerman	262		
Usher	61		
Vardaman	116, 262		
Velleius	104, 162-163, 174, 179		
Vermes	109, 194, 200, 205, 208		
Vespasian	110, 218		
Vincent	30		
Virgil	8, 12, 54		
Wacholder	206, 248, 250, 252, 254, 258		
Weymouth	60		

279

Other books by
Dr. Ernest L. Martin

Restoring the Original Bible

Secrets of Golgotha

The People that History Forgot

The Place of the New Third Temple

The Tithing Dilemma

101 Bible Secrets that Christians Do Not Know

The Biblical Manual